THE VALLEY BOYS

The Story of the 1958 Springs Valley Black Hawks

W. Timothy Wright

ISBN: 978-1-4834-7850-0 (sc)
ISBN: 978-1-4834-7852-4 (hc)
ISBN: 978-1-4834-7851-7 (e)

Library of Congress Control Number: 2017919513

Lulu Publishing Services rev. date: 04/28/2018

CONTENTS

Preface: The Valley Boys xi

Prologue: The Valley Boys xv

Chapter 1   The Vale of Two Cities 1

Chapter 2   The Boys 12

Chapter 3   And the Twain Shall Meet 30

Chapter 4   And Two Become One 40

Chapter 5   A Match Made in Heaven 48

Chapter 6   Let the Games Begin 61

Chapter 7   All Aboard Who's Gettin' Aboard! 73

Chapter 8   The Hawks Take Flight 91

Chapter 9   Yea, Though I Walk Through the Valley 104

Chapter 10   All for One and One for All 122

Chapter 11   Providence 157

Chapter 12   Towns (and a Team) Turned on Their Heads 178

Chapter 13   The Perfect Season 196

Chapter 14   The Sectional 207

Chapter 15   Regional, Here We Come 219

Chapter 16 More than a Game 236

Chapter 17 The Big Show 244

Chapter 18 Game Number 26 261

Chapter 19 Back Home Again—in Southern Indiana.................273

Epilogue 283

From the Bleachers..297

From the Coach 301

Acknowledgments...305

About the Author...307

This book is dedicated to the memory of
Frankie Self, Ronald "Butch" Schmutzler, Billie Jo Harris Sayler,
Beverly Runyon Condra, and Billy Rose

*"It's not settled happiness but momentary
joy that glorifies the past."*
—*C. S. Lewis*

PREFACE

THE VALLEY BOYS

The story of the 1958 Springs Valley Black Hawks basketball team

"When it comes to revise the already tradition-steeped history of Indiana High School basketball, there will be a special chapter for Coach Wells and his miraculous Springs Valley Black Hawks." —W. F. Fox Jr., Sports Editor, *Indianapolis News*

This story has intrigued me since I was a first grader in 1958, when the goings-on in the "twin cities" of West Baden and French Lick had trickled down even to us "wee ones." All of us, and particularly boys with big brothers and fathers who were basketball fanatics, overheard many conversations on the subject. We could tell that something very unusual was happening in this community during the now-hallowed year of 1958, when two archrival high schools consolidated and experienced a rocky beginning to this first season as one school—one team.

It was a year of historical events taking place on both the world and national stages. It was early in America's and Russia's "Race for Space," and we had successfully shot Explorer 1 into orbit on the first day of the year. Arnold Palmer won his first Masters golf tournament, and President Eisenhower signed the Alaska statehood bill. Legos building blocks, the Hula Hoop, and the classic 64-colors box of Crayola Crayons all made their debuts.

Events such as these were helping U.S. citizens get a good glimpse of the future as this decade of prosperity and postwar growth neared its end. However, I don't recall ever being fortunate enough to own the 64-color box of Crayola Crayons! That was terribly extravagant for any little boy in French Lick, Indiana. The box with the 18 colors seemed to get the job done quite well. And who needed a built-in crayon sharpener when you had access to your grandpa's Barlow knife?

One of my earliest memories of school days was taking my black and orange crayons and drawing the head of a black hawk on one of my folders. I was so fascinated with the depictions of this powerful bird that I had been seeing everywhere in our small town. Posters in store windows and in my grandpa's barbershop told me that something quite unprecedented was occurring—and it was all because of the brand-new basketball team, the Springs Valley Black Hawks.

I heard these ballplayers' names spoken around our kitchen table and my grandma's Sunday dinner table. I heard these boys' names so often that now, 59 years later, I could recall them with ease before starting to write this story. These names had been floating around in my head my entire life. They were the names of boys who changed a town—or should I say, two towns—forever.

In the state of Indiana, basketball is as revered as hockey is in Canada, baseball at Yankee Stadium, or college football in Alabama. The game of putting a ball through a hoop was a very powerful force in every community, especially the smaller Indiana schools. Basketball held such an emotional grip in small towns in the days before the Indiana High School Athletic Association folks got together in the late 1990s and chose to end one-class competition, creating divisions within the high schools to "even the playing field." I'm sure these intentions were all well and good, but it sure took the wind out of the sails of this Indiana tradition. When schools began playing for separate state championships in varying divisions according to school size, the days of those dramatic games between powerhouses and small-town schools were over.

The popular movie *Hoosiers*, telling the tale of how tiny Milan overcame all odds to win a state championship, revealed to the world this love affair we folks in Indiana have for this high school game and what it can do for an entire community. So much of our own self-esteem seemed to be inextricably attached to the local team's fortunes each season. The emotions of an entire town could be swayed by the outcome of these games, and entire populations would suffer agonies or thrill to victories from one Friday night to the next. This was the way of life for those citizens of West Baden and French Lick, Indiana, during each basketball season.

Although their combined population was only 3,500, two separate schools were built in the 1930s as part of FDR's Works Progress Administration. The separation of the two towns had begun at the turn of the century when the grand hotels were built so the nation's elite could enjoy the supposed healing properties of the water from the local mineral springs. (West Baden's teams were dubbed the Sprudels, a German-language reference to its waters. French Lick's teams were the "Red Devils," based upon the town's marketing of Pluto Water from the springs surrounding their hotel.) Life had carried on this way until the summer of 1957, when the high schools from West Baden and French Lick decided to consolidate. This merger set up immediate conflict.

While *The Valley Boys* is based on real people and events, I've taken a writer's creative license to embellish this saga. It is a real-life story with its own color and conflict—and a first-year high school team's sometimes rough-and-tumble journey through its inaugural season. As to the personalities I've painted onto this canvas, I've used the team's and coach's real names in relating actual events and circumstances. Based on my own knowledge of the people and events in French Lick and West Baden, I have invented certain events and conversations between real-life characters and speculated on relationships that truly existed.

The people in this story have been living the years of 1957 and 1958 in my head for the past ten years. I've tried to imagine seeing them and hearing them in their day-to-day lives during basketball season. I've come to know these boys (now men in their mid- to late 70s). I have based the players' personalities in *The Valley Boys* on my conversations with them and the stories that their now-85-year-old coach has shared with me.

I've listened to brief interviews that these men have given at various times. I've attempted to take what I heard in those interviews and imagine what these men may have been like 60-some years ago, when they were just teenage boys; what they might've said, places they may have gone, and how they may have reacted to the hoopla that was surrounding their young lives during this one special basketball season.

Not long ago, my cousin Jerry Denbo, a former state legislator from French Lick and perhaps the greatest 1958 Black Hawks fan, organized a reunion to honor these players. Most of them showed up for the event, including the coach, Rex Wells. Jerry summed it up best when he said, "We didn't need Mickey Mantle or Johnny Unitas. We had Marvin Pruett, Frankie Self, Paul Radcliff, Bob McCracken, and Butch Schmutzler, and the rest of the entire team."

He's right. These boys and their young coach, not much older than his senior players, were the role models in this community. They showed two towns what can happen when very good ballplayers come along at the right time in the right place, with the right coach and set of circumstances. Ten boys and a 25-year-old coach formed a synergy, creating a story that looks as if it were created by a Hollywood scriptwriter. But these boys and this team were real, and proved, once again, that God is the greatest dramatist. So, here's my take on what took place during this very real period. They were typical small-town boys who, although they didn't know it at the time, were soon to become a very atypical team of destiny: the 1958 Springs Valley Black Hawks.

PROLOGUE

THE VALLEY BOYS

1941

Tonight, the first basketball game of the 1941–42 season was raging between two rival schools, and it was late in the fourth quarter. It was a very tight game, as most of these contests seemed to be back in the '40s. The West Baden Sprudels were in the lead against the French Lick Red Devils on their home court. To say that there were bitter feelings between these two town's teams would be quite the understatement. In fact, these two teams hated each other as much as two basketball teams could.

World War II was approaching, but it was another type of war on the home front when West Baden's Sprudels took on the Devils, and it had been this way as far back as anyone could recall. These two towns were not ordinary burgs. Nor had they been at the turn of the century, four decades prior. Dubbed the "Twin Cities," French Lick and West Baden shared a mile-and-a-half stretch of a valley that cuts through the rural part of Orange County in Southern Indiana. You could drive through these two towns, nestled in the Hoosier National Forest, and not even realize when you're leaving one and entering the other.

The competitive spirit had begun way back when two of the grandest hotels in the entire USA, the West Baden Springs and the French Lick Springs Hotel, had been built—only a half mile apart.

Each town had always tried to get the jump on the other with its resort. In their heyday, both of these landmarks were drawing large crowds of visitors from far and near. Movie stars, politicians, and even gangsters visited the valley to take advantage of the natural mineral and sulphur springs found there.

The rich and famous of the era, including Howard Hughes, Lana Turner, the great Joe Louis, FDR, and John Dillinger, all made these resorts near the crossroads of America their destination for rest and relaxation.

Gambling had been a part of the draw, but at one time, the West Baden hotel had even been considered the "Eighth Wonder of the World" as the largest unsupported dome structure anywhere. French Lick and West Baden both had something quite grand to be proud of.

Sadly, the Depression brought on the sales of the two hotels. The West Baden Springs was sold to the Jesuits for one dollar; the French Lick hotel came under the management and ownership of the Sheraton chain. (This was quite convenient, as the new Sheraton hotel operators didn't have to change the initials emblazoned on everything from towels to marble floors. The FLS logo of the French Lick Springs was easily adapted to that of the French Lick Sheraton.)

The folks in French Lick had kept their landmark hotel, but West Baden had lost theirs. This was just one more bit of history that stuck in the craw of most of West Baden's folks. It was obvious by the late '40s that the town that had kept its hotel was the one that continued to have some measure of growth and vitality. West Baden had become something like a suburb of French Lick. It seemed to have lost its identity.

Whenever the West Baden high school basketball team could put a whippin' on French Lick's team, it was always a bit of sweet revenge. Now, these folks had been carrying on like this for quite some time, and tonight was just another round being fought for one town's pride and bragging rights. The Sprudels held on to their lead, beating French Lick by two points.

"Here, take back your ring. I never want to see you again!" Gertie Willoughby could be heard above the din of West Baden fans cheering for their Sprudels. Harold Self just stood there, accepting the angora-covered ring with a bit of a smile on his face. His team had just won the contest. Gertie's team had gone down in another bitter defeat.

This teenage drama had played out more than once before. This was part of a ritual, it seemed, between boys and girls from West Baden who dated someone from French Lick. Normally, the one from the losing school's team would break off the relationship, almost as if it were some sort of official requirement instilled by generations that had gone on before.

This night was no different. Harold and Gertie were breaking up—again, and for the umpteenth time. In a week or so, they'd be back together, at least until the French Lick Red Devils and the West Baden Sprudels met once again.

Harold Self was a senior at West Baden High School, going steady with Gertrude Willoughby, a senior at French Lick High School. The two schools were a little more than one mile apart, but separated by a lot more than railroad tracks.

1954

Rex Wells had grown up in West Baden and starred on its Sprudels basketball squad during his high school days. He played for Hanover College in Southern Indiana and had recently graduated. He'd returned to his hometown, fully expecting to hear from Uncle Sam now that he was out of school. So, he took on the job of coaching the West Baden seventh and eighth grade basketball team—for free. Rex simply loved the game of roundball and he realized that he would likely not be able to complete the season. The young graduate volunteered his services to coach the team until he was drafted.

Frankie Self, Marvin Pruett, Paul Radcliff, and Jim Conrad all played on the West Baden junior high team. Bob McCracken was one year ahead of both Marvin and Frankie and two years ahead of Paul and Jim, and he was now on West Baden's Sprudels high school team. Rex enjoyed coaching these boys. He could also see something special in the way they interacted with each other. None of them were from families with much money. In fact, there were hardly any families living in the French Lick/West Baden area that could be considered "well-to-do." The towns were economically depressed, located in one of the lowest-income counties in Indiana. Hills and valleys don't make the greatest farmland, and since the end of the resort hotel's boom days, everyone just seemed to get by.

Husbands and fathers who didn't own or run a store, sell insurance, work at the bank, or teach school, drove considerable distances to work. Some would travel south to the Crane munitions factory, the big city of Louisville, or even as far away as Indianapolis to earn a living.

These boys loved playing ball for young Coach Wells. There was just something about his personality that clicked with them. Rex never hollered, but he did demand their full attention as he taught them about running a pick and roll, setting a screen, getting position for a rebound, or making a sharp, clean pass for a fast break. His close-set, narrow dark eyes told them he meant business, and he wasn't going to waste his time on players who didn't want to give the game their very best.

Winning games was important, but what Rex wanted most from his players was their best effort. The boys understood this and they delivered by winning their first 10 games with their young volunteer coach.

Then, as expected, Rex received his marching orders and had to leave for his "further education" in the U.S. Army.

The West Baden junior high basketball team went on to win every game but two that season. They were defeated twice by the much larger Huntingburg Junior High, each time by only one point. This was only a foreshadowing of things to come. These same boys from these two teams would meet on the hardwood in a few years in a much, much bigger contest.

Frankie, Marvin, Bob, Paul and Jim showed an unusual understanding for the subtleties of the game, and they could play team basketball together very well, even at this early age during many pick-up games at the Jesuit College outdoor court.

"We got to that jelling point at an early age," Marvin Pruett later observed. Ten wins in a row with Coach Wells was a memory they'd take with them into future competitions. They would draw from their early experience many times.

In only a few years, the time spent with Coach Wells would come into play in a unique way.

·CHAPTER 1·
THE VALE OF TWO CITIES

The seventeenth day of August 1957 was a sweltering day, and William Jennings Andrew's barbershop was full. One man sat in the green leather barber chair, awaiting a shave and a haircut. The lone barber had a full day ahead of him. All five molded wooden seats, carved arm rests attached to scroll-patterned iron legs, were filled. These waiting chairs were connected in one row and bolted to the floor.

The Sulphur Creek Evangelical United Brethren Church had bought several of these chairs for their "amen corner," and Bill Andrew had arranged to buy a row of seats from the church. And while these seats were filled, just as the EUB's would be tomorrow, the "amens" rising from the chairs today were of a different nature from those that would be voiced in the next day's Sunday morning service. These men were all in agreement on a topic well outside of theological discussions.

Saturday was the busiest day of the week for the hard-working barber. His day would not end until 11 p.m., when he swept the floor, sterilized the combs, and counted the day's earnings before heading home.

Flattops were the style of the day, and for most men, this meant frequent visits to the small building with the red, white, and blue striped barber pole twirling outside the door. The barber shop was located across the street from the French Lick High School, on the front side of a house's "walk out" basement. Just like most houses in French Lick that were built into or upon a hill, the barber's house was built into the side of a hill, and the one-time garage on the ground level had been turned into a barbershop. The Eskimo-brand window fan, sitting on the floor and going full blast, was blowing the hair clippings into one corner. This was not the type of day that evoked patience in anyone, and the dripping sweat from determined faces indicated that something more than humidity was hanging in the air. Some of the men in the waiting chairs were letting off a bit of steam, while still trying to remember why they were waiting for a haircut on this stifling day. Since the 40s, men had been getting their hair cut on a regular basis, particularly on a Saturday so they could look their best on the Lord's day. These fellas didn't have much money, but they did take pride in their appearance. You could set a clock by their weekly grooming habits. Folks went to church around these parts, and sprucing up for the Almighty was just something everyone believed was the proper thing to do.

This Saturday was no different, but for one thing: all the usual talk in the shop was now being driven by a new topic. Instead of tales from years gone by, the weather, or whoppers about the size of a fish someone had caught, all the men were discussing a word that had just entered their vocabulary—consolidation.

The two schools in this small valley were consolidating. The French Lick and West Baden high schools would become one this year, and many of the folk from both towns were not keen on the dramatic change. For most towns and cities, two schools consolidating would not garner that much attention, but something more was at stake here—something more important to most of the citizenry than any academic advances or potential tax advantages.

"I just don't know how this is going to all work out," Hobby Gibson growled, as he sat in the waiting chair.

"I just don't understand why they have to go and change things all around," the man in the barber chair answered. "We have our ways here in French Lick, and those West Baden folks have theirs.

They should just leave things the way they've been ever since I can remember."

"Yeah, it just won't be the same no more without the Sprudels takin' on the Red Devils," added a younger customer awaiting a Hollywood burr.

All the men lamented what this consolidation portended: a new basketball team. Only *one* basketball team. Even as the wonderful aromas of the rich vanilla and clove of the Clubman aftershave, Clubman talc, and Amber Lion hair tonic wafted through the shop, a bitterness hung in the air.

The conversation continued over the slap-slap-slap of a straight razor being sharpened by the barber on a leather strap that hung at the side of the barber chair.

"I hear they done hired Rex Wells, the Sprudels coach from last year," Hank Harrison offered while chewing on the toothpick he always had at the side of his mouth.

Hobby Gibson piped up again. "He's just a pup! What does he know about basketball, anyway? He's only coached high school ball one year. We need a coach like Marvin Wood." Jokingly, Hobby added, "Whatever happened to him, anyway?" This comment elicited a chuckle from all the men in the barbershop. Everyone knew that Marvin Wood had coached the French Lick Red Devils just one season prior to becoming the Milan Indians coach, and leading their team to the Final Four—two years in a row, 1953 and 1954.

"Yeah, can you believe that we had Marvin Wood coaching here in '51 and '52?" another man asserted. "Maybe we'd have won it all four years ago instead of Milan if Coach Wood had stayed here."

"I don't know if that could've happened," Hank asserted. "Bobby Plump and Ray Craft and all that starting five played for Wood both those seasons. They had a strong enough squad to even beat Oscar Robertson's Crispus Attucks team. I ain't sure the Devils had that kind of talent."

"Oh, yeah. You're probably right. Plump's been tearin' it up for Butler the past three years. Why'd we get rid of Marvin Wood anyway?"

"Who knows why school boards do what they do," Paul Grigsby complained. "Look what they're doin' now."

"This consolidatin' stuff will never work out," Hobby said. "The Sprudels and Devils can never come together successfully as one team. There's just too much rivalry between 'em. It'll be one big mess on the hands of that young whippersnapper of a coach."

The barber, Bill Andrew, usually kept silent when he heard the talk heating up a little, and wisely stayed out of the fray, just doing his job. But today, he decided to get in on the chatter.

"I think it might just be a good thing in the end—this idea of bringing the schools together," he said.

The barbershop grew strangely quiet at this comment from the low-key, humble man wielding the razor. Bill continued, "I think that these two towns have been at odds for long enough. Maybe it's time that we become one community, and leave all of the bickerin' and fightin' in the past."

But after a few more moments of silence, the talk resumed as if he had not said a word.

"Let's just see what happens," Hank Harrison finally offered. "This is already too far down the pike for any of us to object. Let's all stand back and watch this whole shebang go down the drain."

Only a mile and a half away from this French Lick outpost, a very similar conversation could be heard at Skeet's Barber Shop—but from the perspective of a male citizen of West Baden. Only the names of the barber and the customers were different. These men, who had once played basketball for the West Baden Sprudels, were echoing the same concerns as the former Red Devils players now getting gussied up for the next day's church services.

The two towns may not have employed all that much brotherly love and forgiveness, but they made sure they'd be in good standing with the Lord by keeping their weekly attendance record going. When it came to resisting being a "doer of the word, and not a hearer only," as the Apostle Paul implored of the new Christians in the first century, folks from both these small towns had simply been fighting for too long to be able to give it up now. It's just the way things were—and it even seemed like the towns derived a certain enjoyment from the ongoing feud that had started way back in 1902, when the two resort hotels were built.

A historic change was coming that no one could see on this hot August day, nor even have the faintest vision of during Wednesday evening prayer services. The times were changing, and it was high time the two feuding towns changed with the rest of America.

☺ ☺ ☺

The summer of 1957 was nearly over. High school boys from both French Lick and West Baden, Indiana, were working their three-month stints. Some were detasseling corn or baling hay. Others were stacking lumber at the Twin City Lumber Co., parking cars at a hotel, or being a gofer at the Orange County Beverage Company. But they were all dreaming of two things: what they would do with the money they were earning from their summertime jobs and what the new basketball season would bring.

For most teen-age boys around these parts, owning their own car was a distant dream—if even a dream at all. Most folks in Orange County in the '50s considered themselves poor. There was no real industry, and wages were low. Most families lived lives of hardship without the luxuries that many in other areas of Indiana took for granted. Most boys living in these towns grew up under a certain handicap, yet they didn't seem to know it at the time. To these young folks, it was just life as they knew it, and that was that. They took what they got, didn't complain, and made the best of things.

So, owning a car was almost as great a fantasy as having a date with Marilyn Monroe. But any boy of driving age was saving either for his own set of wheels or for gas money to feed his old man's Ford or Chevy. There was no such thing as a free ride, and the boys knew that if they were lucky enough to borrow the family car for those frequent spins to the Chatterbox drive-in hamburger joint or the Springs Valley movie theater, then they'd better put gas in the tank.

The prospect of finding their own thrill—as Fats Domino had

crooned about in "Blueberry Hill"—was the only incentive teenage boys needed to keep working hard all summer long. If they weren't earning money for the upcoming school year, they'd be out shooting a basketball. Sometimes they practiced by themselves on a goal attached to the side of a barn, or scrimmaged at the two towns' best outdoor court at the Jesuit college. If they weren't at the college court, they'd be playing at the park in French Lick, where the rusted rims usually had no nets.

At the park, the half-court line of the concrete surface was located almost parallel to the city limits sign marking the boundary between the two small towns. This seemed appropriate. Basketball games revealed a greater divide than did any sign or line of demarcation between the neighbors populating the two towns. Local businesses such as the Twin City Dairy and the Twin City Lumber Company used this moniker in their businesses' names without irony.

This "Twin City" title may have been a bit inflated, given that the combined population of the towns never exceeded 3,500. One hundred miles south of the state capital of Indianapolis, this sleepy Southern Indiana community seemed almost in a different era altogether. In most respects, the people there still appeared to be living in the decade prior to the 1950s. Change didn't occur too quickly around these parts, and folks were just fine with that.

Oh, everyone knew what was going on in the world, all right. Alaska was getting ready to become a state. Elvis was still on the radio with "Hound Dog" from the year before, and his movie *Jailhouse Rock* had just been released. Soon the king of rock 'n' roll would be inducted into the U.S. military and singing "G.I. Blues." The Wham-O company had invented a new toy called the "Pluto Platter" that would later become known as a Frisbee. Even hula-hoops had made it to Frank and Bee's variety store and the Five and Dime located on the downtown stretch in French Lick, next to the drug store. The Ford Co. had launched its Edsel. Eisenhower was practicing his putting on the White House lawn, and all was well with the world.

But outside of the sighting of an occasional pair of black and white Oxfords, senior corduroy pants, letter sweaters, or rolled-up T-shirt sleeves with a pack of Pall Malls tucked neatly inside, life in these little towns in the valley still seemed much like the 1940s in many ways.

Frankie Self, a 16-year-old boy from West Baden, had gotten the best summer job a Twin City teen could have, stocking groceries for Mr. Ellis at the Star Store. Mr. Ellis had asked him to stay on part time during the coming school year. Frankie was the number one stock boy in this store, which had sat at the corner of Maple Street and Highway 56 since the '20s.

Most of the boys in West Baden and French Lick had to find work each summer. In Frankie's case, however, this "summer job" was an absolute necessity. His father had passed on, leaving the family pretty much destitute. Frankie and his older brother had to find work to keep food on the table for the family.

Frankie loved working for Mr. Ellis, and now, as an employee, he could take home food that was nearly expired. Mr. Ellis always let him take home a bag of apples or oranges every week.

🌏 🌏 🌏

The Star Store stood as a connection to an earlier time, much like many of the establishments that were so much a part of the fabric of life in the two towns. Its storefront always sported a fresh coat of red and white paint—one of Frankie's duties. Back in the '30s and '40s, red-and-white-striped canvas awnings had adorned all the shops and storefront windows up and down Maple Street's one-block "business district." These awnings now were gone, but Mr. Ellis liked tradition, and he continued the red and white color combination—perhaps as a sort of tribute to the French Lick basketball team, which shared these same colors.

There was ample evidence of deliverymen having bumped their hand trucks into the store's lower shelves. The floor was a grayish-light brown from years of being mopped and scrubbed with strong cleaning agents, and Frankie was well acquainted with the original tongue-and-groove oak flooring that had been laid when the store was built. He knew well the soundtrack of shopping carts rolling on the creaking hardwood. Any person weighing more than 100 pounds could feel this well-worn floor giving a little beneath their feet as they entered through the bright red, wood-framed glass door and encountered the floor's many ruts and gouges—the evidence of decades of shoppers trudging up and down the narrow aisles.

Entering the shop was always pleasant. The aromas of recently delivered Colonial bread and sweet rolls, just-picked produce, fresh-ground coffee, and myriad spices hung in the air. The essences of these foodstuffs all mixed with that of the aged wood and the meat counter, scrubbed frequently with Bab-O cleanser.

While the bigger city grocery stores by this time had tile floors on concrete slabs and automatic opening doors for both entering and exiting the store, this grocery's eight-foot-high wood frame doors with plate glass windows still boasted the original brass handles— the kind with the thumb piece you had to press down on to open the latch. These were worn smooth from the thousands of hands having grasped it to open the door through the years. But the Star Store was never very crowded these days.

During basketball season, to the delight of Frankie and his friends, the store would offer promotions for town folks to save their milk bottle caps from the Twin City Dairy and exchange them for tickets to the next ball game or the movie theater, just a few doors down from the Star Store.

Mr. Deremiah's corner drug store, too, still stood where it had for the past four decades, on the corner of Maple Street and College Street. This was the perfect place to take a Saturday night date for a soda or ice cream sundae. The staff would fry up great hamburgers and French Fries as well, and many a high school boy and girl meandered past this corner on a Friday or Saturday night, each with hopes of catching a glimpse of one of their heart-throbs who was usually in the same vicinity, doing the same thing.

A typical Saturday evening would find the boys walking up and down on one side of Maple Street, while the young ladies nonchalantly strolled up and down the other side, each knowing full well that they were being checked out. There was much more talking about the opposite sex than there was actual contact. There was still a bit of mystery left back in those days when it came to romantic matters.

The movie theater, where the boys from decades past had watched Tom Mix in Saturday morning Westerns, was still going strong. Movies like *Gone with the Wind* had played years before; the current film, *The Blob*, was catnip to teenage boys. A horror film about a meteor filled with a purple, gooey, oozing mess consuming everything in its path was a must to see.

At times when the theater couldn't obtain the most recent movies, the proprietors would pull out their own reels of the 1938 Errol Flynn film, *The Adventures of Robin Hood*. Little boys were not aware that this was not a current movie, nor would they care even if they understood. They left the theater as thrilled as did the generation before, going home to pretend to be that hero with his band of merry men who robbed from the rich and gave to the poor.

The Catholic, Baptist, Methodist, Wesleyan, Christian, and Assembly of God churches, too, all stood where they had for many years. The American Legion Post and the building where grandmothers and aunts attended the Eastern Star, a female version of a Masonic Lodge, stood where they had for years. The Eastern Star was the one place in town where ladies-only meetings were held, in a very old two-story structure with tan-colored, tar-shingle, faux-brick siding. The sign with the organization's multicolored star emblem above the door appeared to be quite mysterious to anyone who wasn't involved, though it was rumored that the ladies mostly played canasta.

The most obvious relics from the past were the two behemoth hotels, one in French Lick and one in West Baden, which had been built at the turn of the century. These once were world-renowned resorts, welcoming the elite of their day from all over America.

Up until the Depression, nationally and internationally known celebrities, politicians, gangsters, inventors, authors, and sports figures all made frequent visits to this valley. Now, those glory days were long gone, remembered fondly by those who grew up seeing the superstars of their day at the unique resort hotels.

By the 1950s, the days of gambling casinos and the opulent lifestyles of the rich folk who had visited the Valley were now mere fodder for nostalgia. Life had settled back into a more normal, small-town pace. Since the Depression years, French Lick and West Baden had hardly changed in the least. Folks were conditioned to a certain monotony and sameness of life, week after week, month after month, year after year. To all of them, this was just as it was supposed to be.

Yet the towns still clung to the special pride they had once taken in their respective hotels, which had once bestowed a booming economy upon the locals. Today the self-esteem of each town seemed rather to have attached itself to the local basketball team as its source of pride.

And so, during four exciting months each year, residents would soak up every bit of town pride and root for their home team. Girls from West Baden who dated boys from French Lick, for example, were still breaking up a week or two after a heartbreaking loss to the Red Devils. The same held true in the event of a Sprudels victory.

The word "consolidation" hadn't been used too often, if ever, in the Valley, though it became home to one of the very first Indiana high school consolidations. But thanks to the *Springs Valley Herald*'s many articles and numerous letters to the editor, it was now a part of everyone's vocabulary. Just how much change was in store for these two sleepy hamlets no one could have possibly imagined.

By the end of July, the two town boards had both met and voted on this great advancement for the community. The meetings were over, the arguing done by both sides—for and against. But the 92 students of West Baden simply didn't merit having their own high school located so close to another, and it simply made good economic sense; state funds would increase because of the larger student body after consolidation. In the end, logic won out, and the two towns combined their high schools into one, Springs Valley High. This momentous decision would affect the lives of nearly every resident of the towns.

The academic aspect of the merger was not foremost on most people's minds. It was the game of basketball.

For years, since the '30s, the two schools had been archrivals, and the place where this rivalry was most evident was on the basketball court. On the hardwood floors of the two schools' gymnasiums, some of the greatest of small-town Indiana's basketball games—feuds, rather—would be played. The contests were fought as if the fate of the world depended on the outcome of these 32-minute contests. In a way, the fate of many people's worlds did in fact hang on the final scores of these games that repeated year after year, as if a kind of pagan ritual to appease the basketball gods.

The fans of both towns would come together to serve up another Friday night sacrifice, screaming at referees, coaches, and even the young players, hoping their cheers, jeers, and chants would have some influence on the outcome of each game. It seemed their most desired result in the world was a victory that always ensured bragging rights—until the young gladiators met once again.

• CHAPTER 2 •
THE BOYS

A hazy, hot August day found four boys skinny-dipping again in their favorite swimmin' hole, where Pigeon Creek meets the Lost River near the bridge on the way into West Baden on State Road 56. The day seemed very remote from the mid-December evening in the old brown-brick West Baden gymnasium that had kept the fans at a ball game comfortably warm and protected from the snow.

Yet that game remained on the minds of virtually everyone in the twin cities. The eight months that had passed since the West Baden Sprudels soundly defeated the French Lick Red Devils was not enough time for the embarrassing loss to be forgotten. Losses were hard to take, but now, there was something else that many citizens from both hamlets felt they were losing. All the townsfolk were still discussing basketball and the future for the community. Consolidation meant one school, not two, and that meant there would only be half the boys playing on a team this coming season. For the best players, this was of no concern, but for those more marginal players who were "bench warmers," this most likely meant that they would be watching from the bleachers this year. The issue had hung in the air all spring and summer, and it was never far from the minds of these boys from West Baden and French Lick.

Frankie Self, Marvin Pruett, Paul Radcliff, Jim Conrad, and Bob McCracken were the best of friends. They had played basketball for the West Baden teams since sixth grade and they knew each other like brothers. These were the boys from "across the tracks" that divided French Lick and West Baden.

They had not only been playing for their school since sixth grade, but also had continued to play in the off-season and every chance they could get at the former West Baden Hotel, now the Jesuit school—with collegiate competition. The Jesuit students studying for the priesthood would shovel the snow off the court every winter, just so they could play against the boys from West Baden. It was a nice asphalt court, and if the boys wanted to use it, they'd have to play against these priests in the making, who were coming in from Catholic universities such as Marquette and Xavier. They didn't let up on these younger players.

Those Sunday afternoon scrimmages had certainly toughened up the boys from West Baden, and as Marvin, in later years, often said, "Man, I think those guys were taking their frustrations out on us!" The youngsters had developed their own style of team play going up against the much taller, stronger players. They had to learn to make the quick pass, move the ball from man to man, and find the open shot.

On this day, three of the boys had been baling hay with their fellow ballplayer Jim Conrad. Jim's dad owned a farm out near Prospect, and the boys were often hired to do some of the farm chores. Baling hay in the heat had Marvin, Bob, and Paul sweating and itching like crazy when they arrived at the creek. Frankie had arrived a bit earlier, after finishing his shift at the Star Store.

Inevitably, their thoughts turned to basketball and the coming season, and between the splashing and diving, they shared what was uppermost on their minds.

"Gee whiz, I just don't know if I'm gonna like this playin' with a bunch of hicks from French Lick," Frankie mused in his quiet voice. As he dove, his buddies whistled and clapped their approval. All the boys had gotten Frankie's joke—they knew they were all considered hicks by most folks living north of Orange County, and visitors to the Valley couldn't even tell where West Baden ended and French Lick began.

Frankie stood a compact 5'7" and his voice had a raspy tone that sounded like he spoke from the back of his throat. His delivery made listeners have to lean in to hear his modest voice, creating an eagerness to hear his next words. He spoke deliberately, choosing his words carefully, and always offered a look that said, "You do understand what I'm sayin', don't ya?" His habit of understatement helped him get his point across—and he always made his opinion known succinctly.

He was good at everything, including making a clever joke in his quiet delivery. When his cohorts saw that grin come across his face with his squinty, twinkling eyes looking sideways, they knew they were in for a good chuckle. Frankie barely opened his mouth and maintained a constant smile when he spoke, giving his little jabs even more of a sarcastic tone. Frankie was also a thinker. He was the one to engage in a political discussion and could hold his own in any argument. His quiet demeanor cloaked a very clever and calculating mind.

While Frankie's manner of speaking was reserved, his athletic abilities were not. There was a reason that he had been the starting guard at West Baden the previous season.

When Frankie bobbed up out of the water, he could hear the other boys still clapping, hooting and hollering in response to his remark as well as his excellent dive. He pretended not to hear. Frankie wasn't a show-off, and he didn't like to stand out from the crowd. His last name, Self, seemed ironic; he was selfless. Playing guard, leading the half-court offense on the basketball team, fit him perfectly. He wasn't the one who scored the most points. His job was to find the open man who could score and get the ball to him. And that other "man," often, was Marvin Pruett.

Marvin loved Frankie, as all the boys did. He and the other two voiced their approval at Frankie's dive and funny remark after he came up from the muddy creek. "Yep," Marvin hollered, "those hillbillies only have a couple of guys who could make the West Baden team."

Marvin was a natural shooter, and he was developing one of the sweetest jump shots that anyone had ever witnessed in Southern Indiana. He would take the ball in both hands and hike his right knee as he went up for his shot, and just before releasing the ball, his right hand took over for a one-handed shot—much like that of the famed Oscar Robertson, who had just finished a spectacular high school career at Crispus Attucks in Indianapolis and was preparing for his first year of college at Cincinnati.

Marvin's style was the opposite of Frankie's. He longed to make that last-second shot and hear the roar of the crowd, feeding off the crowd's reaction. He didn't mind receiving the glory in the least—and his jump shot was accurate enough to back up his swagger.

Of all the boys, Marvin was perhaps the most "worldly." His dad had worked at the Bedford stone quarry his entire adult life and had passed a few of his habits to his son early on. The Sunday school teachers in town would say that the Pruetts were a little "rough around the edges," thanks to some of the coarse language they were known to use at times—though they didn't go so far as to take the Lord's name in vain.

While most boys in the Valley refrained from profanities, this was not so with Marvin. If something happened on the ball court or when hanging out with his buddies, the expletives would fly. This habit, along with his accurate jump shot, set Marvin apart a bit from the other boys. They viewed him as sort of an older brother who had been out in the world longer than they. Besides, the boy who puts the ball in the basket always gains profound respect from his peers. Marvin was respected by his teammates and by everyone who knew him.

"We sure beat the devil out of those Red Devils last year," Paul Radcliff quickly added. The tallest of the boys though he was only going into his sophomore year, he always played center. Paul was a straight-A student and mature beyond his years, always seeming to be a stabilizing force. He was grounded in many ways, looking at life through a more theological lens, and therefore coming to conclusions that the other boys had never considered.

Paul realized this was God's world and he knew his place in it.

He often whistled "Onward, Christian Soldiers," knowing well that he was in "the service of the Lord." Paul's father never let him miss a Sunday morning sermon or a Wednesday evening prayer service at the local apostolic "full-gospel" church, and Paul had never known a time when he hadn't heard the gospel message and responded to God's Word. In fact, he'd been baptized at 10 years old in this same creek. And if Paul's father had known he was swimming and splashing around in the exact same place he was lowered backwards under the water, he would not approve. Paul would be feeling the paddle on his back end if his dad ever found this out. To his father, this creek had become a sacred place where it would be sacrilegious to skinny-dip, even on one of the hottest days of the summer.

"I think we poured some cold water on them Devils last season. They only won six games," Marvin threw out, laughing. He scrambled up the bank atop the highest limestone slab to try to out-do Frankie's dive. "We'll have a strong team, don't you worry."

He then climbed to the top of the old covered bridge abutment to make his dive even more memorable. "I've been working on my jump shot a lot this summer," he continued. "I'm planning on doing some scoring—no matter what team we're playing for. After all, we won the first three games in the sectional last year, and big ol' Jasper only beat us by seven points in that final game."

Bob McCracken was the introvert of the foursome. But it was Bob who always got things done when push came to shove on the court. He was tough inside and out. Bob lived on a farm outside of town, and he was used to roughing it. He would often hitchhike into town after his chores were done, and walked the four miles to and from school each day. Many evenings he ran home after basketball practice.

Bob was raised in a home that didn't have the same luxuries as some of the other boys—luxuries like electricity and indoor plumbing. The house was lit with kerosene lamps and heated with a coal-burning stove. Water had to be brought in from a well. The absence of indoor plumbing also meant using an outhouse, and having to take a bath in a galvanized metal tub with water heated on the coal stove. Many meals at the McCrackens would be made from a chicken that Bob would kill, whacking the head off and then hanging the carcass on a clothes line to bleed out. He'd then have to dip the bird in boiling water before plucking the feathers. Bob and his brother would shoot a squirrel early in the morning, then skin and gut it so their mom would prepare it for their breakfast. Bob's lunch at school would often be a bacon grease sandwich. Spam, the tinned meat product, was considered a delicacy for the McCrackens. The greatest treat for Bob was when his mom indulged him with a quarter so he could buy peanuts to put in a Coca-Cola.

It was Bob who was the most anxious about who their coach would be in the upcoming season. Coach Rex Wells had become his mentor during the last basketball season, and Bob wanted that relationship to continue.

Work was scarce around these parts for grown men to make a fair wage, so Bob's father, Merle, made the three-hour drive to Indianapolis, where he worked at the Roselyn Bakery. Making it home late on Friday nights, his dad missed most every game, though his mom always made it. His dad, like many from that era, was not close with his sons. The act of simply working to provide for a wife and eight kids seemed to take everything out of him. Working out of town and being away all week didn't allow for much "father and son" time. Bob needed a father figure, and Coach Wells fit the bill for the hard-working forward.

Bob talked only when he felt he had something to say, and everything he said seemed to convey a sincere finality. His eyes revealed a gentle, intense soul, and he spoke with them as well. Anything outside of the actual game was of not much concern to Bob McCracken. His intensity was evident even now, as the boys splashed in the creek.

"It all don't make a dang bit of difference to me," he offered. "I don't care what the team is named, or what they call the school, or any of that junk the school board is thinkin' about doin'."

The four boys didn't know who the coach would be or even the name of the new team. But they knew they were four of the best players. The Sprudels' last season had been a winning one with a

15-7 record, and young Coach Wells had proven to be a good match for the team.

The previous year, Rex had just returned home from a two-year hitch in the Army and had been looking for a job coaching. He was given the job at his alma mater, West Baden High. He had coached the junior high team earlier, and Frankie, Marvin, Jim, and Paul had played on that team. They had earned 10 straight wins with Rex as coach before he was called into military duty.

To the West Baden city fathers, 25 years was plenty old enough to coach a team. After all, Marvin Wood had been coaching the French Lick Red Devils only a couple of years before he went on to coach Milan, the small-town Indiana team that had won the state championship in 1954. Wood was only 25 years old that year. Rex wasn't much older than his players, and the boys and he had gotten along famously the season before, nearly winning their sectional tournament.

"But man," Bob added, "wouldn't it be great if Coach Wells was hired?" The boys all knew that it was truly a good match, and it seemed like the perfect and logical thing—though the boys weren't counting on this dream coming true. Still, they'd hoped and prayed that somehow, their coach would lead them again in a successful season, even while realizing that was a long shot. The school board was composed mostly of French Lick residents.

Marvin, who had been perched precariously on the old covered bridge abutment, now made his usual attention-getting Tarzan call as he began his swan dive into the stream below, hoping to outdo Frankie's previous dive. Next it was Paul's turn to try to match his good friend's dive. The sophomore center climbed up on the highest point of the bridge abutment, and as he launched his dive, his buddies realized that he was not in the middle of the limestone block structure. Just as Frankie tried to holler a warning that Paul wasn't over the deepest part of the creek, he saw him going head first into just four feet of water from at least 15 feet above the creek.

He splashed hard, and the boys laughed at first. Then, as they saw his writhing legs, they realized he was in trouble. Paul's crew-cut head was completely buried in the muck. He was drowning in mud.

Bob and Marvin simply stood on the bank, stunned at what they were witnessing. Frankie, however, calmly swam over to where the two legs were frantically kicking the air, dove under the brown water, and came up with a sputtering Paul. Spitting mud, coughing, and gasping for air through the dripping gray and brown mud on his face, Paul looked like the "Creature from the Black Lagoon" in the movie they'd seen a couple years back. They burst out laughing, so relieved their friend hadn't broken his neck or drowned.

Paul, though, was more serious. He was thoroughly convinced that a miracle had just taken place, and that Frankie had been the instrument of God's hand, saving him from sure death. Paul, coming from a Calvinist home, was convinced that nothing ever happened on God's green earth that wasn't planned by the Creator and for a certain purpose. Paul considered Frankie his guardian angel from that day forward. When Paul pledged his undying friendship for life to his little buddy, Frankie just said, "Aw, forget it. You'd a done the same for me."

After Paul had regained his composure and cleaned off the mud, all the boys lay on the bank for a while, simply taking in the moment.

"Damn, Paul, that was really crazy what you just did," Marvin chided his buddy. Paul, who had never uttered a cuss word, always ignored his friend's colorful language. His parents had taught him that using this language was surely the first step toward Hell, and now Paul tried again to convey that lesson to Marvin. But he couldn't bring himself to say "Hell"; he said instead, "H-E-double hockey sticks."

Marvin exploded with laughter. "H-E-double hockey sticks!? Are you shittin' me? You can't even say 'hell'? What do you do when you come across that word in the Good Book?" Marvin asked sarcastically.

"Aw, knock it off," Frankie scolded Marvin.

"Sorry, just curious," Marvin replied.

Frankie jumped back into the creek, trying to splash the other boys. Just as he hit the water, Marvin screamed, "Snake!" A water moccasin was trailing just behind Frankie. Paul immediately dove in, grabbed the snake by the tail, swung it in the air twice, and threw it to the opposite bank.

"Jeez Louise, did you see that?" Marvin hollered. "Are you shitting me? Are you shitting me?" Marvin would always pronounce the "g" at the end of his favorite phrase when he was really trying to make a point, as he was now. Frankie didn't even realize what had happened, it had all taken place so quickly.

Paul kept repeating, "Thank you, Lord, thank you, Jesus," over and over as he swam back to where the rest of the boys were still staring in disbelief. Marvin started in on Paul. "That last dive isn't the first time you've landed on that head of yours, is it? I know you go to a church where there's a bunch of tongue-talkin' and snake handlin' goin' on, but that was ridiculous! Those water moccasins are poisonous, ya know!"

Paul, shaken, acted as if he hadn't heard. "Paul's church don't handle snakes no more," Frankie informed Marvin, referring to the Mt. Zion Apostolic Church of the Tabernacle Saints as he climbed the bank. "When ol' Mase Willard got bitten by a big old copperhead that a traveling preacher had brought to a tent revival a few years back, they gave up the snake handlin'," Frankie shared. "Though, I think the congregation still speaks in tongues when the Spirit moves 'em," he added. (Mase Willard was already a bit of a Valley celebrity. When crossing the Ohio River for the first time, he had hollered, "Good-bye, good old U.S. of A.!" The fact he had somehow survived a poisonous snake attack only added to his legend.)

Paul just smiled. "Did you guys know that the Apostle Paul was bitten by a poisonous snake and he threw it right into a fire? It didn't even hurt him a bit, according to the Book of Acts."

Marvin laughed and said, "Well, I can see that you take after the disciple you were named for."

After all the excitement, the boys just lay back on the bank again. Bob, who always felt obliged to insert the latest hit song to mark any occasion, started singing "All Shook Up" in honor of Paul's recent brush with death. Marvin gazed skyward. "Man, look at those hawks just a floatin' around up there." In silence, the boys stared up into the sky. "Wouldn't that be cool to be able to do that?" Marvin thought aloud.

"Hey, what do you think they'll call us . . . uh, I mean the new team?" Frankie suddenly spoke, attempting to divert attention from Paul, who was still visibly shaken.

"Man, I can't imagine anything but the Sprudels or Red Devils," he continued.

"It'll be the 'Springs Valley Something-or-Others,'" Marvin quipped as he stared at the birds circling above. "I heard the town boards were going to use the name of the Springs Valley *Herald* for the new name, since we're combining the two schools."

"Yeah, the 'French Lick and West Baden Somethin'-or-Others' would be too long a name," Frankie added.

Paul piped up. "I heard my dad say he overheard at the barbershop that a couple of the school board members and principal Katter want to call the team the "Grasshoppers," and have green and white as our team colors. Don't mention this to anyone. My dad told me to keep it under wraps."

"What?! *Grasshoppers*? *Green and white*?!" Frankie blurted out. "That's the dumbest thing I've ever heard in my life. I've heard of Hornets and Bees and even Yellow Jackets as a team name, but *Grasshoppers*? They can't even sting!"

Marvin repeated his usual line when in disbelief. "You've gotta be shittin' me!"

"Nope, it's true, and old man Katter has plans on pushing this through," Paul added.

"And by the way, Marvin," Bob said, "we'd never shit you—you're our favorite turd."

"You are hi-lar-i-ous," Marvin shot back.

"Oh, my God—uh, sorry Paul," Frankie exclaimed. "We can't be called the Grasshoppers. We'll be laughed off the court before we even do our warm ups. I mean what is the mascot gonna be? A big old, spittin', bug-eyed green insect that jumps around on the sideline rubbin' his legs together?"

"Uh, I think those are crickets that do that," Marvin laughed.

"Buddy Holly's band is named the Crickets," Bob observed. "Who cares whether it's crickets, grasshoppers, or cicadas? Geez, that just ain't cool—it's so stupid-soundin'.

"Guys, we've gotta do somethin' about this," Frankie urged as he stood, now too upset to lie down any longer.

"Green and white? How about black and white? Now that would be cool colors for our uniforms. Green? That's great if you're the Fighting Irish of Notre Dame or the Ireland Spuds," Frankie said. "Black is serious. Think about it; Zorro wears all black. Johnny Cash wears all black. Black intimidates. Green will make us look like we're just a bunch of plants."

He picked up a rock and skipped it across the creek in frustration. "Gosh, maybe it's just a big joke."

Bob, never one to be too concerned about things he didn't believe he could change, began hopping around from a crouched position, doing his best grasshopper imitation. "I can see every jump ball call now," he quipped. All the boys began laughing at seeing Bob, just an inch shy of six feet tall, hopping along the creek bank. They all began hopping and laughing uncontrollably, imagining each other crouched around the jump circle as the Fighting Grasshoppers.

"We'll mutiny."

"We'll go on strike."

"We'll eat nothing but leaves!"

"We'll spit!"

"We'll refuse to hop!"

All the boys were chiming in at once. "I can hear the radio announcer's play-by-play now," Paul cracked. "The Grasshoppers have swarmed the Rams and are spitting some sort of brown juice as the Paoli team swats frantically at the green insects!"

By now, they had all put their jeans and T-shirts back on and were walking along the county road together back to their homes.

They began thinking up fight songs and cheers that could be sung and chanted at ball games.

"Two bits, four bits, six bits a dollar, all for the Grasshoppers hop up and holler!" "Nobody can out jump the Grasshoppers."

"No one stops a team that hops!"

Each boy took his turn, then Marvin chimed in again. "Wait, wait. I've got a good one. Check this out. 'Them Valley boys are sure ass-whoppers, cause they're a bunch of jumping grasshoppers!"

"Okay, Marvin, you win," Frankie said.

The ideas at last running thin, the subject matter seemed to have run its course. Then, after a long silence, Marvin began singing one of their favorite songs, and they all chimed in. "Let's go to the hop. Oh baby, let's go to the hop. Ah, ah, let's go to the hop." Then Marvin took the verse: "You can really stick it to 'em, you can really out-shoot 'em when you hop," as the other three, through their laughter, tried to sing the background vocal line "At the hop, hop, hop."

As the four walked along, the teen anthem became their farewell to each other for the day. As they came up to each of their houses, the song would lose one part. Paul and Frankie walked alone after saying "Adios" to their buddies.

"We'll just have to fight and pray for what we want," Paul said reassuringly. Frankie just answered, "Or fight for what we don't want!"

At last, Frankie was walking by himself up the old French Lick road to Mt. Airy, where he and his older brother had moved in with their aunt. He walked in silence, lost in his thoughts. He could see again the big black hawks that always seemed to be hovering high above the hills and valleys. The thermal inversion, their science teacher had informed his class, enabled them to glide effortlessly while barely flapping their wings.

"Black Hawks! Now that would be a cool name for the team," Frankie said aloud to himself.

He finally reached his aunt's house. Frankie was hungry after the boys' time at the swimmin' hole. He smelled an apple pie cooling off in the window as he jogged up the long gravel drive. Aunt Edith saw him coming and repeated her usual directive before their evening meal.

"Wash up for supper, Frankie. Food's on the table at six."

Family Matters

Neither Frankie nor his older brother, Benny, lived a very easy life. Their dad hadn't left much to the family, leaving Frankie and Benny to make ends meet. The brothers were offered the job of sweeping the school's floors and cleaning restrooms during the coming year. This was a significant help to their Aunt Edith. Two growing boys can put away a lot of food each week.

The Self family had always seemed to move every 30 days, when the rent was due, and ever since Frankie's dad had died, there just wasn't enough money at the end of each month. The two boys and their mother had been living in the Homestead Hotel in West Baden, when Gertrude Self received a call from Vida Wright. The women had worked together at the Sheraton Hotel. They were both widowed, and the local resort was about the only place a woman could get a job in town.

Vida had informed Gertie that there were some good-paying jobs for the summer up at the Grand Hotel in Mackinac Island, Michigan. The hotel agreed to take them on, and both ladies received their bus tickets and made the trip together to northern Michigan. Once she had settled in, Gertie met a man in Mackinaw City, and she stayed there. The boys, who originally were going to live with their mom's sister only for the summer, were now there permanently.

Aunt Edith made the best attempt to have a family life and provide for her sister's boys. She was always in her freshly ironed, blue-and-white polka-dot house dress with a white apron. Most of the time, she seemed to have flour on her face from her many hours of baking. She relished the idea of taking care of her nephews. She had never married and had children. To Edith, this was not an easy task, but it was a pleasant one. She spent most of her days doing those motherly chores of cleaning the house and shopping for and cooking the family meals. But without a husband around, it was difficult to provide. So, she began baking pies and cakes to bring in money. Frankie loved her baked goods, especially her apple pie, which made him think of his mama.

Suppertime, when he'd join his aunt and older brother around the kitchen table, was special to Frankie. There they connected after another day had taken them all away on their own individual tasks. Frankie took a deep whiff of the pork chops and green bean casserole cooking on the stove. Aunt Edith had recently discovered this new casserole recipe on the back of a Campbell's mushroom soup can. The Selfs and most of Southern Indiana, it seemed, had taken to this dish all at the same time. The new concoction seemed to show up at every pitch-in dinner at church events, social occasions, and family gatherings throughout the year.

This was Frankie's favorite meal, and he couldn't wait for that apple pie. It was the best he'd ever tasted. He had always told his mom that she was the best "cooker" in the world, but now it was his aunt who received his plaudits for her culinary skills.

As they sat around their kitchen table, Frankie rocked back and forth. Tapping his fingers nervously on the yellow Formica table, he kept looking at the casserole. The sight of the green beans had once again brought grasshoppers to his mind. Finally, he blurted out, "They're gonna name our team the Grasshoppers!" He'd decided to share the secret with his brother. Benny just laughed and said, "I wouldn't worry too much about the name of the team. It's how you play that's gonna count—no matter what they decide to call our team."

"But don't ya think the team should have a say-so in what our name's gonna be? I mean, we're the ones with the name on our jerseys. Who's gonna take us seriously?" Frankie argued.

Aunt Edith, between bites of pork chop, just said, "Time has a way of taking care of things. Why don't you wait until school starts and see what all the students think of the new name? If enough people are opposed to the name Grasshoppers," she added, suppressing a chuckle, "then most likely it'll have to be something else. You wait and see, Frankie. Just wait and see."

Benny agreed. "Yeah. Just wait and see, little brother."

Meanwhile, at Paul Radcliff's home, a familiar scenario was playing out at the supper table—green bean casserole included. Like Bob's father, Merle, Paul's dad rarely came to his games, but he had different reasons. Whenever Paul would venture to ask his dad if he would make it to the next one, his dad would say, "It's just a game," and give his pat answer: "When I was a child I did childish things. Now I'm a man, and I've put away childish things." And Paul's mom would always add, "Remember, patience is a virtue."

Paul was tiring of always hearing a Bible verse in answer to his questions. His parents would spout off the memorized scripture, and that was the end of the conversation. Paul didn't like the way his dad used the Apostle Paul's admonition to the church of Corinth to put away childish things as his reason for not attending his basketball games; Paul preferred the passages that alluded to persevering and winning the race.

And despite his mother's admonitions, Paul was not patient. He wanted things fixed immediately and didn't care to wait around to see what someone else was going to do—about anything. Paul knew better than to bring up the new name for the basketball team to his parents. They probably would've started quoting the Old Testament about the plague of locusts visited upon Egypt when Moses was saying to Pharaoh, "Let my people go." Paul just wanted his folks to go to his games and be proud of him.

Not far away, halfway through supper, Marvin Pruett mentioned the new team name to his mom and dad. They didn't respond at first. Marvin, nearly shouting, reiterated his concern. His dad stared straight ahead—but not because he didn't care.

Just a year earlier, Chester Pruett had been blinded in an accident at the Bedford stone quarry, where he had worked his entire adult life. They had been blasting a side of the limestone wall, and Chester hadn't gotten far enough away from 18 sticks of dynamite that had gone off accidentally. The blast cost him the use of one of his hands and both his eyes. Chester would never see his son play basketball again. The colors of the team's uniforms were not going to bother Chester Pruett. He just sat, smiled in his boy's direction and said proudly, "The way you can shoot a ball through that hoop, it won't matter what the name of the team is." Just make those jumpers . . . and keep practicing!" That settled the issue at Marvin's house.

Marvin knew his dad was proud of his abilities on the basketball court. Just last season, Marvin had averaged 25 points per game on the West Baden High School team, which he'd been on since his freshman year. Perhaps his dad was now reliving his own teen years vicariously through his talented son, as Chester had played for the West Baden Sprudels back in the early '40s. Oh, how he now loved to attend those Friday night games, reliving his days of glory, back when he was on the team that won the 1941 Holiday Tournament. "Oh, those were the days," his dad was reminded every time he came to one of Marvin's games.

Mrs. Pruett was known for having become very good at describing the plays during Marvin's games. She was so good at it, everyone said, that she could've easily become a play-by-play announcer. Delilah Pruett would sometimes take her husband to the grade school, where the older trophy case now stood, just so he could touch the trophy with the team's names inscribed on it, and hold that piece of net that he had cut from the hoop after that memorable game. Most of all, Chester enjoyed the way Delilah would recount that game to him, play by play, just as she had become his eyes at Marvin's games.

The dynamite accident had happened in the fall of 1956. Marvin's dad could no longer work, and that put some pressure on the boy— just as in Frankie and Benny's cases—to take the responsibility of bringing in money to keep the family going.

Marvin had played a stellar season for Coach Wells at West Baden during his sophomore year. Shortly after his dad's accident, Marvin ran into the coach at Dad Moore's Drug Store in West Baden one afternoon after school.

"Coach, I'm not going to be able to play this year," he said. "My mom needs help since my dad's been disabled, and I've gotta find a job."

There is nothing much worse for a coach than to hear that the star player will no longer be playing. Coach Wells and Marvin walked together back up the steep hill toward the school.

"Marvin, I think you have a future in basketball," the coach said. "You have the gift. You're the best all-around player I've ever coached—or played with on a team. Please give this some thought. I understand your concern, but don't quit. You'll get by. I'm sure you will. Please know that continuing to play ball could open a lot of doors for you in the future. There are lots of colleges that will want to recruit you, I am certain." Rex left it at that.

Marvin knew that there was no way his folks would be able to afford to send him to college. He decided then and there to just continue working on his game so he could increase his chances at a full-ride scholarship. Rex's advice may have been the best Marvin had ever been given.

As much as Marvin loved to play the game, he could empathize with his dad's love of the game he had once excelled at. On game days, as his son was heading out the door to school, Chester would always holler, "Let's see that jumper work for ya tonight!" Marvin loved his dad and appreciated the special connection that their love for the game provided. And Marvin's mom never missed a game. She could always be heard in the stands after Marvin hit a jump shot. "That's my boy!" This didn't bother Marvin one iota.

Frankie Self, meanwhile, was finishing his apple pie on the front porch. He heard Aunt Edith speaking to someone on the phone. "Whatever they name the team, it's gotta be better than the name Sprudels or Devils," she said. Frankie realized his aunt was on his side.

Frankie thought about what his brother had said to him at the supper table throughout the evening. He decided to sleep on it and not worry any more about something he had no power to change anyway—at least for the time being. Still, he dialed up Paul later that night.

"Paul, remember what we was talkin' about at the swimmin' hole today? I know you're in good standin' with the Lord. Please pray that our team won't be named 'The Grasshoppers.'" Frankie thought that perhaps Paul's connections with the Almighty could get the earthly powers to come to their senses and come up with a better name for their team.

"I promise I'll pray, and keep on prayin'," Paul assured Frankie, then added, "Hey, thanks again for pulling me out of that mud at the swimmin' hole today."

"Ah, forget it. I think you may have saved my life today too," Frankie reminded Paul, then ended the conversation with, "You took care of that snake pretty handily. Pray hard Paul, just pray hard."

He hung up the phone. Still, he couldn't help but worry—not just about the team name but also about the upcoming season: who would make the team, who their coach would be, and what their playing schedule would look like. They would most likely be playing bigger schools now. Frankie whispered a prayer as he was falling off to sleep after an energy-draining day.

"Lord, please take care of all of this. Please Lord."

• CHAPTER 3 •

AND THE TWAIN SHALL MEET

The last month of summer inched along at its usual crawl. The four boys stayed close, continuing their scrimmages, swimming, and discussing the upcoming season. By now, word had gotten around town about Principal Katter's fondness for grasshoppers, and it had become a bit of a joke among the folks around town.

Meanwhile, there were a few boys in French Lick who would meet the West Baden boys for a pick-up game in the park—that "no man's land" between the twin cities. The players truly had respect for one another. They had been competing against each other since sixth grade and knew each other well. While the other students and the parents of each town had a tough time getting along as a result of the ongoing rivalry, the players themselves usually left their aggressions out on the court, having a straightforward, "may the best team win" approach.

On the other hand, during past seasons, most boys from West Baden wouldn't venture into French Lick without numbers on their side. If they decided to cross the railroad tracks and go into French Lick, they would always travel two or three together, just in case there were some Red Devils fans there to give them a rough time. They would rarely get out of their cars for fear of a fight breaking out. Bob McCracken would always remind the boys that during the Centennial, he had bloodied Jimmy Gibson's nose in a fight that occurred inside a replica of a covered wagon that sat just down past the stores on Maple Street. It seems that Jimmy had made fun of West Baden, and that's all it took to get Bob's dander up.

"It was hard-core hate, I tell ya," Bob would say. The hatred was starting to simmer once again as fall approached.

French Lick's Red Devils ball team had not done nearly as well as the West Baden Sprudels the previous season. There was still some pent-up animosity over the losses the Red Devils had suffered, and there had been more than one incident down on the Wells lot on Saturday nights.

French Lick had the movie theater and the corner drug store where a guy could take his gal to get a milk shake, so the West Baden boys had to watch each other's backs when entering enemy territory. Especially during basketball season.

The Chatterbox burger joint was centrally located near both towns' city limits signs, close to the park's outdoor ball court where the French Lick boys usually played throughout the summer. The Chatterbox was the perfect place to go, seemingly neutral territory. Kids from both towns could be seen together at this teen hangout, and it became common ground for everyone. At the Chatterbox, there was nearly always a peace treaty.

The French Lick Fellas

Butch Schmutzler's story was very different from those of the West Baden boys. His dad was the local mortician and ran the Schmutzler Funeral Home up on College Street. The family had money, and Butch drove a '56 Chevy Bel Air—two-toned red and white, the Red Devils' colors—to school each day.

He would usually drive around the school a couple of times to show off his car before he parked. At the end of the day, he would jump in his Chevy and peel out, laying rubber as he made his way home—one block away.

He was a very handsome boy and quite popular with the girls. The other very important consideration was that Butch lived in French Lick. But this was something the boys from West Baden were getting used to—playing ball with a couple of the French Lick players, whom they had always deemed to be the enemy. After a few Sunday afternoon scrimmages out at the Jesuit college's ball court in West Baden, they were getting used to the idea of a blended team from the two schools.

However, Bob McCracken and Butch Schmutzler had to get something straightened out from the get-go. Bob could see that Butch dressed in the finest of clothes, purchased at Rud Bledsoe's clothing store. He had money to spend at the Chatterbox that the other boys didn't. He had a car—a nice, newer car. Bob, on the other hand, wore an old pair of jeans with the legs rolled up at the bottom and a hand-me-down gray sweatshirt to school most days. He didn't care for Butch right off the bat. Bob just thought that Butch had life way too easy—the type of guy Bob thought he would just enjoy punching.

It was these two boys always under the hoop, fighting for rebounds. One day in a pick-up game, Bob gave a hard block to Butch when fighting for a rebound.

"Hey, if you do that again, I'm going to have to do something about it," Butch, the "city boy," complained to his country counterpart. Bob, without any hesitation, answered, "Well, here, let me help you," as he walked over and put his shoulder into Butch, pushing the 6-foot senior backwards.

"Damn, you're one tough son-of-a-bitch, aren't you?" Butch stammered.

In Bob's mind, that got things squared away right then and there.

There may have been a bit of jealousy involved. Butch, having money, a car, and good looks, earned the nickname "Mr. Popularity." But soon Bob would come to appreciate his fellow forward, and they would nearly forget their rough start. Later. Bob confided to Butch, "I was really just looking for a reason to punch you."

Bob, always one to stand his ground, had gained his new teammate's respect, and in the weeks and months ahead, Butch came to know that Bob would always have his back on the ball court. Always. From then on, Butch called Bob "the Enforcer." And that's just what Bob's role became. He wouldn't put up with anyone slacking. Everyone would have to work as hard as he did on the court, or else they would hear from him. He expected every teammate to give 100 percent, 100 percent of the time. Because *he* did.

Mike Watson was Butch's best friend, and they had played basketball together since the sixth grade in French Lick. Mike had one of those likeable faces with a great big smile. He had a space between his two front teeth that Butch always said "you could drive a truck through"—and Mike said the same thing about the space between Butch's two front teeth. Although Mike didn't come from as well-to-do a family as Butch, he let Butch borrow a pair of boots that the "rich boy" really liked. This may have been Butch's way of knocking down any barriers between them, making Mike feel equal.

Frankie and the West Baden boys were aware of Mike's prowess on the ball court, as they were of Butch's. Butch had scored up to 30 points a game for the Red Devils the past season. Paul would speak of the times in earlier seasons when Butch "tore us a new one!" The West Baden boys had played against Mike and Butch many times. Mike, like Frankie, was a 5'7" guard. They were very much alike. Both boys were humble, hard workers. Mike had spent the summer parking cars at the Sheraton Hotel.

One more French Lick boy who would see playing time in the upcoming season was Jack Belcher. Jackie had been a standout on the freshman team the year before, and Mike and Butch expected him to be on the new team as well.

Cruisin'

Tonight would bring a new experience for all the boys. Butch was going to pick them up and they were going to drive up to Paoli—which most folks there in Orange County pronounced "payola"—then to the South Fork drive-in to see what the girls up there were doing on this muggy August evening. Butch and Mike had decided it would be a good thing to get to know their former nemeses better if they were going to be playing on the same team in a couple of months. School would be starting in a couple of weeks, and the boys were eager to do a little cruising to scope things out before books and ball practice slowed what little social life they had.

So he and Mike invited the foursome from West Baden to come along for the 10-mile trip up State Road 56 to the county seat. Mike had called Jackie and Jim Conrad, too, but their parents thought it better that they stay at home. Both boys were only going into their sophomore year, while Butch and Mike were seniors.

The two French Lick fellas picked up Frankie first, then Paul. On their way to Paoli, they picked up their soon-to-be fellow senior Bob McCracken at the Prospect filling station, where he had walked from his farm out past State Road 150—the Northwest Township.

As they drove along, they listened to a Louisville radio station playing Mitch Miller's "The Children's Marching Song," more commonly known as "This Old Man." They chatted about how stupid the song was.

"'With a knick-knack paddy whack, give your dog a bone, this old man came rolling home.' Man, I don't get those words at all. That's a little kid's song," Butch complained. "What'll they play next, the 'Davy Crockett' theme song? Why don't they play some Elvis or some Everly Brothers?"

"My aunt watches 'Mitch Miller,'" Frankie offered, and the other boys all voiced their opinion of the TV star they described as being a "goofy guy with a mustache" who directed a men's choir as robotically stiff as a human being could possibly be.

"Man, that guy could give Ed Sullivan a run for his money on being stiffer than a carp!" Marvin added. Bob remained quiet. His family didn't have a TV.

As they drove on, they talked about the future of their basketball team. Butch Schmutzler and Mike Watson, the French Lick boys, mostly listened to their new West Baden friends, who had all been starters for the Sprudels. They knew these four were exceptional ball players, and they were eager to play on the same team as these boys. They had all taken to each other as if they had always played on the same team, and all realized there would be no problem with blending the two teams into one strong unit. Butch and Mike, however, did

34

wonder how many other former Red Devils would be picked to play on the new Springs Valley team.

The French Lick boys wished that Jackie could've come along. They wanted the West Baden boys to get know him as they did. Jackie Belcher was always good for a laugh and was never too serious.

Mike shared a story that Jackie had told him and Butch. They had recalled one game in the prior season when the West Baden freshman team was putting the hurt on the Red Devils. Every time a West Baden player went to the foul line, Jackie would cross in front of them and pass gas, then say, "This is the *foul* line, isn't it? Don't shoot it short," in hopes of interrupting their concentration.

The Valley's mineral springs were famous for their laxative properties, and Jackie had aimed to capitalize. He knew that the Sprudels would provide another tough game, so he came prepared. Jackie, at 6'1", played center, and he ended up with a lot of jump balls. Before the game, he drank a few sips of the renowned "Pluto water"—just enough to get things churning in his intestines but not enough to keep him from playing; an entire bottle would have kept him hovering near the locker room. Every time he went to the jump circle, he shared the results of the powerful elixir with the opposing player. By the second half, no opposing player would even get in the jump circle any longer.

The boys laughed and laughed, imagining just how bad the entire court must've smelled, as there was no escaping Jackie's silent but deadly "strategy." They all knew they were going to have fun being on the same team this coming season.

"Now, if we can only get Principal Katter to change his mind about our team name," they agreed. The boys from West Baden shared their comedic take from the day at the swimmin' hole regarding a team named Grasshoppers. This caused Mike to make his own joke about the six of them cruising around Paoli's courthouse square, whistling at girls wearing bobby socks and poodle skirts.

"I guess this makes us "lass-shopper grasshoppers," he mused. The West Baden boys all burst out laughing. Butch liked these former rivals more than he thought he would. They had already played a lot of basketball together—just on opposing teams.

This little get-together was good, Frankie thought. The former rivals already felt like teammates. They all realized this was going to work out just fine.

They imagined picking up some Paoli girls, but this never got past the talking stage. They settled for burgers, fries, and cherry Cokes at the South Fork drive-in, then drove back home.

"Hey, let's get together tomorrow and run some plays," Bob suggested as he got out of the car. Frankie answered for all. "Sure, see ya after church."

The Indiana High School Athletic Association had a rule that high school basketball players could not play in a gymnasium on Sundays. But the boys loved to play basketball and Sundays seemed to be as good a time as any to play. So, they would meet at the Jesuit school court. Ball players from several small towns around the area would show up for these games. The IHSAA rule simply made no sense to them; they only wanted to play the game on their "day of rest." So they did—many times.

When all the boys had been dropped off at their homes, Butch parked at the side of his house that was attached to the funeral home where his dad, Ben, worked as the town's mortician. As he got out of his cherry Chevy, he thought, "Tonight went pretty well. Those guys aren't so bad after all."

"Man, that's creepy, living in a house with a bunch of dead people laying around all the time," Marvin once commented as the West Baden boys were taking another swim before the days grew cooler.

"Aw, knock it off. I think your brain is dead," Bob chided his friend. "Somebody's gotta do it—take care of the old folks dyin' off," McCracken added.

Paul spoke up. "My grandma's funeral was there. It was so strange to see her with all this makeup on and with her hair in some sort of hairdo that I'd never seen her wear before. I just wish we didn't have to look at our dead relatives. I just wanna remember my Grandma the way she was when she baked her raspberry cobbler and stood at her stove, cooking those Sunday dinners!"

"I'm with you, man," Frankie chimed in. "Death is too weird. It just don't seem like it should ever happen. Man, I never wanna die. I wanna live forever!"

Paul reminded everyone that they could indeed live forever if they believed in Jesus as their savior.

"The Bible says . . . " Paul began, but Marvin interrupted.

"We know already, we know already. Damn it, you get to preachin' every chance you get."

"Truth is truth," Paul whispered quietly as he got up to leave.

"Yeah, and bull crap is bull crap," Marvin said to himself as soon as Paul was out of earshot.

The next day brought the normal routine of playing a pick-up game after they'd all attended their church services—except for Marvin. His family didn't go to church except on Christmas and Easter. This made his family different from much of the rest of the community. Everyone knows everyone's business in a small town, and this family's sparse attendance at church was known and discussed by all.

The boys didn't mind this a bit. They just liked Marvin for who he was—he was real, and he would always speak his mind. And they sure loved that jump shot of his, especially when that ball swished through the net. A high-scoring guard can make up for a lot of personal and family idiosyncrasies. One could look past what some might perceive as a character flaw, especially when the player could consistently put the ball through the hoop, and Marvin had proven for years that his calling on this earth was indeed hitting those outside jump shots. He had practiced this so many thousands of times that it was just a natural thing to do, almost without thinking. His one-handed jump shot and form were automatic. As some old-timers said, "He could make those strings sing," often hitting nothing but net.

At times Marvin demonstrated his colorful vocabulary on the court. The other boys didn't share his habit, but they had come to know this part of Marvin's personality and even found it somewhat enjoyable. At times when Marvin would let off steam with a few choice words, it seemed to work as a pressure valve for the rest of the team, which was feeling the same frustrations. Marvin would color the air a light blue occasionally after a missed shot or a bad pass, and the other boys just looked past him, as if these words had been spoken by an invisible coach lambasting them for a botched play. This made sense, because Marvin was the go-to man on the court. He was the all-around best ball handler and shooter. This arrangement concerning his language seemed to work well for everyone involved, although during the actual season, Marvin would have to bite his tongue to avoid being thrown out of a game for unsportsmanlike conduct. It was a good thing he sank most of those outside jump shots.

But Marvin never cussed in front of Rex Wells. He had too much respect for his coach.

Each Lord's day, however, the other boys sat through their Sunday school and church sermons alongside their parents. Frankie always felt good on Sundays after church, having just visited God's house and heard the familiar hymns and messages. He always felt as if he'd just received a pat on the back from the Creator. He liked attending the Baptist church of his own accord. No one was making Frankie go to church. Each Sunday he just wanted to be assured once again that there was a God who was hearing and seeing every detail of every life on this planet. He always felt this contentment when leaving the church grounds and heading home for Sunday dinner, feeling that all was right with the world and that he and God were on good terms.

Still, Frankie couldn't help but believe that the result of any endeavor in this life was up to the individual involved. God gives us the tools to work with, he thought; then it's up to each person to figure out how to make the most of things in life with the gifts we're given. In this respect, Frankie and Marvin shared the same philosophy— and they practiced basketball as hard as they did because of it.

Today, one more time, the boys were going to make the best of the daylight hours they had left on the ball court. This is what they loved to do the best.

The Valley Boys

It was a warm sunny afternoon, a day to work up a real sweat and play some good outdoor basketball. Something just felt so right about running plays and playing the game for these boys, who knew each other well. It was as if someone had put a plan in their minds, and they all knew it. Basketball was what they were born to do in their young lives, and their skills were being honed for something that lay ahead. What, exactly, they weren't sure, but nevertheless, something was telling them to practice, practice, practice.

They all knew that the upcoming season would be different from all past basketball seasons. In the back of their minds, a voice seemed to be whispering to each of them: *1958 will be a year you'll always treasure. Live it to its fullest. Play your hardest. Practice relentlessly. Do your best. Something big is at stake.*

These words were never spoken aloud between the boys of the Valley, but they each heard this same voice within, and they were preparing accordingly.

· CHAPTER 4 ·
AND TWO BECOME ONE

Sacrifice and Rebellion

Frankie's brother, Benny, was only a year ahead of his younger sibling. Benny was a very good ball player as well, having played for West Baden in the past and participated in those scrimmages at the Jesuit school as often as possible. However, he missed most of the scrimmages, as he was usually working somewhere for someone, trying to keep the family's head above water.

"Hey, little brother, you know that both of us can't play this year, don't ya?" Since the boys had recently landed the janitorial job every day after school, that meant they couldn't be at the basketball team's practices.

"Yeah, I've been wonderin' about that too," Frankie said, stoically. How were they going to keep food on the table during basketball season? Only one of them would be able to play; the other would keep the janitorial job.

"Why don't we toss for it?" Benny suggested. "I'm heads, you're tails." He didn't even wait for Frankie's response. He quickly pulled a quarter from his pocket, tossed it in the air, caught it, and slammed it down on the back of his hand. "Dang it! You win, Bubby," Benny said, not even showing the coin to Frankie.

Frankie was speechless. He just looked up to his older, taller brother curiously, his eyes full of love and gratitude.

"Thanks, Benny," was all he could muster.

"Hey, just play your butt off out there this year, okay?" Big brother ended the conversation.

Frankie didn't realize the coin wasn't even a quarter, but a metal slug Benny had found. Benny knew how badly his brother wanted to play, and something inside just told him to control the issue before them. Benny would keep working.

Frankie recognized the import of what his brother had just done, and he would never forget it. He would be the one to keep playing basketball. It was truly an act of brotherly love. Benny Self, it turned out, may have been even more selfless than his little brother.

Protest

"Say NO to Grasshoppers—Yes to Black Hawks" could be read on signs and placards throughout the halls of the high school. In parades, up and down the corridors and at rallies after school, the students voiced their opinions—loudly. They were even marching on the lawn of the high school, which like most of French Lick, sat on a hill. The way these kids were behaving so feistily since the two schools had merged was the talk of the town. The protests were all too common a sight the first two weeks of the 1957–58 school year.

The French Lick High School building now housed the two schools' student bodies as they struggled to adapt to consolidation. Now, one segment in particular was speaking out. Since it was the West Baden High School that had been forced out of its building, and it was the kids from West Baden who'd had to leave their school behind, there were a few holdouts. They were probably hearing too much negative talk from their parents about this consolidation.

However, the boys on the team understood what was going on, and they believed it was up to them to help pull everyone together. Frankie had made his rounds and implemented his debating skills, talking up the negative aspects of a team named "the Flying Grasshoppers" and team colors of green and white, chosen by Principal Noble Katter. Fighting for this cause was something that every student could join in on.

But the young people were amassing quite a campaign. Posters depicting an insect being devoured by a black hawk were everywhere, since the art teacher sided with the students. There was even a drawing of the mascot the students wanted. Frankie had given his brother's sketch to a gifted art student, Phil Beaver, who produced a fitting Black Hawk symbol. The profiled head of a black hawk, with a very determined look in its beady eye, couldn't have been a more proper mascot image or more appropriate to the Valley.

"That black hawk my brother drawed up looks great," Frankie informed Bob McCracken as they passed each other in the hall.

"Yeah, with those beady eyes, it kinda looks like you," Bob answered.

But all the students agreed with Frankie and the other players' assessment of the new mascot and team name. That is, all but Principal Katter's son, who was a senior, and greatly outnumbered.

Daily, more signs appeared at the school. A movement had begun. In the eyes of many teachers and parents, these agitated young people seemed to be changing.

"It's that damn Elvis the Pelvis who got all of this started," Ben Schmutzler remarked one day, as he sat in Bill Andrew's barber's chair. He was getting his weekly shave at the barbershop that sat just across from the high school, and he was certainly in a lather.

He continued to gripe. "I been seein' kids paradin' around the school grounds carryin' signs, hollerin' 'We are the Black Hawks!'"

"Yeah, it's that rock 'n' roll devil music that's getting inside these young'uns, gettin' 'em all riled up," added another man. "Maybe some drill sergeant will whip that long-side-burns-and-Brylcreem boy into shape now that Uncle Sam has him serving his country."

"You can only imagine what he was doing on 'Ed Sullivan' that first time. He was vulgar," Hank Harrison growled. "He was moving below the waist so much, they couldn't even show it on TV!"

"Yep, I think you fellers are right. Elvis has infected our kids' minds. They think they can rule the world with rock 'n' roll music," Paul Grigsby remarked.

"Just wait a couple of years," another man said, not even looking up from his *Field and Stream*. "This craziness will blow over. It's just another fad."

The consensus in the barbershop that day was that the adage "Children should be seen and not heard" had long ago disappeared, much to their chagrin.

There was a bit of history at play for the students. Both schools, the French Lick Red Devils and the West Baden Sprudels, had always had to deal with jokes about their mascots' names. Both names were linked inextricably to the towns' efforts to market its sulphur springs, which for many years had been one of the main drawing cards for the two luxury hotels from yesteryear. From the Valley's underground springs bubbled forth waters that emitted a foul odor, but folks from far and wide would visit the Twin Cities spas to bathe in and drink from these springs for their purported health benefits. The "Pluto Water" marketed by French Lick was in reference to Pluto, who, in Greek mythology, was the god of the underworld. He was generally rendered simply as a powerful man with a full beard. But as Pluto's image was unfamiliar, a more recognizable image of the god of the underworld was substituted to market Pluto Water: a red devil, complete with horns and a tail.

(The French Lick team name had once been changed to the "Pluto City Wonder Boys" when a certain coach had agreed to coach there only if the name would be changed. Many a churchgoer in both towns had believed it was high time to rid their teams of names that evoked the underworld. An earlier iteration of the mythic Pluto, in fact, was named Hades. Nevertheless, for one season, the French Lick team name did indeed become "the Pluto City Wonder Boys," but as soon as the coach left town, the team went back to being called the Red Devils.)

Where French Lick had Pluto, West Baden had "Sprudel," a wood gnome character chosen as the symbol of their bottling company. (*Sprudel* is the German word for mineral water.) Years ago, both towns had statues carved in stone of these images, and these mysterious creatures had become ingrained in the minds of the older generation. Through the years their beloved basketball teams had become strongly linked with these ancient symbols.

But these images were certainly not going to be missed by the younger generation. French Lick fans had long ago tired of the joke poked at their Red Devils about the "Beelzebub Booster Club" and the cheer, "Fire up, big team, fire up!" Sportswriters, in their attempts to write colorfully, went on to employ every other name possibly associated with Red Devils—including "Imps," "Satans," and "Demons." The Sprudels, meanwhile, had to deal with their own problems. The name did not exactly inspire fear, and it was excellent fodder for jokes. Their opponent's fans would whitewash "The Sprudels are noodles!" or "We'll be brutal on the Sprudels!" on their cars, although it was usually the Sprudels who brutalized their opponents. These and other insults had been a part of every game for years, and the Springs Valley students weren't going to allow another team name to be chosen for them—especially one that could so very easily be turned into a cheap punch line.

Could the two towns now trust a bunch of kids to come up with something as important as the new school's team name? After all, practically everyone in the "Twin Cities" felt they had a stake in this decision: their very own heritage, their past, their memories, their lives.

Coach Wells realized that the students were serious. He called the Indiana High School Athletic Association and asked for a complete list of all the high school mascot names in Indiana. He and the students did not want one of the same old, worn-out animal names that other teams tend to have. They wanted something new—something fresh.

Principal Katter called an emergency meeting of the school board.

"This is getting out of hand, and we must put a stop to these youngsters' rebellious spirit!" The balding, bespectacled administrator was almost shaking as he made his declaration to the other men sitting across from him.

"Well, maybe the kids have a point." Bank manager Bill Cave spoke first, after an excruciating minute of silence. He went on.

"I think that maybe some consideration should be given to the students. After all, it is their school, their team, their image that they want to project to the rest of Southern Indiana."

Ed Beaty spoke up next. "I think they may be onto something with the Black Hawks name. Those birds are pretty plentiful a-flyin' 'round these parts."

"Yes, I agree," piped up Burel Conrad. "'Black Hawks' does sound a bit more intimidating as a team name than 'Grasshoppers.'"

"Now, just a minute here." Principal Katter tried to take control of the meeting. But it was too late. By this time all the school board members were in total agreement about the team's new name. They all liked the sound of "Black Hawks." It simply sounded more like a team that had some fight in it as opposed to an insect that can be squished underfoot.

"I believe it's time for a vote." All agreed with school board president Bill Cave's suggestion. The vote was indeed taken in the next minutes, and then it was official: the school board would allow the students to vote on the new name for the Springs Valley team. "Mustangs," "Grasshoppers" and "Black Hawks" were the three choices.

This decision had been unanimous—almost. Principal Katter stuck to his guns and sat stunned that not another man in the room had agreed with his dream name and colors for "his" school's team. He left the meeting in a huff, mumbling something about how "everyone knows that green is a more positive color than those 'non-colors,'" black and white.

"They're not even on the color wheel," he mumbled as he raced out the door.

The school board understood what their decision would do for the merging student body, and letting the students vote was a brilliant move on their part. The men must have known that this would solidify the consolidated school and create unity going into this year of change. The students welcomed this news as true validation. This was the students' school and team, and they would be the ones to choose their image. The students had believed in something strongly enough to stand up and rally for it, and now they would see their vision come into being.

Frankie called Marvin Pruett that night to tell him the news as soon as Butch Schmutzler called him with the scoop. Butch's dad had been at the school board meeting and shared the outcome of the gathering as soon as he got home. Within five minutes of Butch hearing the word, three of his new West Baden buddies were breathing sighs of relief.

When Frankie called Paul, the 6'1" center replied calmly to the news. "I knew we'd never be the Grasshoppers," he said. "I prayed about it—earnestly."

"Keep those prayers comin' Paul. I think you're onto somethin' there," Frankie said rather seriously. Paul just kept saying, "Praise God from whom all blessings flow."

Frankie called Mike Watson and told him the good news. Bob McCracken would have to wait until tomorrow to hear; his family had no electricity and no phone. When Frankie first shared with Marvin that he'd tell Bob of the school decision tomorrow, Marvin joked, "Can Bob read smoke signals?" Everyone would be delighted for this good news about the team name—except Bob. He just didn't care. He'd be the one who'd always say, "Let's just play ball, okay?" And play ball that boy did.

The news spread among the student body the following day. The vote was taken immediately during a convocation announced by the vice principal. Noble Katter wanted nothing to do with what he viewed as an impending disaster.

The student body vote was nearly unanimous; it was settled. The new name was the Springs Valley Black Hawks. The students' demonstrations had worked, and now their passion for the newly formed team name had created an energy that no one could ignore.

One more thing had to be decided. What would their team colors be? Black, at least, did seem to be the obvious primary color.

One diplomatic art student came up with an idea one day in Mrs. Ellis's art class. He wondered what would happen if purple and red were mixed together? Maybe that would satisfy the holdouts who had wanted to keep their old school colors. Mrs. Ellis told the imaginative student that he had a clever idea. The mix created a dark color—almost black. At least that's what the art student told everyone of the results of his experiment. It was a very dark fuchsia, close enough to black to be promoted as the new school color and helping to appease the older students and fans of the teams from each town.

Still, there was discussion about the complementary color until it was decided: white with gold and black trim would be the new school colors. The boys on the team, as well as the other students, were certain they had made the right choice in both the team name and their colors. It was simply meant to be.

There was one suggestion the students took from Coach Wells. He was the one who suggested gold trim to go with the black and white. When Coach Wells was ordering uniforms for the team, the salesperson he spoke with showed him a gold fabric and it was chosen for one of their uniforms. The team would wear gold for their away games and white with black for their home games. These were great school colors. The black and white seemed to serve as reminders that this was all new and something untried in this part of Indiana. The gold? This color was also meaningful. There would be much "gold" to mine in the next few months.

Springs Valley students wanted to stand apart and be their own school, their own team, their own image. They got what they wanted, and were soon to get a heck of a lot more.

Now their first battle was over, but there were to be many more battles ahead for the young players.

• CHAPTER 5 •
A MATCH MADE IN HEAVEN

The Team

A crowd of boys gathered around the gym door bulletin board reading a recently posted notice.

Basketball Tryouts
Monday, October 1st

Twenty-five boys showed up that day with high hopes of making the team. Fewer than half of them would become Black Hawks. Of course, the standouts were Marvin Pruett, Paul Radcliff, Bob McCracken, Mike Watson, Butch Schmutzler, and little Frankie Self. These guys were already a team that was jelling, thanks to those pre-season scrimmages. Plus, their old coach, Rex Wells, much to the delight of the West Baden boys, had been voted to lead the new Springs Valley team. It had been the consensus on the school board that anyone who had won 15 games the year before deserved to be the coach of this newly formed team—even if he was only "25 years old and wet behind the ears," as some of the French Lick fathers had noted more than once during those barbershop conversations.

Wells, who had coached the West Baden team the previous year, had decided to start working on his master's degree at Indiana University. He'd had no idea that he was being considered for the job. After all, he had been the coach of the French Lick Red Devils' greatest nemesis. Why would they even consider him to enter their "hallowed grounds"? The board members had asked for opinions of former players, going all the way back to the sectional champ Red Devils teams of 1943 and '46. All the former players agreed: Rex Wells was the man for the job. Plus, he was young, and that made him affordable.

The day after tryouts, the names of those picked for the team appeared on the bulletin board. Five seniors, two juniors, and three sophomores were chosen to be the first Springs Valley Black Hawks basketball team. Butch Schmutzler, Mike Watson, Jerry Breedlove, Bob McCracken, and George Lagenour were the seniors. Frankie Self and Marvin Pruett were the two juniors, and Jim Conrad, Paul Radcliff, and Jack Belcher were the sophomores who made the cut.

Two other boys who didn't make the team became part of the organization as student managers. Billy Rose and Bob Trueblood chose this route rather than not be around basketball the upcoming season. They loved the game as much as the boys who made the team; they simply didn't have the same level of talent. They became an important part of the organization, showing up for every practice, and sometimes even taking part in the dreaded running of laps and sprints.

Being a student manager was certainly better than not having anything at all to do with the team. Their duties were to make sure the uniforms and towels were cleaned regularly, keep water on the sidelines for the players, and have the first aid kit handy for any cuts and sprains that occurred during games. They both adjusted well to not playing. In fact, the two boys recognized the importance of their positions. They liked being around the coaches and overhearing the discussions about various players, upcoming games, and strategies in the inner sanctum. The title of "manager" attached to each of their names felt good, and the two boys believed they were as much a part of the team as Frankie and Marvin.

The boys who made the cut were called together for a meeting and first practice after school. Coach Wells spoke.

"Fellas, this is *our* team. Not West Baden's. Not French Lick's."

Rex, like most folks in the area, tended to pronounce the word "French" with a bit of a long "e," making it sound more like *Freench Lick*. "We're Springs Valley Black Hawks now. Forget the Sprudels and Red Devils. Those days are gone. You can honor those teams of the past now by becoming the best team you all can be."

Rex then brought out a large pad of art paper with some sort of drawing on it. He pulled the top sheet over the easel it sat upon, and the boys saw the drawing of their mascot for the first time—the emblem that would soon appear on every notebook in the school and on bumper stickers around town. It was a cartoon-like drawing of an anthropomorphic black hawk, standing in a basketball jersey, shorts, and Converse high-tops while spinning a basketball on the tip of his wing.

The boys all applauded.

Rex had decided on his own to have this mascot created.

"Hello, is this Walt Disney Studios?"

The coach had made a call to the world-famous cartoon and animated movie department in California, more than a world away from his hometown. He simply thought, "Why not? All they can do is say 'No.'" He reached one of the artists on the phone and made his request.

"Say, I'm a coach of a high school basketball team here in French Lick, Indiana. You may have heard of it: French Lick, Indiana. It used to be a famous resort town in the Midwest. I'm calling to see if I could get someone out there to draw a picture of a Black Hawk—you know a bird, but make it look somewhat human-like—uh, you know, kind of like Woody Woodpecker."

The artist he was speaking to on the other end, nearly 2,000 miles away, was probably smiling to himself, wondering about the chutzpah of this young coach—not only contacting the world's most successful cartoon film creators at Walt Disney Studios but also mentioning Woody Woodpecker, who was not even a Disney character. This project might even borrow time from an artist working on the next *Cinderella* or *Bambi* animation.

Yet the artist agreed. The drawing of the new mascot was in

Rex's hands a week later—still another in a chain of serendipitous events—and the season hadn't even begun.

This drawing encompassed what the team and students wanted: a stronger, cooler image that certainly represented youth and change. The Disney Black Hawk was drawn with a serious determination in its eye, a look of confidence, almost cocky, yet appearing to be having great fun at the same time. This was different from any other school's mascot, and it fit this unique team quite well: sure of itself, determined, but having the time of its life.

Rex began his talk. "This is a new beginning for all of us. We don't have anything to live up to but our own pride in what we can accomplish together as a team. I picked you guys for a reason. I didn't choose some of the players who played last year on the Sprudels and Red Devils. You've noticed I have chosen four out of the Sprudels' starting five and Jim Conrad from our freshman team from last year. I only went with what I could judge from what I saw on the court during tryouts.

"I chose you for your athletic abilities and talents. I chose those with the best skills, and those with a good attitude. That's it. I didn't feel pressure or a need to have a balance of players from each school, although, that is exactly how it turned out—five boys from French Lick and five boys from West Baden made the team. That may have sounded like a fair idea to some, but believe me, I simply chose who I believe are the best players. When we're battling in some of these games this season, you'll be glad we have the strongest players on this team. Now let's get out there and run some laps, and then we'll do some sprints. We'll repeat that until you're dog tired, then we'll divide you up into shirts and skins for some scrimmages—after a little written test."

No one groaned; they simply obeyed their young coach. After the players ran 20 laps around the gym, they "ran the lines"—a drill that many players refer to as "the suicide drill." They would run from the baseline under a basket to the foul line and bend over to touch it, run back to the baseline and touch it, run to the mid-court line and touch it, and then return to the baseline again. While some coaches would keep the sprints contained to one side of the court, Coach Wells kept them sprinting to the opposite baseline, then repeat the process from the opposite side. It is a very grueling exercise, but it gets a team whipped into shape.

Rex Wells was known for being more of a teacher of basketball than a coach. He wanted to know just how much these boys understood about the game—so he asked questions and they got out their pencils and paper. After the short test, the coach collected the papers. Then he told them, "Our schedule will be posted for you to see after practice. Now, get running laps. Let's get in shape!"

The boys—even as they ran their laps and seemingly never-ending sprints—were glad to be back on the hardwood and playing ball again. Even the familiar smells put them in their comfort zone: locker rooms, sweat-drenched T-shirts, wintergreen salve for sprains. They were gym rats.

For Frankie, in fact, and for any high school boy who played for his team, life couldn't get much better. It was the only credential he needed. The echo of a coach's whistle, or the booming voice calling plays and rumbling throughout a high-ceilinged gymnasium, were siren songs to all the Valley Boys. The fluorescent lights reflecting on the polished floor, players scrimmaging and shouting, "I'm open!" or "Way to go!" or "Good pass, man!" and the incessant squeaking of rubber-soled high-tops—it was all intoxicating, a heady mixture of sights and sounds that welcomed Frankie home every fall, his favorite season of the year.

The junior guard loved the camaraderie of the team and putting together both a good offense and defense. Words couldn't describe his elation at a good play, when he'd dribble the ball down the court, penetrate to the basket, and fire a bullet pass to an open Marvin Pruett for his patented jump shot. So many times, he'd make a quick dish-off to Paul at the center position or Bob at forward, each getting around his man for an easy lay-up.

Only 10 boys had been picked to be on this team—just enough to have a second string. The "bench-warmers" made up a very good team themselves, and they would get better and better scrimmaging every day against the starting five. The second string always gave the starting five a tough scrimmage. The first and second string made each other stronger, practice after practice.

Coach Wells could tell that these boys had been playing together over the summer. He was pleased to see their familiarity with each other and the ease with which they moved the ball up and down the court. It was as if he had discovered something rare and stumbled upon a gold mine of talent, and all he had to do was extract the gold within each player. Coach Wells liked what he was seeing already. He knew that this would be a fun team to coach. He did have something to prove to some of the townsfolk who weren't sold on the idea of a 25-year-old coach.

At the end of practice, the coach blew his whistle and gathered the boys around him. "Guys, listen up. Sit down for a minute before you hit the showers. I'm liking what I'm seeing here. I know we have some potential. So, now for a minute or two, I'm going to be serious with you.

"I just want you to know a couple of things. I want you to ask yourself, all of you, 'What is possible? What is truly possible?' I want you to always remember this: Never give up. Never give up. All things are truly possible to those who believe and direct their energies toward positive goals. The difference between being good and being great is giving that little extra effort toward a job . . . choosing to be a builder and not a destroyer. And of course, always being honest with yourself."

The coach paused.

"Well, that's it, fellas. This is what I expect from every one of you, and you can expect the same from me as your coach. Now, hit the showers and go home and eat a good supper."

The boys jogged into the locker room, tired enough to refrain from speaking until after their showers. This had been a tough first practice.

"Man, did you see the teams we're going to be playing this year?" Butch lamented to Marvin when reading their posted game schedule.

"Yeah, I can read too, Bozo," Marvin informed his new friend.

Frankie overheard and smiled. "We'll be ready for any of those bigger schools," he said quietly. The other boys, viewing the schedule for the first time, just whistled through their teeth or remained soberly still when reading the schedule.

"My gosh, Jasper is four times our size," George Lagenour sighed. "They usually play French Lick as a warm-up to their regular season," he added.

Frankie sensed the others' worries.

"Guys, we've been playing ball together and against each other since we were in sixth grade. We'll have a strong team this year. I just know it. Let's just take 'em one at a time, practice our hardest, and do our best to play team basketball. Whaddya say?"

Frankie Self was an anomaly. He was only 5'7" tall, but he could nearly dunk the ball—something that hardly any high school basketball player of any size could do in the 1950s. Coach Wells nicknamed him "Jumping Jack." Frankie would take the ball "to the hole," hit the rim, duck under the backboard, and land on the stage that was just past the goal. It looked nearly impossible.

But Frankie was very athletic—and he demonstrated this as well in his speed and his ability to play defense like no one else. Whereas Marvin's defense was limited—his expertise was hitting outside jump shots (which today would all be three-pointers)—Frankie was so quick that he could guard two opposing players. During scrimmages, Coach Wells would holler, "Pruett, I couldn't play you if Self wasn't guarding your man for you."

Frankie usually let his actions speak for themselves, but he was hearing too much worry in the voices of even some of the upperclassmen. Frankie may have been only a junior, but he was wise and tough beyond his years. He was a born leader, with a quiet strength on and off the court. The rest of the team knew it and they listened to him. Marvin understood that Frankie had a certain way about him that invited people into his world. Everybody loved Frankie.

October's first three weeks went by with hard practices every day after school. Coach Wells even called a couple of optional Saturday morning practices that everyone attended. Every player could see the team getting better, stronger, and more confident with each passing day. They'd be ready for their debut as a team November 8 against the Shawswick Farmers—just two weeks away.

The Coach

Rex Wells was a humble man with a quiet demeanor—something like Frankie, but with a few more years on him. He had just returned from his two-year hitch in the Army, and he'd just gotten married in August to the girl he fell in love with during his years at West Baden High. In fact, August proved to be a monumental month for Rex Wells. He signed his contract to coach Springs Valley High on August 1 for a $4,250 annual salary. He was married on the 18th, honeymooned, turned 25 on the 22nd, and began coaching on August 31, the first day of school.

Rex and his beautiful wife, Margaret, were happy to be living in their hometown, known for its love for basketball and historic hotel. Their wedding at the local Methodist church was very small, with just family and a few friends attending. The newlyweds left the ceremony, hopped in Rex's 1956 two-door Oldsmobile, and drove to New York for their honeymoon. Where else but Niagara Falls, the most popular honeymoon destination in America? Rex wanted to have the greatest honeymoon possible, so Niagara Falls it had to be.

Rex's Aunt Harriet had phoned ahead and had the hotel management leave a bottle of champagne in their honeymoon suite, but they both laughed when they entered the room and saw the bottle of bubbly on ice. They were not drinkers, and didn't feel they needed any adult beverage to relax. The couple was rapturously in love—intoxication was unnecessary.

Margaret believed in her husband like no other living soul.

"Honey," Rex would confide, "I don't know what I'm doing coaching this new team. I don't mean that I don't really know how to teach this game. I only mean that I didn't think I had even a small chance at getting the job. But here I am.

"I have so many people mad at me already—and the season hasn't even begun. That Wilson boy's father has called me a dozen times asking why his son didn't make the team," he went on. "I don't know if I can take any more disgruntled parents walking into my office complaining that their boy should be starting or playing another position. One of the mothers walked in today, threw her son's old jersey in my face, and started cussing me out!"

After a few of these confessions, Margaret would lean over, rub her husband's head lightly, kiss him, and then whisper, "You may be young, but you're a good coach. Don't forget, you nearly won the sectional last year for West Baden and led the Sprudels to 15 wins. You always make good decisions. You married me, didn't you?"

Rex would smile at her oft-repeated joke, yet he did need to hear it. He knew so many people were looking to him to lead this new team. So many had made dire predictions. "This will never work." And, "There'll be too much conflict." Rex was feeling the conflict already, as unhappy parents called him to share unsolicited advice. Someone even wrote a comment that appeared on the *Springs Valley Herald* editorial page. "*If God wanted one team and one young coach, then he wouldn't have made these two towns.*" This logic didn't make much sense to Rex, but it still hurt to be thought so little of—even from someone who apparently believed that God himself had formed French Lick and West Baden, just as He had the Grand Canyon.

Many of the locals wanted things to remain just the way they had always been. Most would've been happy seeing about as much change in their way of life from year to year as occurred in that great big hole in the ground out in Arizona. They didn't cotton to so much newness surrounding their game of basketball. Plus, at least a dozen families were now seeing their boys coming home after school and moping around, instead of being at basketball practice every day after school.

🏀 🏀 🏀

"How could that young whippersnapper of a coach not have my Daryl playing?" one father was overheard at church saying. "My boy was first string last year! This year will be a disaster."

At the barbershop, Earl Wininger was overheard making dire predictions about Coach Wells. "This kid got lucky last year, but wait till he faces those bigger schools' teams, like the Loogootee Lions or the Jasper Wildcats. He'll get eaten alive!"

These types of comments were heard all around the community at supper tables—particularly those evening meals of the families of boys who had failed to make the team.

"I'm not receiving too many 'Good luck, Coach' cards in the mail, honey," Rex joked to his wife during supper. Margaret, who had continued going to Hanover College in Jefferson County, down on the Ohio River, had had a late class. Rex had even beaten her home after practice. So, their late-evening meal had called for a modern-day invention—the frozen TV dinner. Television sets, now in nearly every American household, seemed to have spawned several unexpected products, including TV dinners and TV trays.

Margaret laughed as she carefully peeled the aluminum covers off their three-course Swanson dinners. "Dang, these things are hot!" Rex exclaimed. "They must be 4,000 degrees! And why are they called 'TV dinners' in the first place?"

"Well, I guess it's because one has to do something to occupy the time while these things are cooling off," Margaret answered. As if on cue, she walked over and turned on their black-and-white Zenith.

"This is Your Life" was on. The program would invite a well-known celebrity into the studio under some pretense, then surprise them with milestones from their lives and careers. The producers would reveal various people from each celebrity's past—childhood friends, teachers, family members, and the like—from behind a curtain, but only after the celebrity tried to identify the disembodied voices offering up tales of the celebrity's former life.

"Good," Rex said. "I like this show," so Margaret got out their TV tray tables, and they sat there watching as their dinners cooled.

Toward the end of their supper, Rex's mind began wandering back to his own life, and his dilemma. Finally, he voiced his thoughts.

"It's as if half the town wants the team to fail just so they can see me go down in flames."

"Rex, honey, they just aren't happy at this moment. They're just angry that their boy or their grandson didn't make the team, or they're just holding onto the past a bit too much. That's all. This will all blow over after a couple of wins. They'll cool off one day—just like these TV dinners eventually did."

Rex laughed. He needed some levity at that moment, and he loved his wife's sense of humor. Margaret's words helped, but reading editorials about his lack of experience and his inability to put the proper players together were taking their toll on the young coach. After all, he was in only his second year of coaching high school boys.

He and Margaret always asked each other about their day, but the conversation lately usually wound up with Rex telling her about the various players on the new team. She loved to hear her handsome husband, dark hair cropped in a crew cut, go on and on about his favorite subject.

Many of the folks in town believed that 25 years isn't enough time to have much experience at anything in life, much less develop the coaching skills required for high school basketball. But Margaret didn't believe this, and neither did a few former players who recognized Rex's prowess as a coach.

Rex would sometimes doubt himself. Coaches need to be psychologists, he knew, while teaching the ins and outs and subtleties of the game. They must understand their players. The profession is as much about human interaction as finding raw talent on the court.

"What if we don't have a winning season?" he would wonder to himself late at night, when his sleep would be interrupted by a dream of being run out of town by an angry mob of red devils taunting him with pitchforks. Yet the next day's ball practice would always bring him back to a comfortable reality.

As he watched his boys running the plays he'd drawn on the

chalkboard at the pre-practice meetings, Rex knew he had a good team that would be very competitive. He knew that his boys knew how to play the game. All they needed was a little direction. And the 10 players respected their coach because he knew how to play the game. In fact, during practices, Rex would say to Marvin, "Hey, Pruett, try to guard me." Rex would give Marvin a fake and go around him and score every time. Rex was "the best player on the team," some of the boys would say. His years of playing college ball had served him well. The team appreciated this about their coach, and they wanted only to be like him—a good ball player. A smart ball player. A good man.

At first Rex was unsure if the star players for French Lick, Butch and Mike, would try to outdo the boys from West Baden. "Would these boys meld into one?" was the coach's big question. "Can they play team basketball?"

The coach's question was soon answered. After a few practices and scrimmages, Rex's confidence grew. Rex was not really an X's and O's type of coach, but he could see that these boys understood his method of playing the game—team basketball. He saw it in Frankie, Mike, Marvin, Bob, Paul, Butch—all the boys. In a way, they were a dream team. Each boy seemed to understand the bigger picture and naturally accepted his role on the squad.

Jack Belcher, Jim Conrad, George Lagenour, and Jerry Breedlove were proving to be good off-the-bench players, but after the starting five, it was hard to determine the best player with the second team. That's how good the second-string players were. Through the season, they would all end up with a lot of playing time, as they played their positions nearly as well as the starters. The boys from the Valley had what is referred to as a "deep bench." They all had heart as well as natural talent. When those two ingredients come together, wonderful things can happen—even when you're the little guy or the underdog.

The young coach hoped that his Hawks could soar this season. How high he didn't know, but he could see they were ready to leave the nest, represented by the safety of their practices and the softer schedules of the past. It was time for them to spread their wings. He was there to push them out of that nest, and the boys were ready. They couldn't wait to get out on the court and do what they felt their jobs were—to play team basketball in Southern Indiana.

As Rex left the last practice before their first game, he smiled as he looked at the poster of the cartoon Black Hawk he had commissioned from the Disney artist. He recalled the recent events with the team name and school colors being supported by the students. He was young enough to relate to the students and he had sided with them. But he realized that he was fortunate at his age to be coaching this new team.

As he paused before the Black Hawk mascot, spinning that basketball on the tip of its wing, he saw the personality of his boys. Tough and confident, but having so much fun at the same time. This was his team, and he felt good about its immediate future.

These boys were ready to play, just as Frankie had assured them—even against those bigger teams.

· CHAPTER 6 ·

LET THE GAMES BEGIN

The First Game:
Black Hawks vs. the Farmers

Friday, November 8, finally arrived, and the entire school was abuzz with excitement and anticipation to see their new team in action. The student body, for the most part, had fully accepted the schools consolidating and forming one basketball team. They all knew how strong the West Baden team had been last year. Five of those players were on the new team, and three were on the starting five for Springs Valley High. Best friends Butch and Mike were the two starters from the French Lick team.

The first game of the new season would be a home game, and a Booster Club rally fired up the students during the last class period of the day. The two female cheerleaders, Billie Jo Harris and Beverly Runyon, debuted their new black-and-white pleated skirts, which they'd made in Home Economics class, and sweaters emblazoned with a big, golden "V" overlaid by the word "Springs" in script. The male cheerleader, Joe Ellis, had the same sweater and carried the three-foot loud hailer bullhorn to be used shortly. Coach Wells spoke briefly, welcoming the students into the Booster Club section. Various posters of Black Hawks were hoisted into the air. Cheers erupted for the 10-man squad as they walked onto the court.

That same week, the new school mascot had been painted by student artist Phil Beaver on the wall above the stage side of the court.

61

But this wasn't the Disney depiction. This was more realistic—more like the actual hawks that always circled the skies above the two towns—and it looked as if it were ready to attack and put fear into any opponent. No one, not even the players, had been allowed to see it before the pep rally; it had remained covered since being painted. Everyone marveled at the striking image. The profile of the hawk's head looked fierce, with its sharp and intimidating beak turned down in a determined fashion. Looking every bit the bird of prey, with its squinting, beady eye seemingly focused on its next meal, made everyone just that much more pumped up for the opening game of the season.

Not only were there drawings and paintings depicting the black hawk mascot—there was a live mascot. The Agan family, who owned the local West Baden grocery store, had an eight-year old son, Jeff. They were close friends with Rex Wells's family. One day prior to the season opener, Rex had commented to his Aunt Harriet how great it would be to have a live mascot at each game.

"Do you think we could get Hoober Agan's boy to wear some sort of black hawk suit?" the coach asked his aunt. The call went out to the Agans and their third-grade boy agreed wholeheartedly to dress up for each game in an all-black outfit, complete with an over-the-head mask of a hawk's head that his mother and Aunt Harriet created. What eight-year old wouldn't love to do that? Most high school teams in this era did not have a live mascot, running around the court during time outs and between quarters, and this would only add to the mystique of this new school and team.

The student paper had been doing its job, enthusiastically promoting the newly formed team. The sports reporter, Billy Ray Wininger, wrote as "the Old Rebounder." Sports reporters for the French Lick school paper had used this pseudonym since the '40s. Billy Ray had attended every practice. He had confirmed Coach Wells's impressions: this was already a very sharp team.

"Two bits, four bits, six bits a dollar! All for the Black Hawks, stand up and holler!" The old gymnasium exploded in teenage bedlam as Coach Wells and the team strode to the center floor jump circle.

While the court had been cleaned to look its best, there were a few flaws. In some areas the wood had swollen, thanks to a leaky roof, and created a couple of high spots. The court was 16 inches narrower than the regulation width of 50 feet, and a foot shy of the normal high school floor length of 85 feet. The wood had long since aged to a light brown.

Still, all the lights were on and the floor had been swept and polished to a warm luster by the team managers. The court's flaws did not squelch any of the enthusiasm on this special day. If anything, it seemed instead to bestow a sense of basketball heritage on the new school. And now the atmosphere was charged with the 335 teenagers stomping on bleachers in unison to the cheer of "Fire up, big team, fire up!"

Once the noise had subsided just enough for him to be heard, Coach Wells approached the microphone. He spoke of school spirit and team pride, and celebrated how easily most of the students had made the switch to the new team after the consolidation of the two schools. He then repeated a few of the things he had shared with the team at the very first practice. "The past is the past. We're not Red Devils. We are not Sprudels. We are Black Hawks!" As he spoke, the coach emphasized the team's name, and the place erupted once again.

Spontaneously, the Booster Club section started to chant, "WE ARE THE BLACK HAWKS!" over and over, and the rest of the students joined in. Finally, the din of cheers subsided, and the coach continued.

"This season is historic already, because two schools that were once great rivals are now one. We don't know what this season holds, but I know one thing for sure. These players representing your school are very good. I've known most of them since they were in junior high, when I had the opportunity to coach some of them. They've only gotten better every year since then.

"I've seen these boys develop into young men, and they play with that kind of maturity—as a team. I shared this with the boys at our first practice, and I'll share it now with you: 'I believe that all things are possible to those who believe and direct their energies toward positive goals.'"

The student body burst into applause, whistles, and hoots of agreement. Coach Wells smiled at the amazing exuberance of youth, then went on.

"Let me just sum up how I feel by sharing this thought: You, the student body, aligning your desires for this team's success, for these boys wearing the uniform, create a collective energy. That is all of you working together to accomplish one thing. Just as you all made your honest feelings known about what to name the sports teams of this school. That too, was a type of collective energy—working together on a shared vision—and that vision has come to pass. Now we have another vision, and that is to have a winning season. I promise you we'll do our best and work our hardest to do just that— win more games than lose. And we hope you'll attend the games to root us on."

With that said, the entire gym became a cacophony of hooting, hollering, cheering, and whistling once again, until finally the students were dismissed from the rally and the familiar school hall clatter of dozens and dozens of simultaneous conversations ensued.

"What are you wearing tonight?" and "Who are you going to the game with?" the girls asked each other. Boys theorized how many points the Hawks would win by. Some couples made dates, holding hands as they walked through the gym doors. Various shouts of "Go Black Hawks!" could be heard above the energized din. In just four hours, they would all return to this place to cheer on their team, to share the experience of seeing their team vanquish a worthy opponent. To accomplish something great—together.

The Game is On

The Valley Boys arrived for their warm up drills at 5:30 p.m.; game time was 7:30 p.m. The team had gathered at Coach Wells's Aunt Harriet's house for what would become the traditional pre-game supper. She would prepare the team meal prior to each home game.

A home-cooked meal was always welcome, of course, and the boys went to her house right after school. This way, they had time to chow down but still let their food digest a bit before the shoot-around.

At 6 p.m. the fans began showing up to claim their seats, and the two teams had gone back to the locker rooms to suit up and absorb their coaches' pre-game pep-talk. The boys could hear the crowd noise growing as they contemplated the game ahead. The muted strains of the pep band, playing down on the stage side of the gym, could be heard above the crowd noise, and the smell of fresh popcorn permeated the building and wafted into the locker room.

The Valley's starting five would feature the tough Bob McCracken and Butch Schmutzler at forward and Paul Radcliff at center. Marvin Pruett and Mike Watson would start at guard. Mike had gotten the nod as starter over Frankie. But Frankie was comfortable with the plan. He knew Mike had played for French Lick's team last year, and he was a senior. Coach Wells, who had to walk somewhat of a tightrope at the start of the season, may have wanted to try to put at least two former Red Devils players in the starting five to appease the French Lick folks. Having four of the five starters having played for West Baden the year before would have caused Rex even more parental complaints. But not starting didn't much bother Frankie. He knew he would get in games, and he would have to prove himself. He was a very perceptive young man. He was a team player—and the Hawks would learn this season what the word "team" meant from the selfless Frankie Self.

Coach Wells gave last-minute instructions and went over a couple of details on the blackboard, attempting to solidify certain new plays in the minds of the players. Then the coach reminded the boys of the true simplicity of this game, looking at each player as he spoke his name.

"Marvin, your job is to guard your man and keep him from scoring more points than you score." Always promoting a man-to-man defense, Coach Wells repeated this instruction to each starting player just as he had told Marvin. The team understood what they were supposed to do. The Springs Valley players felt a sense of invincibility in their home uniforms of white jerseys and shorts with the black and gold lettering and new Converse basketball shoes. They felt like young gladiators dressed for battle.

The boys were a bit nervous. Coach had told them that no matter how well a team plays, the players should feel those nerves and that adrenaline beginning to pump through their veins before a game. Marvin threw out the first lighthearted remark.

"Well, I think we'll plow through those farmers tonight." Then Schmutzler weighed in. "Yeah, who's their mascot—Mr. Green Jeans? Amos McCoy?"

Coach Wells overheard the quips. "Boys, boys, don't ever do that again. Don't ever underestimate your opponent or belittle them in any way. All you need to be thinking about now is how you are going to play tonight—nothing else. Don't forget, you could've been called the Grasshoppers. So no making fun of another team's name. And never make boastful predictions about the outcome of a game.

"All I want you to do is play your hardest, and give that one little bit of extra effort on the court. It's okay to be confident, but you know what the Good Book says about pride coming before a fall. Treat the other team with respect, but play as if they're your enemy. Play to win, but play fair. Play intelligently. Play honestly. But play hard!

"Now, let's get serious about winning this first one."

The Past and Present Collide

The boys were ready to play. The Hawks formed a line and ran out onto the court, breaking through the large paper hoop bearing the image of their Black Hawk mascot. The Booster Club and students went crazy when the first player, Mike Watson, burst through, dribbling a ball to the basket to begin the layup drill. The show was on at last.

Everything seemed to be as it should be, with the familiar rituals at the beginning of a high school basketball game all coming together in a prelude of anticipation. Nothing else could compare to this blend of excitement and anxiety. The Shawswick players were already on their side of the court, getting their pre-game warm-up shots in. The players could hear the shouts of students and the stomping of feet on the bleachers. They could smell the popcorn. They could see the cute cheerleaders jumping up and down, waving their pom-poms in the air as the Booster Club, led by Billie Jo Harris, Beverly Runyon, and Joe Ellis, were all standing and dressed in black and white, clapping and cheering.

Frankie dribbled the ball in for his first practice layup. Sophomore Jack Belcher was under the hoop, grabbing the ball and passing it to the next player in line.

But still, something wasn't quite right. Then it hit Frankie what was wrong. The school pep band was playing the French Lick fight song.

"That's weird," Frankie said to Paul as they stood together in the layup line. "Yeah, maybe they didn't learn the new song yet," Paul answered. "Maybe they could at least play the old Sprudels fight song after the Devils song."

Bob, after his layup, just shrugged his shoulders and raised his eyebrows, then quickly suggested, "Hey, remember this is French Lick's gym. Let's just play ball."

"Well, it's Springs Valley Black Hawks' school now!" Marvin shouted as he took the pass from Bob.

Paul had guessed correctly. The band had not had time to learn the new fight song. So the pep band opted to go with the song they knew best, the song that had been blasted throughout this gymnasium for many years, the same melody as "On Wisconsin!" The band instructor, Mr. Aylsworth, figured that playing the old French Lick fight song was better than playing no song at all. After all, this was a time of transition and the band hoped all would understand.

But there were a lot of people in the bleachers who felt that this was absolutely as things should be. These were the same folks who had come to the game wearing the Red Devils colors.

As the boys continued their shoot-around, they started to notice something else rather strange. One side of the Booster Club was a sea of the red and white of the French Lick Red Devils. On the other side of the Springs Valley Booster Club, who were decked out in black and white, were former West Baden Sprudels fans, dressed in purple and white. It was glaringly obvious: change can be difficult.

"Oh my gosh," Frankie said, "all the old folks are wearing their old school colors—both West Baden's and French Lick's." It was as if every former student on the home side of the court had been told to wear their alma mater's school colors.

Marvin dribbled by just as he let go a jumper and said, "Those old farts just don't get it." His practice shot hit nothing but net. Then he added, "Do they think the Sprudels and Devils are playing tonight?"

Jackie ran by and repeated his favorite line from his favorite TV show. as uttered by William Bendix in every episode of "The Life of Riley": "What a revoltin' development!"

Whether the townsfolk understood that this was a new team didn't matter. The boys on the team knew it. The students knew it. Time and events would just have to play out.

"Talk about being stuck in the past," Jim Conrad said as he dribbled by Frankie and Paul.

The ref blew the whistle to signal that the teams should go to the bench as their starting five began to take their places at center court. Coach Wells offered one last word.

"Go out there and play the game the way you always have—as a team. Don't forget, it's all about teamwork. Move the ball, make that extra pass, find the open man. Set your screens. Use your heads out there. Think ahead. Anticipate those rebounds and play defense. Stay on your man like flies on a cow pie."

The boys chuckled nervously, put their hands together in a circle and together bellowed, "TEAM!"

The Shawswick Farmers had some size. They were a bunch of big ol' country boys and they were even making comments now about which team they might be playing. One smart aleck Farmer tried to provoke the boys as the centers stood in the jump circle. "Are you guys the Devils, the Sprudels, or the Black Hawks?" Marvin just pointed up to the painting on the wall of the menacing head of the hawk.

68

The referee, his whistle at the side of his mouth, reminded the boys, "Fellas, you're here to play a ball game, not have a tea party!" He blew his whistle and tossed the ball between the two centers jumping for the first possession. The Farmers won the opening tipoff. They missed their first shot and Paul Radcliff rebounded.

Mike Watson could see that Paul had grabbed the missed shot and was already running toward the Hawks' basket. Paul in turn saw the fast-breaking Mike and made a football-like pass to the senior guard. Mike caught the ball, dribbled a couple of times, and took it in for a layup—the first basket made by a Black Hawk. In the first minute of the game, the first two points had been scored for Springs Valley.

"That's my boy!" Mike's father stood and yelled. As he sat back down, he continued, "Way to go, Mikey boy!"

Shawswick took the ball out and came down and missed their next shot. They got a good bounce, and their forward took another shot from three feet out that bounced off the front of the rim.

"Man, these guys can't hit the broad side of a barn," Frankie, sitting on the bench, thought. Frankie almost laughed aloud when he realized what had run through his mind. Most of the Shawswick players, as well as many of the Springs Valley boys, had grown up shooting a basketball through a backboard and hoop attached to the side of a barn. But the Farmers were certainly missing the bucket.

"Maybe I'll get in the game soon if we get a big lead on these guys," Frankie thought. He wished he could be on the court, but he didn't complain.

Shawswick scored on their next two possessions. On the next Valley possession, Marvin, playing right guard, ran toward the foul line and took a pass from Mike. Mike turned his back and set a pick against Marvin's defender as Marvin dribbled around the top of the key.

Marvin, at the 11 o'clock position, turned and faced the basket. As he had done thousands of times before, he went straight up, both hands taking the ball above his head, then switching mainly to his right hand as he let go of the one-hand shot from 15 feet out. Swish. Nothing but net—just like in warm-ups.

Bob signaled "way to go" as the Black Hawks ran back on defense. "Keep 'em coming, Marvin," Butch called out.

But Bob's first game was short-lived. On the next Valley possession, he took an elbow just above his right eye and began bleeding profusely. He had to come out of the game. Sophomore Jim Conrad went in the game for him, moving Marvin to the forward position. Jim couldn't believe that he was already playing, in the very first game of the season. Bob's injury wasn't an entirely terrible thing, since it gave Jim confidence early on that he could compete on the starting five. He scored six points in this first game; Bob got 10 stitches.

The scoring in the remainder of the first quarter seesawed until Valley surged ahead with a couple of quick fast-break baskets, a steal, and a two-shot foul that put them ahead in double figures.

The score at the break was 30-20, Springs Valley in a comfortable lead. Just before halftime, the coach decided to rest one of his starters, calling for Jack Belcher to go in for Butch. As Jack kneeled at the scorer's bench, he waited for a foul to be called or for a time out so he could go in the game. No fouls were called and the end of the first half came. This was unfortunate for Jack, sitting just beneath the man holding the .32 caliber pistol that would signal the end of the period.

Not many schools in Southern Indiana could boast an electronic buzzer to signal the end of quarters. The official timer, Elmer Benson, was eyeing the clock while holding the firearm down at his side. Unfortunately, Elmer didn't see the player kneeling just below him, waiting to go in the game.

The final seconds ticked off the clock and Elmer fired the blank cartridge in the gun, hitting Jack just behind his knee. The gun was so close to the boy's leg it gave him a bad powder burn and left him bleeding.

Jack yelled, "I've been shot! I've been shot!"

The timekeeper put his arm around the injured boy, trying to calm him, saying, "No bullets! No bullets! It's just a powder burn." Still, Jack was shaking as he clutched his burned and blackened leg.

As the teams went to their locker room at halftime, the team managers helped Jack leave the court. Doc Sugarman and Dr. Keseric attended both Jackie and Bob in the locker room during the 15-minute intermission.

Aside from the bizarre circumstance of one of his players being shot right before the halfway marker and another player being bloodied by a flying elbow, Coach Wells liked what he was seeing during the first two quarters. Now he made sure Jack was OK as he confided his disbelief that such a thing could have happened.

"Maybe this will cause the school board to get one of those electronic buzzers like they have down in Loogootee. I hope this is the last time any of you will be in danger of being fired upon with a lethal weapon."

The coach reminded the boys not to let down and to keep playing aggressively. All the players had scored and contributed.

During the second half, Frankie went in the game for Mike Watson when Mike sustained an ankle sprain. Both guards were 5'7" and this was a great two-man rotation at that position. You could hardly tell them apart from up in the bleachers. They both handled the ball well and were strong playmakers. They both knew how to get the ball to co-captains Bob and Butch at forward, Paul at center, and, of course, Marvin, the man with the outside shot.

However, Frankie got sick just after he went into the game. It was either nerves or something he had eaten that had disagreed with him. So, with Mike already out of the game with a sprained ankle, Butch went to the guard position for Frankie, and George Lagenour came in the game at forward. The battle for points continued as it had the first three periods, and Springs Valley pulled ahead in the fourth stanza, winning 55-40, a relatively easy first win.

Everyone in town expected the team to handle Shawswick without too much trouble. The true test for this team would be the very next game against the much bigger Jasper—in only four days. Perhaps they'd get lucky and no one would be injured while playing—or not playing—the next game.

Coach Wells silently tallied the injuries.

"Let's see . . . a player with a gunshot powder burn, a player with

10 stitches, another player with a sprained ankle, and one with the stomach flu," he mused.

"I hope someone's not trying to tell me something about this coming season."

• CHAPTER 7 •

ALL ABOARD WHO'S GETTIN' ABOARD!

The Afterglow

"Good game, Frankie."

Mr. Ellis complimented Frankie's team on Saturday morning as he unlocked the door to let his young employee in. Frankie had been employed at the Star Store during the summer, and now he worked part time at the corner grocery. His family needed every penny he and his brothers could bring in. Even though Frankie had hardly played in the game because of his stomach flu, he politely answered, "Thanks a lot, Mr. Ellis." He walked to the back of the store to begin unboxing the produce that had been delivered earlier that morning.

Saturday was the busiest day of the week at the grocery and Frankie enjoyed how fast the time went by. He also liked running into folks who'd been to the game the previous night. Compliments about the team and particular plays were always good to hear. Sometimes a game went by like a dream, and hearing a spectator's perception of the previous night's events brought certain moments in the game back to Frankie.

The young guard could feel that sense of community, being part of something that most folks held in high esteem. He knew that for many folks, this was more than just a game. It had been this way in the whole Valley for many years.

Frankie was just glad to be on the team, although he did miss being on the starting five with the boys he had been playing ball with since sixth grade. Still, he was content to sub for Mike and very glad Mr. Ellis kept him on, working Saturdays. Things were working out as well as possible, and he was thankful.

As Frankie stocked shelves, he daydreamed about repeating the kind of season that the Sprudels had had last year. Sometimes, Frankie would stop and just stare at the trophy case. He would gaze at the winning game ball from long ago, signed by all the players, along with the piece of net and team picture that sat behind the sliding glass doors. Perhaps it was to make a break with the recent past, but the game ball and pieces of net from the long-ago French Lick sectional victories were nowhere to be seen. Now, too, the glass case that held French Lick's past triumphs had been moved to the French Lick grade school.

The trophy case was like a shrine for the townsfolk who held onto great wins of the past like a kind of religious experience and worshipped at the altar of the five-on-five. The joy of winning was not soon forgotten. These physical reminders of having brought home the great prize escorted many former players and town folk back in time to that wondrous event. As precious as any ancient historical artifacts in a museum, these relics of the team's past were on constant display. Even grown men could be seen staring at the ball and sighing as if to be saying, "Oh, if this could only happen again! If we had players like Marvin Cave and Billy D. Wright again!" (These boys had played for the 1943 Red Devils who had won the sectional championship.)

But today Frankie was in work mode: white shirt, bow tie, and full-length white apron and paper hat, as required by Mr. Ellis. "A uniform makes you look professional," Mr. Ellis reminded his stock boy each time he would stop and straighten Frankie's crooked bow tie.

Mr. Ellis had relatives up north in the capital city of Indianapolis. He often made trips, 100 miles north, to visit the bigger grocery chain stores that were being built there. The small-town store owner had recently brought back a great idea: piped-in music for the shoppers. Frankie was elated when his boss brought in his 1952 model Philco radio, set it up in the office window in back, and turned the volume up. Pat Boone's "April Love" could be heard drifting through the entire store. Listening to the current hit parade, Frankie thought, made the hours go by much more quickly.

Love at First Sight

About 10 a.m., Frankie looked up to see a girl staring at him.

"Oh, it's the girl who works behind the counter at the drug store," he realized. Frankie's mind was racing. He smiled sheepishly and went about his job of stacking soup cans the way he had been taught.

When Thelma McFarland saw Frankie almost making eye contact with her, she quickly said, "Nice game last night, Frankie, you played really well."

"Uh, thanks," was all Frankie could muster.

Frankie had seen her working as the "soda jerk" at the French Lick City Drug Store several times, but he was too nervous ever to speak to her, much less to ask her name. To Frankie, she seemed so mature, so much older, with the kind of job that an adult usually had. Thelma was a very responsible girl, and the drugstore owner, Mr. Deremiah, had given her the job during her freshman year.

Thelma wore her blonde hair short, somewhere between a "bubble" and "bouffant" style, with short curls and bangs. Frankie thought she looked like a blonde Loretta Young, the starlet who always made a grand entrance on her weekly TV show. Even though Thelma was a junior, just as he was, all of this made Frankie feel that she was much older than she really was.

It seemed there truly could be such a thing as "love at first sight." Frankie thought she had the kindest eyes and the sweetest smile he had ever seen. And when she spoke, her soft, gentle voice sent his heart into a flutter.

The girl of Frankie's dreams had attended French Lick High, and until this year, the stock boy and basketball player had never gotten closer to her than the drug store's big aluminum soda counter allowed. Now, they even had a couple of classes together.

Thelma's family lived about as far from West Baden as one could be and still be in French Lick's "city limits." Her house was way out on Adams Street, on the outskirts of town, heading toward nearby Birdseye. This morning, she had come into town with her mom to do the Saturday shopping. Frankie was beginning to realize that there were more things to life than basketball and stocking shelves.

Immediately after work, Frankie ran up a block and across the street to the corner drug store, in hopes of seeing Thelma behind the counter. She was there. Frankie took a seat on the swiveling red leather-covered stool.

"Hi Frankie, can I help you?" Thelma asked. Frankie got tongue-tied at hearing her say his name again. He immediately thought, *"You sure can! You can be my girlfriend!"* But the words had no chance of leaving Frankie's mouth. Stuttering for a second, Frankie just said, "Yeah, uh . . . yeah, can I get a cherry Coke?"

"Sure can," Thelma answered, as she poured the cherry syrup in and pulled the Coke lever. Frankie could only stare as she set the big green-tinted glass on the counter.

Frankie couldn't speak. He sat there guzzling the drink, the straw never leaving his lips, never taking his eyes off Thelma—that is, until she looked his way.

"Can I get you anything else?" she asked.

"Uh, sure . . . can I have a refill?" Frankie needed an excuse to sit there a bit longer. He downed the second soda in about the same record time in which he'd finished the first.

"Another refill?" Thelma asked.

"No, I'm fine. Uh, thanks."

Frankie couldn't take the pressure any longer of not knowing what to say to the lovely girl behind the counter. He heard the sucking sound of his straw against the bottom of the glass. He put a quarter on the counter, slid off the stool, and left in a hurry. Thelma looked up from her work to see him going out the door. She just smiled that sweet smile.

Frankie knew that he would see her in class on Monday, He

thought, "I'll make sure to say 'hello' to . . . Dang, I didn't even ask her name!"

Up until this point in his young life, Frankie hadn't been too interested in girls. There were so many other things to fill a boy's day with that he couldn't see how anyone had the time to just hang out with the opposite sex, or even give them that much thought. However, he was beginning to understand how he might be able to squeeze in some time for this girl.

Girls were still quite mysterious to Frankie. His attraction to them was something he'd been very much aware of since first grade, when he'd kissed Sally Owens during recess on the playground. He also knew something was going on even in grade school. Every Valentine's Day one of the girls in his class had always handed him the biggest Valentine card and looked at him kind of funny. It seemed to Frankie that his attraction to girls had always been there, but, now at 16 years old, this mystery was beginning to take on a new significance.

Frankie was glad that he and Thelma shared a couple of classes and that she'd come into the Star Store that morning. He tried to imagine her perspective of the ball game, sitting in the stands, cheering the team on from the Booster Section. "She must like me a lot," he thought, "or she wouldn't be in here telling me how well I played last night. And I didn't even play all that much."

Frankie's hunch was right on the money.

The following Monday, Frankie got up the nerve to talk to Thelma. He could feel his face flushing as he walked over to her desk, but he had to get to know this girl.

"Uh, I'm sorry I don't know your name," he stammered. "I know I should by now, but there's a lot of new kids here now . . . and I, uh, I . . ."

"I'm Thelma McFarland." She smiled.

The ice was broken, and at the end of their class, Frankie walked Thelma to her Home Economics class. Well, he didn't exactly walk with her. He walked a step ahead and two feet away, looking back awkwardly to ask her if she'd be coming to the next ball game. Even making eye contact with this beautiful, mature girl was a little way down the road for Frankie.

Romance can move quickly for juniors in high school. By the end of the day, Thelma had Frankie's name written in black ink on her blue, three-ring notebook. Frankie could see this when he ran into her after school.

"Hi, Thelma, how ya doin'?" She smiled, which got Frankie all tongue-tied again.

"Um . . . I've got to get to ball practice, uh . . . but would it be okay . . . uh . . . if I gave you a call tonight? I mean, would your parents mind?"

Thelma smiled that kind, gentle smile, her blue eyes sparkling, and just said, "Sure, I can't wait. You can tell me about your practice."

Frankie floated all the way to ball practice, feeling like he had more energy than ever to run that half-court offense and defend. He started whistling "Wake Up, Little Susie." He day-dreamed about what it would be like to take Thelma to a drive-in movie.

Game #2: Jasper

The Black Hawks had a full schedule, so the first few games had to be squeezed in just before fall break, a week and a half before Thanksgiving. Their second game was on Wednesday, only four days after their home opener. This was an away game with one of the bigger schools in the area. Although they were playing Jasper, a team that had always been a very challenging opponent for both French Lick and West Baden—neither had beaten its team in years—they nonetheless felt confident.

This game would be played on the Jasper Wildcats' court. Coach Wells looked forward to it, believing that traveling to an away game this early in the season would help toughen up his boys. With their first win under their belt, the players were feeling good about their team. Each player understood his role, and they all played for each other and their coach. These boys understood the very delicate balance of personal drive, pride, and selflessness. They were the definition of the word "team."

The midweek pep rally was a big hit with the students, who were looking forward to the second big game.

Paul Radcliff's parents complained of this Wednesday game conflicting with the weekly evening prayer service at church, which they never missed. But he begged them to not file an official complaint and to let him play.

"Please, Mom and Dad, we always go to church. Can't I just miss this one time? I've gotta be with the team," he implored them. "I can't tell the coach that I can't be there until the second half."

Mr. and Mrs. Radcliff understood their son's dilemma, and they understood that for most folks around these parts, attending basketball games was a close second to visiting the house of God. As much as they hated to see anything interfere with church attendance, they were certain that God would understand. They told Paul he didn't have to be at this week's prayer service—but that they would all be praying for "God's will to be done" regarding the outcome of the game. (In this church, no one had the gall to ask aloud for God to take sides. However, most in attendance probably let this request be known in their silent prayers.)

The Hawks arrived in Jasper around 6 after their pre-game meal and traveling down State Road 56. The Valley Boys had reason to feel a little bit intimidated. Besides being a much larger school than Springs Valley, Jasper had won the regional last season, a big deal for any team. The Wildcats' gym was newer, much nicer, and twice the size of the Springs Valley gym. Everything was so much brighter and shinier.

Nervousness aside, all of this seemed somehow to fire the boys up that much more. They realized they were the underdogs, and they were set on this game being an upset.

Bob McCracken, who had gotten the gash above his right eye during the Shawswick game, still had his stitches in. On top of that, the night following the first game, he had gone to an outdoor hayride party. He had recently found a Zippo lighter and was asked to light the bonfire, a part of most every get-together during the fall around the Twin Cities. Unbeknownst to Bob, someone earlier had doused the cornstalks, brush, and dead tree limbs with gasoline, and when he leaned down to light the highly combustible material, it blew up in his face. He was taken to the hospital for his injury. The starting power forward now had a cut above his eye and a burned face, his eyebrows practically gone.

"Man, this hasn't been such a great week for me," Bob observed to Marvin during warm-ups.

"Yeah, you kinda look like Boris Karloff in *The Mummy*," Marvin joked.

"Thanks, that makes me feel so much better," Bob retorted. Marvin smiled as he shot another practice jumper that swished through the net. He leaned in close to his singed teammate.

"Bob, I think our manager Billy has some black pencils he could draw your eyebrows back on with."

"Ha, ha, Pruett. You're so funny, I forgot to laugh," Bob shot back as he shoved Marvin away with his shoulder.

The boys were unrelenting in joking about Bob's recent accident. Butch walked by, and without even looking in Bob's direction, did his best impression of Smokey the Bear. "Remember, only you can prevent forest fires!"

"Watch it, Schmutzler."

But Bob knew that all this talk was coming from a hard-earned male camaraderie. All the boys would give each other a hard time every once in a while, and it just happened to be Bob's turn. It had taken a long while, for example, before Paul Radcliff could live down the day his head got stuck in the mud at the swimmin' hole. It was just guys being guys. They could laugh at, and with, each other.

"Aw, knock it off, fellas," Frankie interjected, while dribbling up to the jokesters. "We've got a big game here to be thinking about. Let's get our heads in this game—right now," he reminded them in his firm but gentle way.

Bob agreed wholeheartedly. "Let's just play ball! Okay!"

Frankie clapped his hands together hard twice, in his own version of a "Fire up, big team!" cheer. He glanced over at Thelma, whose eyes were fixed upon her new boyfriend. Frankie blushed, and then grabbed a rebound—getting his own head back into this game. He did a practice fake one way, then a quick turn-around as he let go of the ball and nailed a fadeaway jump shot. He hoped Thelma was still watching.

Even though the Black Hawks hadn't had much rest since their first game, they came out hot. Marvin let loose the first two shots of the game, sinking them both. The scoreboard read 4-0, the way a coach likes to see a game begin. The Hawks guarded the Wildcats in a rotating man-to-man defense. On Jasper's third possession, they finally scored their first bucket. Springs Valley had already scored four times.

It was 8-2 when the Wildcats put up another jump shot. It took a "friendly bounce" high off the rim and dropped in. Then the boys from the Valley started making mental errors. As they inbounded the ball, a Jasper player stole it and put up an easy layup, making it 8-6. The Hawks' lead had been cut to two points. Then, as Springs Valley brought the ball down, the Jasper guard smothering Mike Watson stole the ball and cruised down the court for another layup. Tie game. The Valley fans grew quiet. The Wildcats fans were going wild for their 'Cats.

Coach Wells called time out.

"Fellas, you're not thinking out there. You're letting them dictate the game. Forget that you're on their court. Just settle down and go back out there and run your plays. Just play better," the coach implored.

"Paul, box out their big man under the basket," he went on. "Bob, you're not blocking out. Take a breather for a couple of minutes."

Bob, who couldn't stand to be sitting on the bench during a game, protested. "But coach, I can't iron out my problems if I'm sitting on the bench! How can I correct what I'm doing wrong if I'm not in the game?"

The senior forward had a point. Coach Wells, who had a long history with Bob, understood.

"Okay, Bob, but start blocking your man out underneath. And fight for those rebounds. Mike, you've got to protect that ball, and everybody start hustling back on defense. And stop dribbling the ball so much. Pass it. Keep it moving and find the open man. Okay? Now go play some Black Hawks basketball!"

The possession was Springs Valley's. Mike dribbled the ball down the court, stopped at the right side of the key, and passed it to Paul, who had come to the foul line. Paul saw Bob behind him, cutting behind his man toward the bucket. A perfectly timed bounce pass allowed Bob to take the ball with one dribble to the basket. Two points for the forward.

Then Valley put on a press and stole the ball again on Jasper's inbounds. Bob was there again to lay the ball in for another two points. He had six points in the game already. As Bob ran back on defense, he thought, "I bet the coach is glad he left me in the game!"

The Wildcats got the ball in on their next possession, came down and sank a jump shot. Then the Hawks advanced the ball to their side of the court. Mike called the play, and once again, Bob McCracken was cutting to the hoop. Mike sailed a pass to Radcliff, who once again saw Bob getting away from his man. Bob had the ball again, going in for his third lay-in. The Jasper center fell back from Paul and took a swipe at Bob as the Hawks forward released the ball against the glass. The ball went in—but the Jasper center's attempt to block the ball was more like a right hook to Bob's eye.

The stitches opened and Bob was bleeding heavily again, looking like a battered boxer. Time out was called. The team manager put an adhesive bandage on it so Bob could shoot the free throw. He somehow sank the extra point, then had to come out of the game to get stitched up—again.

The guys who had been joking with him now felt bad that they'd given him such a tough time during their pre-game warmups. Bob, who had gotten burned in the past week, was "on fire" tonight. And he was burning the boys who were attempting to guard him, and proving to the coach why he had to stay in the game. He got 23 stitches at intermission and was back in the game for the second half, the wounded Hawk still fighting under the boards. Indeed, the coach was glad Bob was in this game.

Rex was pleased with how his team was playing, for the most part, but he was seeing things that needed to be improved upon. The boys, some of whom had switched positions this year because of the merger of the two teams, were making some mistakes. He realized they'd be experimenting with assigning positions and the starting lineup for each game. But the coach was increasingly certain he had the luxury of a deep bench.

The Wildcats and Hawks exchanged baskets for the rest of the second half and well into the fourth quarter. With only 4:17 left in the game, the score was tied, 35-35. That's when Valley began to pull ahead. The players seemed to know when to apply the pressure and put the game away during the remaining minutes, although only four of the Hawks scored in the game.

Jack Belcher came off the bench to put in a bucket. Bob's four baskets and a free throw contributed nine points. Butch scored his last two baskets underneath for 17 points, and Marvin got his 17 when he put in three more jumpers in a row that put the dagger in the Wildcats' chances.

When the gun—pointed toward the ceiling this time—went off at the end of regulation, the scoreboard read: Springs Valley 45, Jasper 38. The Valley Boys had been victorious now in their second game, and only four players had scored. The coach was happy but would have liked to see the scoring spread out a bit more.

The young team knew now that they could compete, and win, against bigger schools—even on the road. Jasper, in the fourth quarter, finally went down without too much of a fight. The Hawks had their second win under their belt.

Doc's Advice

One of the referees in the previous season's contests had been Warren "Doc" Keyser. He had driven down from Indianapolis to interview for the job coaching the Red Devils when the coach from the previous year, Bill Bright, had been called into the service. It so happened that one of the referees for that night's game didn't show up. They asked Doc if he would ref the game. After the game, the French Lick High School board was so impressed that they held a meeting that same night and hired him on as coach for the remainder of the 1956–57 season.

He was familiar with most of these boys since he'd coached the games between French Lick and West Baden. He had been happy to accept the position of assistant coach of the Springs Valley Black Hawks and the reserves' team coach for the 1957–58 season.

Doc and Rex Wells had clicked from the first time they met, having quite similar backgrounds. Doc understood the chemistry that Coach Wells had with the boys who had played for him in their earlier years. He didn't mind taking a back seat and doing all he could to help the younger Rex. He had a hunch that something unusual was occurring in these two towns, and he was happy to be a part of it.

Doc could see something special in the way this Hawks team played. He had played high school and a couple years of college ball at Indiana Central College in Indianapolis, and once basketball is in your blood, it never leaves you. So, he was happy now to be on the coaching end of things. Doc was one more ingredient that blended well in this new team mix.

The school board was growing more and more confident in their young coach, but most of the teams nowadays had an assistant coach. If the head coach ever lost his temper and got thrown out of a game, there needed to be another coach there to take over—even though the chances of Rex Wells losing his temper during a ball game were about the same as Marvin Pruett not hitting a jump shot in a 32-minute contest. Still, Coach Wells didn't mind the extra pair of eyes evaluating the players, and helping with strategy during a game.

Margaret's Advice

That night, Rex confided in his wife when he arrived home late from the out-of-town game.

"Honey, I think we have an unusually good team here. We have never beat big ol' Jasper before tonight! I know we're only two games into the season, but I'm seeing some great play. It's too early to really know, but I'm getting the inkling of a feeling that this is going to be a very good season.

"The board voted in Doc Keyser as my assistant. Just think; me, Rex Wells, having an assistant coach who played college ball at Indiana Central. This is getting kind of 'big time.'"

"You know I believe in you," Margaret assured him. "You're a great coach and you have some special boys out there playing for you. If both towns can only get behind the Black Hawks and leave their precious past behind . . . if they just begin looking ahead, I know it'll only help the team, and the two towns." Margaret spoke with wisdom beyond her years.

"You know something, honey," Rex answered, "I think this team is going to teach our community something about how strong we can be when we all pull in the same direction. You know these towns have languished for too long in the past, always referring to 'the good old days' when the hotels were doing well."

"The players and students understand what's going on here," she said. "I think you're right, honey. From the mouths of babes . . . "

Rex just smiled at his lovely wife. She was truly a treasure.

Young Love, True Love

Sometimes Frankie would walk Thelma home after school, then run back to the gym for practice. But it was a long distance, so he could only walk with her halfway to her house. This meant they usually just spoke with each other at school.

During lunch one day, Frankie asked, "Thelma, what do you think about during a game? Do you get just as caught up in the game as most of the others in the Booster Club?"

"Hmmm, I think it's mostly just being excited to see our team hit a basket—you know, the team that hits the most baskets wins."

"Yeah, I heard that someplace," Frankie responded as they both laughed. Thelma went on, "Billie Jo and the other cheerleaders lead us really well after you score or somebody makes a great play. We just join in with them."

"Uh, I was just kind of wondering . . . uh," he faltered. "Do you really watch the game closely?" What Frankie meant was, "Do you watch me when I get in the game?"

Thelma looked up at Frankie with her head tilted slightly in her shy way.

"I never take my eyes off you," she confessed, intuiting his meaning. "In fact, I dream of you."

As they walked along, she began to hum the recent Everly Brothers hit, "All I Have to Do Is Dream." This was quite forward for Thelma, but the melody just seemed to be tumbling out of her. She was falling in love. Frankie was the perfect guy for her.

Frankie smiled and took her hand in his as they walked to class. He asked her, "Would you like to go to a movie sometime? I hear *The Silken Affair* is playing at the Valley Theater next week."

Frankie spoke in his soft Southern Indiana drawl, pronouncing theater, as *the-ay-ter.*

"I would love to. That would be swell, but my parents have already said that the title of that movie doesn't sound like something I should see."

"I think it's a comedy," Frankie told her, "but that's okay. It sounds stupid anyway. We don't have to go to a movie. We can just go up to Bedford and get a pizza at Grecco's," he suggested.

"That will be loads of fun!" Thelma spoke with great glee. It was set. Their first date was firm—that is, if her parents would allow her to go that far away on a date. To her great surprise, they did. Thelma assumed it was because Frankie was on the team, and reputations travel quickly in small towns—good and bad. Frankie was known around town as a hard-working kid who went to church. When Thelma's parents had met Frankie, they wondered if he and Thelma would ever be able to keep a conversation going, as quiet as they knew their daughter was, and they could see that Frankie was a rather shy boy.

Grecco's was the only pizza place within 50 miles of the Valley. It was located 30 miles away in the next county north. Bedford and Grecco's had become quite the destination for the French Lick pizza connoisseur since opening in 1955. This delicacy was a pretty new dish for most folks in Southern Indiana.

The pizza place sat on a corner—literally—where two streets met at a point, just like a slice of pizza. The store sat where the old State Road 37 angled by 0 Street as it ran through the heart of Bedford. The Grecco family had recently bought this building and their unique recipe included unusually high mounds of mozzarella with sausage mixed with anise spice, giving it a special flavor all its own.

The young couple arrived at Grecco's after their drive to Bedford. They entered the building that overwhelmed them with the most wonderful aroma they had ever experienced. The scents of rising pizza dough, tomato sauce, crumbled Italian sausage, garlic, and oregano permeated the room. The ovens, full of pizzas to go, warmed the room. Tonight, Frankie and Thelma were the first customers to sit down in this intimate, romantic space.

The red and white checkered table cloths and the juke box playing the music of Dean Martin and Frank Sinatra transported them to a place far, far away from French Lick and West Baden. Thelma and Frankie ordered the "Grecco Special." This was indeed going to be a special date if they could just figure out how to keep the conversation going.

They continued to look over the menus while drinking their Cokes. Frankie was nervous, and he began to move the salt and pepper shakers around, as if he were in an intense chess match. Thelma found the napkin holder and began tearing pieces into little balls and rolling them between her fingers. Frankie broke the silence.

"Uh . . . do you like the pizza here?"

"I've never had it before, but I'm sure it's wonderful," Thelma answered.

Then another full minute of silence as they both began looking around them and pretending to survey the room, as if memorizing the layout for future reference.

"Nice music," Thelma offered.

"Yeah, those guys can sing," Frankie agreed.

"I love Frankie's—uh—I mean, Sinatra's voice." Thelma tripped over her words, aware she had revealed her feelings about the boy sitting across from her. Frankie just smiled, and said, "I like Sinatra too!"

At last, they settled in, having found a common denominator in the music.

Frankie asked, "Did you notice the colors that the old folks was wearing during the first home game?"

"Yes, I did notice that most of the parents were wearing the Devils and Sprudels colors," Thelma answered. "I wonder if they're fantasizing that the Hawks are their old school's team," she went on. "I hope they figure it out soon and start wearing *our* school colors." She acknowledged how hard it is for old folks to change sometimes.

"The adults will finally come along," Frankie replied. "I just wish they could see all of this from our point of view."

Just then, their minds were abruptly taken off that subject. Someone had put a nickel in the jukebox and played "All I Have to Do is Dream," which was now "their song." They just listened, shyly looking into each other's eyes between bites of pizza.

Near the end of their meal, Frankie reached for Thelma's hand— and knocked over her Cherry Coke.

"Oh gosh, I'm so sorry, I'll get it," the nervous young man told his date. He emptied what was left in the napkin holder as he cleaned up the spill. He leaned over the table, dabbing up the last drop. He was face to face with this beautiful girl whom he had so recently wondered about and looked upon only from afar.

"I'm sorry," Frankie said for the fourth time, flustered. Thelma's eyes met his.

"It's okay," she said softly. "Don't worry about it." They were inches apart, their eyes locked, and then it happened. Their lips met in a rapturous moment. It was the first kiss for them both. (Frankie didn't count kissing Sally Owen in the first grade.) It was quick but effective. Even if measured in nanoseconds, it was a first kiss. It was a date they would both remember for the rest of their lives.

Life was good for Frankie, and getting better all the time. When he arrived back home, he decided it was time to tell his aunt about his new girlfriend. She was happy for her young nephew, who had always been shy when it came to girls.

Along with most of the French Lick and West Baden parents, Frankie's Aunt Edith was reliving her younger days as she watched what the kids were achieving during this new and exciting school year. Their youthful exuberance had spilled over to parents, teachers, and some of the townsfolk, who were just beginning to feel the change in the air. Every citizen in the Twin Cities would soon be breathing it in deeply, offering a new lease on life for these forgotten hamlets. As if a spring rain had been washing across the land, a much-needed cleansing was taking place.

Having told his aunt of his feelings, Frankie next wrote his mom a letter, telling her of his newfound love.

"I guess there's more to life than basketball and apple pie," Gertrude Self thought when she received her son's letter. She mentally traveled back in time, hearing a voice in her head: *"You better believe it, woman,"* her husband laughed. *"He's a chip off the old block."* Thinking of what her late husband might say, Gertrude almost said aloud, "Oh, Harold, does this remind you of anything? A girl from French Lick dating a boy from West Baden?" Her mind drifted back to high school, when she and her boyfriend would break up after a heartbreaking basketball game loss. She smiled, reminiscing about those wonderfully innocent days.

She quietly began humming "I Could've Danced All Night." Gertie (as Harold had called her) remembered their love, and just how much God had blessed them with their strong and healthy sons. She missed her boys, Benny and Frankie, so much. She knew they were now carrying the load of providing for the family since their dad's passing and her move to Mackinaw City. Gertrude sent home what little money she could, knowing that her sister and the boys barely got by. But as tough as things were, there was always something to be grateful for.

And Frankie had found someone to be quite thankful for—Thelma McFarland.

• CHAPTER 8 •

THE HAWKS TAKE FLIGHT

Game 3: The Loogootee Lions

For years, the Loogootee Lions' name had always instilled a bit of fear in the two teams in French Lick and West Baden. Now, the Black Hawks felt they could hold their own with the Lions—especially on Springs Valley's home court. Three wins in a row and more sportswriters—not just the local writer for the *Springs Valley Herald*—might begin taking notice. Winning tonight against Loogootee would really have a special meaning. Their fans were as crazy for the game of hoops as the Hawks fans, and the tickets for tonight's contest were sold out.

Once again, the interval between games was short; this contest was only three days after their last. The following week, the students would be on their fall break just before Thanksgiving, the holiday to give thanks "in all things for everything," as Paul would always remind his teammates.

The Hawks ran out of their locker room and onto their dark, old, warped maple court for their second home game. Frankie noticed that the fans were still wearing their old school colors: purple on one side of the student rooting section and red on the other. It was evident that the Red Devils and Sprudels worshipers weren't going away easily.

"They're still playing the old French Lick fight song," Frankie mentioned to Marvin as they began their layup drill.

"I can name that tune in three notes!" Jackie Belcher's joke about the NBC radio show could hardly be heard above the din of the pep band and the 1,100 plus spectators crammed into the old French Lick gym, eager to see this game get started.

Bob McCracken also had noticed the band hadn't learned the new school song, but only said, "Let's just play ball. That song won't make any difference how this game goes." And it didn't.

The Springs Valley team was still a mystery to other teams, which didn't think much of the Black Hawks until after they had played them. The boys in black and white came out strong once again. It was almost a repeat of the previous game. But in this contest, more players scored. Frankie, Butch, and Jack Belcher all put in 11 points each, and Marvin and Paul 9, while Bob led the way with 18 points.

Senior guard Mike Watson had scored a free throw in the game, but because of his relentless defense, he fouled out of the game.

"Frankie, get in the game for Mike," the coach yelled down the bench. Frankie was now back on the court with the three boys he had played ball with for so long now. Coach Wells liked what he saw from his junior guard; he now had another scorer on the floor. Frankie hit five of 11 field goal attempts and one of two free throws for 11 points, hitting 50 percent.

"Good decision Coach, putting Frankie in," Doc told Rex after the game.

The Hawks gave their best game to Loogootee. The Lions "lay down and were reduced to pussy cats," was the verdict of the local sportswriters in their columns the following day. One wrote, "The Lions roared on only 17 of 57 tries, giving them a .298 average." Inevitably, the writers seemed determined to employ as many tortured references to a team's mascot as they could. It was irresistible, apparently.

But already, the Black Hawks team was really coming together, and some began to take notice.

"The Valley Boys hit 27 of 62 shots from the field for a 43.5% average, and 16 of 28 free tosses," the local sports columnist, Jim Ballard wrote. "The scoring for the Hawks was well balanced, with four of the boys hitting double figures and two totaling nine points each. The distribution of the scoring will make any opponent pull his hair. The reserves played throughout the 32-minute fray—demonstrating the depth of this team from the bench."

The glowing praise from the sportswriter of the *Springs Valley Herald* was beginning to sound like that of "the Old Rebounder," Billy Ray Wininger, who wrote for the school paper. People were beginning to believe in this team that had now won its first three games.

The team continued to sharpen as it kept up its daily practice schedule during the fall break. Passes were quick and accurate, shots were going in, and fast breaks from great rebounding were common occurrences in practice scrimmages. This team was finding its playing style. It didn't hurt that for four of these players, this style had been forged long ago during their junior high days and those tough summer and winter scrimmages against the Jesuit priests.

Frankie, Bob, Marvin, Jim, and Paul had played together for five years, and now, with the high-scoring former French Lick star, Butch Schmutzler, they began to jell as a team.

The game was a faster game now than in their earlier years, but this team was never in a big hurry. They knew how to work the clock. When they wanted to, however, they could get the ball down the court fast, thanks to the speed of Frankie, Mike, and Jack Belcher. One writer, in fact, once referred to Jackie Belcher as "the human rocket."

This team set up plays, running pick and rolls, setting screens, blocking out bigger players, and passing—either to the sharp-shooting of Marvin, the pivot man Paul, or the high-scoring Butch or Bob. Frankie's specialty was defense, but he was great at moving the ball up the court and opening the lanes with his ball penetration and quick passes. He had earned a spot in the starting lineup, in fact. Mike Watson now would come in the game for Frankie. At all the practices, however, it was Mike's challenge to guard Marvin Pruett. He was the only player who could stay on Marvin, and this only made Mike a stronger player.

Everybody Loves a Winner

Game #4 was another home game, this time against Medora, a small school west of the Valley. Seven o'clock arrived and the Hawks took to the hardwood after the usual pep talk from Coach Wells. At times, the boys and their coach seemed more like buddies. Perhaps it was Rex's age or the fact that this was a new experience for everyone involved

This time, when the Black Hawks ran onto the court, they immediately noticed something they hadn't experienced. All the students and alumni, parents, grandparents, and other relatives sitting on the Hawks' side were now wearing black and white. What's more, during the pre-game warm up, the team heard their new Springs Valley fight song.

"All right!" Frankie hollered.

"Yeah, now they've got the right song!" Marvin chimed in.

The fans didn't know all the words the way the cheerleaders did, but they were standing and clapping louder than the last time a tent revival came through town. People were jumping on the Black Hawks bandwagon.

Some folks had noticed the shift even before tonight. Instead of referring to the new roundball squad as "young pups" who were coached by "another kid," people were beginning to use the phrase "our team." Springs Valley had a team to be respected and reckoned with. They were making believers out of many former naysayers.

Just as the game was to begin, Mike Watson looked into the stands. "That black and white looks pretty good to everybody now!" he observed.

Marvin answered, "Yeah, but is Principal Katter wearing our colors? I wonder if he would still like to call us the Grasshoppers."

They wondered aloud whether the principal, who had resisted the team name and the black and white colors, was even in attendance.

"Hey, Principal Katter is a good guy," Mike reminded Marvin. "He's driven me to my scout meetings and church many times. He just thought 'Grasshoppers' was a good name. You know how grasshoppers are small, but jump high. I think that was his thinking. Coach mentioned the possibility of 'the Mustangs' as a name too remember?"

"Well, I'm glad we're not wild horses or insects," Marvin replied.

Looking to their side of the court, the players saw a sea of black and white as the fans began to cheer as one.

"Go Hawks, Go!" This was something the boys could get used to.

Win #4

It was no contest at all. The Hawks more than doubled their rival's points, with a final score of 74-36. In the locker room after the game, the team started singing the Black Hawks fight song. When that song ended, one of the guys started singing "Dre-ee-ee-ee-eam, dream, dream, dream," the chorus to the Everly Brothers hit, in a high falsetto. Thelma had told one of her girlfriends about the song that was so special to her and Frankie. Now, the whole team knew, and they weren't going to let Frankie forget it.

"Ah, knock it off guys," Frankie laughed. "Can't a fella have any privacy?"

Mike Watson shot back, "Hey, our team has a dream too, don't forget!"

"Yeah, four games into the season and we've won all of 'em," Butch said. "This ain't no dream! Let's keep winning!"

Coach Wells overheard the conversation. "Don't forget what won this game tonight," he reminded the boys. "It's *team* effort. It's okay to have dreams, but don't get your heads so far in the clouds that you forget what your feet and hands are supposed to do.

"It's all fundamentals," he went on, "and implementing what you know how to do. So far, that's exactly what you've all done. Just keep doing it. My daddy used to say, 'The harder you work, the luckier you get.' Dreams are great, but preparation and hard work are what make dreams come true. Don't ever forget that!"

The cheer from the 10 boys went up and they started singing their fight song again. The locker room was full of the joy that comes from winning basketball games in Southern Indiana. Could they keep this up? Rex didn't know for sure, but his own confidence in his team was growing more and more as the gun fired at the end of each game.

Thankful

The next day was Thanksgiving. There would be no practice today, but they had an away game on Friday. Rex was glad for the day off to spend with Margaret and relax, going to his Aunt Harriet's for their Thanksgiving feast.

That morning, Rex was reading the sports pages in the *Herald*. At the top read the headline: "Sprudel + Pluto = Dynamite."

"Honey, listen to this," Rex exclaimed as he began to read aloud. "Credit belongs to Wells. There can only be one answer for the success of the Blackhawks."

Rex stopped reading for a second. "Why do they keep spelling our team's name as one word? I keep telling them that we're not an Indian tribe, we're birds! Why can't they get it right? We are the Black Hawks. Two words—*birds*! Not Indians."

Margaret laughed and said, "It doesn't matter all that much, does it? What matters is that you are winning games—and that goes a long, long way around these parts."

Rex had to agree. "It still bugs the tar out of me," he groused. He continued reading aloud.

"There are very few men around our community who could've taken a bunch of boys, who just one year ago were rivals, and mold them into one smooth working machine. When we say 'smooth,' we mean smooth. If you haven't seen Bob McCracken run his arm up an elbow's length above the hoop for a rebound, then you haven't seen anything. If you haven't seen Butch Schmutzler or Marvin Pruett stop, spin, and throw in a two-pointer on a fade-away jump shot, then you haven't seen anything. If you haven't seen Paul Radcliff display some of his pass work as well as his rebounding ability, then you haven't seen anything.

"If you haven't had a glimpse of little Frankie Self, then folks, you are just not a basketball fan. Frankie is a bundle of dynamite all by himself. Jim Conrad and Jack Belcher are a pair of sophomores who are showing a lot of improvement under Coach Wells. Mike Watson is a mighty good scrapping guard, and Jerry Breedlove and George Lagenour a couple of good rebounders."

Rex finished reading the article about the last game to himself. Margaret just watched her husband, who only a few weeks ago was concerned about being the coach. Now, after four wins in a row, she saw a confidence in him she had never seen before.

"I told you things would turn around as soon as you got a few wins under your belt," Margaret reminded her husband.

"I remember well, Mrs. Wells." They kissed and hugged.

"Hey, we've got to get ready and get over to Aunt Harriet's," Rex said.

"We do have much to be thankful for, don't we?"

Having married in August, these newlyweds were on top of the world just four months later. When it came to Springs Valley basketball, the climb up the mountain may have only begun, but the ascent was feeling quite comfortable already. And to be experiencing all this with the love of his life, Rex could say only one thing to his lovely bride.

"I'm as happy as a pig in slop," he told her.

"Oh Rex, you are such a poet!" Margaret laughed aloud.

The boys on the team had a lot to be thankful for as well—a winning season so far, a great coach they all loved, and a sense that they were part of something just beginning to happen. They had no idea of what lay ahead, but the momentum was building. They felt as if they were being pulled by the current of a fast-moving river and picking up speed.

Love is Found on the Other Side of Town

Frankie wasn't the only love-struck ball player from West Baden. Marvin had found the love of his life as well. The dead-eye jump shooter had met Barbara Love. He had noticed this girl the year before when the West Baden team played French Lick. Barbara was a cheerleader and Marvin couldn't help but notice her. When he saw her cheering on the sidelines, he knew he had to know this girl.

"Love at first sight" is an often-misused phrase, but in the case of Marvin and Barbara, it had happened. Just as Frankie and Thelma had, these teens had found their one great love in life. Of course, at the time, they didn't even have a hunch they were destined for marriage and many years together. They were still just teenagers, and there was so much of life that they were living now—exciting times in discovering this amazing attraction to someone, while hitting a very high mark on the high school social ladder.

Barbara had been in Marvin's heart since he had seen her cheering for the Red Devils. He'd first noticed this cheerleader with the dark-brown hair two seasons earlier when West Baden played French Lick. He'd always thought she was so beautiful. It was as if the Disney superstar Annette Funicello had joined the cheerleading squad, performing somersaults and doing back flips on the sidelines. He had hoped that Barbara would be a cheerleader for the Hawks, but it hadn't happened.

Marvin had been quite happy when he first learned that the schools were merging. The odds of getting together with Barbara had increased by leaps and bounds. Barbara had of course noticed the star basketball player when her team had gone down in defeat at the hands—literally—of Marvin Pruett. But now, with the schools having merged, she would not be considered a traitor for going steady with the sharpshooter.

The "jocks," the boys who excel in sports, especially basketball, are usually the stars of the school—the ones everyone looks up to and respects. If the players are high school royalty, their girlfriends are princesses as far as their classmates are concerned. It's natural for a certain "pecking order" to emerge.

Some people, of course, peak during their high school years, which then become the high-water mark in their lives, but this would not be the case for these Black Hawks. Being forged in the competitive fires seemed only to prepare them for the realities of life. There are winners and losers, and the only way to win is through challenging work.

Marvin Pruett knew he was a winner. He had been hitting those wonderful jump shots since he was in junior high school and hearing the roar of the crowd as the ball slipped through the net. And he loved the feeling of success. Marvin realized the countless hours he had put in, throwing up those thousands of shots to the goal on the side of his house and on the ball court at the Jesuit college, were now paying off for him in a big way. He was part of a very strong team, and he had a girl he could confide in.

He simply loved his life. He loved Barbara Love—and the fact that she appreciated and understood basketball and came to every game. Just knowing she was in the crowd inspired him. Just as Frankie did, he liked the fact that his girlfriend was keeping her eyes on him during games.

Marvin had never experienced this funny feeling inside before. Neither had his heart felt this unfamiliar ache—that feeling of being so powerfully drawn to someone, as if she were the source of life itself. He adored everything about his girlfriend. Barbara was a year older and a senior. Marvin thought she was the most beautiful and sophisticated girl he'd ever seen. The very sound of her voice touched a deep chord within him. Something in her tone, even her slight Southern Indiana accent, made him fall more deeply in love with her with every conversation. She was soft and gentle whereas Marvin was a bit rough around the edges, but, of course, opposites attract.

But Marvin was always ready for a laugh or a good joke, and so was Barbara. It seemed they laughed more than anything else when they were together. The fact that Barbara thought Laurel and Hardy were the funniest comedic actors ever to have graced the silver screen endeared her even more to Marvin. Barbara was one of the drum majorettes, and Marvin thought she looked like a movie star in her outfit.

Once, he asked her, "What's the difference between a majorette and a drum majorette?"

"Well," Barbara replied, "A drum majorette has a whistle and marches in front of the other majorettes."

There was a pause after Marvin said, "Oh, so it's having a whistle, huh?" Then, they both erupted in laughter, which they had become used to doing together. Marvin could relate to the lyrics of the rock 'n' roll song "Susie Q": "I love the way you walk / I love the way you talk." Barbara had a certain musical cadence in her speech and in the way she simply walked through the halls of school. Her confidence drew this boy to her even more. Yep, everything about this young lady told Marvin that she was his gal.

Double Dating

As many of the ball games were on Friday nights, Marvin and Frankie decided to take their ladies out one Saturday night to see *The Seven Voyages of Sinbad,* the film playing at the Springs Valley Theater. The girls didn't care much for the movie, but the guys loved every minute—especially when the Cyclops begins to roast the captured sailors over an open fire.

"I can't watch this!" Barbara whispered.

"Hey, they're just a bunch of actors on a Hollywood set," Marvin reminded her. "Relax. No one is getting hurt. I don't think."

"Next movie we see will be the new Debbie Reynolds movie we saw the advertisement for," Barbara whispered back. "*Tammy and the Bachelor.*"

After what the girls considered a dreadful movie, the couples walked up Maple Street to the corner drug store for an ice cream sundae. The boys hoped that since Thelma worked there, they would get special treatment in the form of a bigger helping of ice cream.

This was the usual order of things for a Saturday night date in the Valley. As they sat at the aluminum counter, twisting back and forth on the swiveling stools, they discussed the merits of the film they'd just seen. The guys only saw greatness in the production: huge stop-motion animation monsters seemed to come to life, and those Hollywood wizards could make a lizard appear to be an ancient dinosaur, even if it pretty much still looked like a chameleon with a fin attached to its back.

The girls listened politely until Thelma finally said, "I sure would like to go see *Tammy and the Bachelor.*" Barbara wholeheartedly agreed.

"That would be a wonderful movie to see."

Debbie Reynolds' latest hit record, "Tammy," had been getting a *lot* of play on the Louisville radio station lately. Marvin started in.

"Oh, that's the song with those incredibly romantic lyrics. 'That old hooty owl hooty-hoos to the dove. Tammy, Tammy, Tammy's in love.' What in the world does that mean, anyway? Does the owl fall in love with the dove? I mean, why is the owl hooty-hooing to a dove—shouldn't it be another owl he's hooty-hooing to?"

"Was Tammy a bird watcher?" Frankie wanted to know. "How did she know the owl hooty-hooed to the dove?"

Both boys began laughing, finding themselves hilarious. The girls just rolled their eyes, then excused themselves to go powder their noses.

"Men. What are you going to do?"

By the time the girls returned to the counter to finish their sundaes, the boys had talked it over. They promised that the next movie they'd take the girls to would be *Tammy and the Bachelor.*

"Just maybe there's a bit of romance in these two fellas after all," Barbara announced, as the girls looked at each other and smiled, proud to be sitting next to two of the best players on the Black Hawks team. Life couldn't get much better for a small-town teen-age girl.

The jokes always went around like this between the couples—whether they were alone or together on double dates. They all believed that verse in Proverbs: "Laughter is like a good medicine." Of course, they had much to be jovial about with the Black Hawks' first season, the new high school, and rock 'n' roll—the world seemed to belong to them.

There is a saying that "Youth is wasted on the young." But it was not true in the case of these kids. These boys and girls, the team and their young coach, were not wasting a minute.

It was early in the season, but it already seemed as if everything had been written by some scriptwriter and that all the stars were aligning. This was the story where the heroes vanquish their foes and in the end, win the girl; the bad guys lose, the good guys win, and everybody lives happily ever after.

They were making memories that would last a lifetime, and they would reap the benefits for the rest of their lives.

Game # 5: An Explosive Team

The Silver Creek Dragons were next on the schedule. This was the second road game of the season, with three more away games to follow. The referee's starting whistle couldn't come fast enough for the young warriors. The Hawks wanted so much to keep their winning streak alive. The boys from the Valley knew that five wins in a row would start turning more heads and improving opinions of the team and their young coach.

During a time-out in the first quarter when the Silver Creek Dragons began outscoring the Hawks, Marvin complained in the huddle, "Man, those guys are all over us. The refs aren't calling fouls!"

Coach Wells quickly addressed his remark. "Pruett, play tougher. You can't control anyone but yourself. Forget about the 'no-calls.' I can see that these refs are amateurs. Just go back out there and play better. Do what you know how to do—play ball! Play your defense. Make those passes. Move to the ball. Block out underneath, and put the ball in the basket. Now get out there and play Black Hawks basketball!"

At the end of the first quarter, the Hawks found themselves down for the first time at the end of the first eight minutes of play, with the score 18-13. The Valley Boys had not come across this strong a team so far in their schedule. The score seesawed during the second quarter with eight ties, and the teams headed to the locker rooms at half-time with Springs Valley having taken the lead, 30-27.

The Dragons proved to be a very worthy adversary for three and a half quarters on their home court. But there were two men "posing as referees," as the local sportswriter had it, who "turned their heads when the going got tough." In the third stanza, the Hawks started to take over the game, outscoring the Dragons 15-8, which led to the sportswriter's tongue-in-cheek observation, "The Dragons were draggin' in the third canto."

The boys and coach realized that playing hard for the full 32 minutes was the only way to win a game. In a couple of their games so far, their opponents had stayed close for three quarters, but when it came to the last eight minutes, the Hawks had seemed to know just when to switch to that extra gear that put them comfortably ahead. On this night, Silver Creek turned the tables, giving Springs Valley fans a scare when they came roaring back in the final quarter to outscore the Hawks, 20-17. But when the timer's gun went off, it hadn't been enough to overcome Valley's lead. Schmutzler, Pruett, McCracken, and Radcliff were all in double figures. The consistent scoring of these four had continued.

The boys hadn't disappointed their coach or their fans on this evening, either. They "slayed the Dragons"—an over-used term in most of the local sports columns the next day—beating Silver Creek 62-55, even though a lack of foul calls seemed to suggest two referees had been looking the other way.

But for now, the Hawks were still winning, and learning, and everyone in the two towns was beginning to wonder the same thing. Could these guys win their sectional? Could they even make it to the regionals? That would be an accomplishment that had never occurred in either French Lick or West Baden.

So far, the sports columnist had had it right. "Sprudels + Pluto = Dynamite." The school consolidation was now looking to the local citizenry like the best idea that had ever come down the pike. The new school colors seemed to be showing up everywhere one looked in the twin towns. The Black Hawks train had pulled out of the station, and folks were scrambling to get on board.

• CHAPTER 9 •

YEA, THOUGH I WALK THROUGH THE VALLEY

Although hills and valleys were not conducive to large stretches of farmland, there were several small farms sprinkled around the area. John Sutherland owned one of the larger farms. John had a daughter, Michelle, but he called her Mickie; he had always wanted a boy. Because John was a successful businessman, having invested in the Twin City Lumber Company, Mickie grew up in an affluent home—like those seen in the idealized family TV shows folks were watching: "Lassie," "Ozzie and Harriet," and "Leave it to Beaver."

Mickie was already driving a tractor by the time she was 10 years old. After her mother passed away two years later, Mickie pretty much ran the household and grew up rather quickly. She always seemed much older to the other kids her age—and in many ways, she was. She was also one of the most popular kids throughout her school years.

Mickie was a senior in '57. She had dated Paul Radcliff the year before—when she was a junior and Paul was a freshman. Mickie could drive, and Paul was all for that. He had already reached his height of 6'1" so there was no incongruity when they walked together. However, the couple only lasted for that year and now, Mickie had dated Butch over the summer.

Mickie loved boys with nice cars, and Butch was one of only a few boys in the Valley with his own set of wheels. However, once the basketball season had started, Mickie had begun seeing a young man from nearby Paoli who drove a souped-up 1950 Plymouth Coupe. It was a hot-rod, and Mickie did love engines and tail pipes that made a lot of noise. It was probably her early connection with tractors, she decided.

The young couple had decided to go to the Rustic, a juke joint down near Jasper. The Rustic's "bring your own beer" policy made it easy for kids under drinking age to gain access to the popular dance hall. Later that night, driving home along State Road 56, the boy driving fell asleep at the wheel.

As sturdy as the old Plymouth was, it couldn't compete with the old oak tree that stood beside the right lane at one of the sharp turns that stretch of road is known for. Both Mickie and her date were thrown from the car, and both their young lives ended on this tragic night. A Saturday night that had begun so routinely had ended in heartbreak and anguish.

Butch heard the news first because his dad was the town's mortician, and the next morning, he called Paul.

"Paul, I've got some terrible news . . . uh . . . some very sad news. Mickie was killed last night in a car crash, coming home from the Rustic."

"No! Oh no! Oh no! Oh God!" was all that Paul could say. This can't be happening, he thought. Stunned, he said to Butch, "I gotta go to church. See ya tomorrow."

Paul buried his head in his hands and wept for Mickie and her family, and that morning, his church prayed for 30 minutes for Mr. Sutherland. They knew that Mickie was the apple of his eye, and he would now have to face this devastating news alone. He had lost his wife six years earlier, and now this.

Mickie's death was difficult for both Butch and Paul, and certainly for all her other friends and classmates, to accept. Just the day before, many had seen her full of life at the Paoli drive-in, laughing and listening to the car radio at full volume in her new boyfriend's car. She had died much, much too young.

The school closed the following Monday. The principal and staff knew their charges would need time to deal with the emotional impact of the sudden loss.

Many students simply couldn't make themselves attend Mickie's funeral. The harsh reality of the tragedy didn't fit into their world of dating, hayrides, bonfires, the Chatterbox drive-in, basketball, and everything else that filled the local teen-agers' daily lives. It was surreal.

It was a very sad time in the Valley—the shadow of death had crossed it.

If We Make It Through December

The sixth game for the Hawks was just up the road, 13 miles to Paoli. It had been a week since the Hawks' last game. The Paoli Rams, in the past, had been the greatest rival for both the Sprudels and the Red Devils—except for their own battles with each other. All the locals looked forward to this match-up. In fact, most of Orange County was anticipating this game.

Paoli's gym was packed to capacity. Every game now, in fact, was standing room only. Basketball fans from all over Southern Indiana were driving to see this team that had come out of nowhere and was just starting to make headlines outside of Springs Valley. The excitement was growing.

Tonight, however, prior to the national anthem, a moment of silence was requested in memory of Mickie and of Henry Brown, the boy from Paoli. It was oddly sobering, as it contrasted so sharply with the exuberance of youth and the festive atmosphere.

As they put their hands together and hollered, "TEAM!" as they came out of the huddle, there were tears in Butch's eyes. "Let's win this one for Mickie!" he shouted.

Butch came out to play like a man on a mission. He was going to ensure that this game was won for the girl he had dated. He racked up 19 points as high scorer in this contest. Bob and Marvin followed close behind with 16 and 15 points respectively. Paul and Frankie put in 13 points between them plus 16 rebounds, and the diminutive Frankie added 10 more.

There were two plays that evoked oohs and aahs from the crowd. On one play, Frankie shot the ball hard from outside the foul circle. When it hit the rim, it took a hard and high bounce back to the foul line. Butch, apparently by instinct, just slapped the ball from there—and it went in.

People couldn't believe their eyes. Bob laughed as they ran back on defense.

"Bet you didn't call that shot!"

"Sure, I did!" The two boys, who had faced off during a scrimmage just before the season, now viewed each other differently. Though they would never be close—the differences in their backgrounds and lifestyles were too great—they were developing real respect and camaraderie on the basketball court.

The other impressive highlight from the game came when Paul was trapped in the right corner, trying to get the ball out to the backcourt. All he could do was give a quick fake as if going up for a shot. Then he turned to the side, away from the two Rams guarding him, and made a hook shot from 15 feet away. It splashed through the net, clean as a whistle. Even the Paoli fans had to appreciate that athletic feat.

The scoring was consistent, with the six main scorers lining up in the same order. Marvin, Butch or Bob usually had the most points, then Paul, Jackie, and Frankie. The same players made the same contributions from game to game pretty much as expected. And it seemed that every time a substitute player came off the bench, he contributed as well. Jack Belcher, Mike Watson, George Lagenour, Jim Conrad, and Jerry Breedlove were the second team, and they had done their job in keeping this team rolling. These boys were strong players who, after all, had to compete against their own starting five in daily scrimmages.

Sometimes the second team would beat the first team. "Mike, you guard Marvin," the coach might say. Or "Breedlove, you take

Bob in today's scrimmage," he might tell Jerry, when no one would volunteer to guard the player known as "the Enforcer."

Rex knew that this would only make his bench players that much better.

The Rams went down in defeat, 85-69, in this first game of December. Another team toppled by the Black Hawks. The Paoli sportswriter, attempting to keep up with the creative headlines by the *Herald*'s Jim Ballard, wrote, "Clean Records Stand as Hawks Claw Rams." It seems that Paoli's young and inexperienced team had suffered their seventh straight loss as Springs Valley had triumphed with their sixth consecutive victory.

The next two games were also on the road, and then there was one more home game just before Christmas.

Standing Nearly Cornered in Winslow, Indiana

The Hawks had faced Paoli on Friday evening. Now, on Tuesday, they were headed to Winslow, Indiana, to take on the Eskimos on Winslow's home court. As usual, sportswriters broke out the puns, with the *Springs Valley Herald* sports page predicting, *"We believe the red-hot Blackhawks will thaw out the Eskimos at Winslow next Tuesday night."*

Now, why a school in Southern Indiana would come up with "Eskimos" as their team name, no one could guess, outside of the rhyme. Perhaps it was because Winslow was near Santa Claus, Indiana, and the proximity to ol' Saint Nick was the only inspiration needed for this moniker. Springs Valley's playing schedule was dotted with quirky team names.

They would take on the Eskimos without help from Bob McCracken, who had badly sprained an ankle in a practice the day before. He was quite frustrated with not being able to play. Bob was very introverted, and Coach Wells could easily see that he was withdrawing into himself. He understood, too, that sometimes fathers and sons can grow distant through no real fault of their own, and that problems can go unrecognized or simply be ignored within a family.

It was clear that Bob now needed some advice. The coach truly cared for his players, and whenever any of them faced a challenge, Rex would write an encouraging note.

When Rex saw him in the hall the day of the game, he handed him a note.

"Bob, please read this when you get a chance."

In study hall, Bob opened the note. The coach spoke to him the way a father would.

"Dear Bob, I know that you're having a tough time right now," the note read. "I understand. Life is never easy. It will always be full of challenges that we must face and overcome. I know how strong a young man you are. I know you'll get through this and come out stronger. Have faith in God. Have faith in yourself.

"You are such a strong part of our team. I know you always give your best out on the court. Now, give this challenge your best. Imagine any challenge like it's just one more rebound you are fighting for, one more bucket you are trying to make, or the next game that you desperately want to win. You will come out better than before. I know you will.

"I have faith in you, Bob. Your Coach."

The note really touched Bob's heart. He had never had anyone address him this way before. It was clear that Rex cared for his team far beyond the confines of the basketball court.

They were family.

The Winslow game was the Hawks' seventh contest, and again, Marvin contributed 25 points, reinforcing his 19.1-point per game average. Even without Bob, the best rebounder and one of the highest scorers on the team, Valley came out on top, 57-50. The Eskimos, competing on their home court, did give Springs Valley a run for their money, losing to the Hawks by only seven points, just as Jasper and Silver Creek had. The Eskimos, Dragons, and Wildcats had all come close to beating the Hawks from the Valley.

Ironically, the biggest snowstorm of the year hit as the team bus and the fans from Springs Valley were leaving the Winslow Eskimos in their rear-view mirrors. It took most travelers two hours to reach their homes on this blustery winter night.

Three days later, on Friday, December 13, the Hawks traveled due north on State Road 37 to Orleans, where they continued their streak, defeating the Bulldogs by a wee-bit-more-comfortable eight points.

At last, the boys had nearly a week off before their next game. Their last contest of 1957, on December 20, was against Washington Catholic. They could use the rest, but they were looking forward to a home game after battling in three straight games on the road. Playing in their own house and feeding off the electricity generated by their fans would make that well-worn gym come alive.

The Games get Tighter

By now, Springs Valley's ninth game, the word was out, and every team the Hawks faced was bringing their best game—"comin' to town to gun 'em down." The final curtain on this game against Washington Catholic, and the 1957 part of this season, still saw the Hawks winning—but by a mere five points. The winning margin seemed to be getting smaller and smaller. But a win was a win, and so far, no one had been able to knock off the Hawks.

In the locker room, after the closest finish the Hawks had endured, Paul casually mentioned, "The Lord was with us tonight. I think some of those boys must've been praying hard themselves. I saw some of their fans with rosary beads in their hands."

"Yeah, that was a close one," Marvin offered. "I saw that group of nuns, with their eyes closed, looking pretty intense. But I sure liked their colors. Black and white! They would've looked right at home on our side of the court!"

Paul thought this would be an appropriate time to invite the team to his church for the Christmas cantata.

"I'm just not a cantata kind of guy," Marvin quipped, then added, "What the heck is a cantata, anyway?"

"It's a musical presentation, Marvin. Christmas music about our Lord Jesus' birth and why he came to earth on that first Christmas Eve."

"Oh boy, here we go." Marvin couldn't help himself.

"You do realize that it couldn't have been December 25th when Jesus was born, don't you? All of those Christmas carols just make up a bunch of stuff to make it sound like Joseph and Mary were trudging through snow drifts, on a donkey, trying to find a place to stay the night."

"Oh, oh—I heard my dad say this one joke," Bob chimed in. "Did you know that Mary was very unhappy as she and Joseph traveled to the place of Jesus' birth? Yeah, the Bible says that Mary rode Joseph's ass all the way to Bethlehem!"

The boys burst out laughing at Bob's joke. Paul didn't laugh, and responded as if Bob hadn't spoken.

"It doesn't matter—those nonessential details," he said. "The reality is that Jesus was born into this world, and came to save us all from our sins." Paul couldn't help himself either. Any time he could stand up for his faith, he did, and tonight wasn't going to be an exception.

He felt that the real reason Marvin always chided him about his faith was that he really wanted Paul to talk about his beliefs. So, these verbal battles had been going on since junior high school. Paul felt that Marvin's heart was softening, thanks to the many prayers he had prayed for Marvin to come to the Lord.

Paul tried the invitation again. "So, let me know who's coming to the cantata. Connie Wright and Cora Hendrix are playing piano and singing a duet," he said, trying to sweeten the pot.

No one answered. But after a few awkward seconds, Marvin said, "Okay, I'll be there. Me and Barbara, we'll be there. I'm not kidding."

Paul just said, "Great," and smiled to himself as he dressed in front of his open locker. A wooden cross hung inside the door.

After this close game, the last of 1957, Coach Wells came home to his wife.

"Y'know, we've got a pretty good team here." Rex was thinking aloud as he climbed into bed.

"We're actually 9 and O," he reminded Margaret—as if she could have forgotten.

"It's going to be a very Merry Christmas this year," she said. "I'm so proud of you," she whispered. She then kissed her husband in a way that always made him forget about everything else in the universe but Margaret. He knew he was very blessed. When the kiss was over, Rex came up for air.

"Yes, I believe it will be," he panted. "I just know it will be!"

When a coach has a winning team, everything is right with the world. He feels "peace on earth and goodwill towards man."

Christmas Love

Marvin and Barbara had a date almost every Saturday night, if there wasn't a game. Now, school was out, and a couple of days before Christmas, the new couple decided it would be fun to attend the annual Christmas concert at the French Lick Sheraton Hotel. Every year, the hotel brought in an orchestra and singers for an hour-long program.

Marvin borrowed his mom's '52 Plymouth Desoto Deluxe and picked Barbara up at 6 p.m. They decided to stop by the corner drug store for a soda and burger before the much-awaited annual concert.

"Hey, Thelma, how's it goin'," Marvin practically shouted as the couple entered the store.

Thelma was just ending her shift behind the counter and took off her apron to sit down with them for a minute before she went home.

"Hey, why don't you and Frankie go out with us on a double date again some time?" Marvin asked.

"Oh, sure . . . sure, that would be fun," Thelma answered. She couldn't help thinking that with this other couple, the conversation tended to come much more easily.

Marvin and Barbara downed their burgers and sodas and left the drugstore, then drove down to the corner, where Marvin parked along the street beside the Star Store. He knew Frankie's boss wouldn't mind if it were his car parked there, blocking the view into the store.

Mr. Ellis was following the Hawks mighty closely since his stock boy was now starting each game. Plus, it was a Saturday night. Marvin could see the lights being turned off in the store.

He and Barbara held hands as they walked along State Road 56, then crossed at the sidewalk entrance to the hotel. They felt very sophisticated, having dressed up in their Sunday best for this special occasion.

As they strolled up the wide walk toward the lobby entrance and climbed the grand, red-carpeted stairway, a pair of avid basketball fans came up to Marvin and asked him for his autograph. Marvin was so taken aback he began to laugh. It embarrassed him. He thought of himself as just another high school student who played a good game of basketball and happened to have a jump shot that usually went in the basket. Getting free burgers and Cokes from the corner drug store was one thing, but this kind of treatment was a bit uncomfortable for the 16-year-old shooting star.

A year ago, he realized, he would've felt just a wee bit on his guard going into French Lick without his buddies. But now he was being greeted with open arms and treated like a local celebrity. Oh, how those jump shots create admiration—when the guy hitting them plays for your team!

Marvin quickly introduced Barbara, and the autograph hounds immediately asked her to sign her name on the Christmas program as well.

"Whoa, Nellie! This is getting kind of strange," Marvin whispered as they walked away.

"Yeah, that made me feel so weird," Barbara agreed.

As they entered the hotel lobby, Marvin tried to imagine whose famous feet had walked over these same inlaid tiles of Italian marble back when the resort was thriving. He knew that FDR had visited here. Marvin's dad always spoke of the time he saw John Dillinger on the hotel's veranda, sitting in one of the big rocking chairs with a cigar in one hand and a bottle of Scotch in the other.

One time, too, when his dad was working at the golf course, he had caddied for Bing Crosby. Marvin recalled how his dad expected the biggest tip of his life for hauling the superstar's golf clubs around for 18 holes. Afterward, however, he had handed his caddy only a couple of bucks. Bing was a bust.

Most of the lobby's former splendor had been painted over by the Sheraton Hotel Corporation, but Marvin and Barbara could imagine how posh the place must've been in 1920. The ornately tiled floor was still in its original condition, and seeing it always caught Marvin's imagination, sending him into the past as he wondered about the glory days the two towns had enjoyed.

The young couple walked hand in hand through the hotel lobby and made their way into the grand hall for the concert. It was very close to starting time, but no musicians were in place yet. Marvin overheard someone say that some of the musicians and singers had gotten stuck in a snowstorm north of Indianapolis.

Everyone sat staring ahead at the two Christmas trees that adorned each side of the stage. Then, the emcee entered stage left and walked to the microphone.

"We've had a bit of a change of plans for this evening's performance. Tonight, we are very fortunate to have some of the best musicians from Chicago with us. They've just finished their engagement at McCormick Place and at LaRue's Supper Club in Indianapolis. They have just arrived, having been stuck in a snowdrift up north.

"However, the singers have been held up somewhere between here and there, due to old man winter. So, we have a special guest singer with us tonight: our own Billy D. Wright."

The 31-year old native of French Lick came out from behind the curtain and made his way to the microphone.

"Oh, great, some local yokel," the teenagers heard a man behind them say.

The young singer walked onto the stage as confidently as Frank Sinatra. With his hands in his trench coat and wearing a Gene Kelly-style fedora, he strolled to the microphone as the band struck up "I'll Be Home for Christmas." A snow machine helped set the mood as the lights dimmed and the spotlight narrowed in on the young crooner, who sang effortlessly as he leaned against a lamppost. It seemed a scene from *Holiday Inn.*

"Wow, this guy's not so bad," the voice behind Marvin and Barbara said aloud. When the song ended, the audience clapped and clapped. Marvin reread the singer's name in the hastily printed program.

"I think he used to play basketball in the '40s," he said. "My dad mentioned him as being the player who made a winning shot in the '43 Sectional. I think Thelma lives in the house he lived in, over on Adams Street.

"If he played ball as good as he can sing, then I imagine French Lick had a pretty strong team back then," Marvin concluded.

The love-struck couple left the concert that night singing "I'll Be Home for Christmas" and sharing the incredible euphoria only a high school romance can create. It was cold outside, and the snow had been coming down hard. Barbara spoke through her chattering teeth.

"Gosh, maybe we'll have a white Christmas."

"Yeah, it's looking that way," Marvin answered as he put his arm around his sweetheart. The snowflakes, illuminated by the street lamps that lined the hotel walkway, were now large, wet, and falling steadily. The snow already on the ground created a stillness in the dream-like silent night. The couple felt as if they were in a dream, walking inside a giant snow globe.

Arm in arm, they strode back to the car, hopped in, and turned on both the heater and radio. The Louisville station was playing the sounds of the season, and Bing Crosby's "Have Yourself a Merry Little Christmas" drifted among the fragments of their conversation as they waited for the car to warm up.

Barbara was certain that Marvin could hear the pounding of her excited heart. Marvin knew she could hear his. This was a new and intoxicating experience for the young couple, so much in love. As they hugged each other, the car slowly warmed. They sat a while in the heavenly glow of the dashboard lights, serenaded by the radio.

"'Have Yourself a Merry Little Christmas,' Barbara," Marvin whispered in her ear.

"Oh, I am. I am!" is all she could say.

They wished this "silent night" could last the rest of their lives—and it would.

A Long Walk for a Kiss

This same evening, Frankie decided he would take a walk and visit Thelma. Just up the steep hill—steeper than all the others, that is—beyond the hotel, and at the top of the winding Old French Lick Road, was Mount Airy, where Frankie now lived with his aunt.

The distance to Thelma's was not a short one, but Frankie wanted to demonstrate just how much he loved his new girlfriend. His three-and-a-half-mile walk began just as the snow was beginning to fall. By the time he reached Thelma's house, on the far side of town, he was looking much like a snowman, totally covered in the wet, sticky flakes.

He knocked on her door. She answered.

"Oh, Frankie! Hi. I wasn't expecting . . . uh . . . anyone. Come in." Thelma could immediately see how much this boy cared for her. But he surprised her again.

"Nah, I've gotta get back home." With that, he leaned toward her, kissed her on the cheek, and turned around to make the walk back to Mount Airy.

Thelma was astounded that anyone would make such an effort, and all for a hello and a peck on the cheek. She was falling deeply in love. She knew in her heart God had brought them together. As she lay her head on her pillow in the soft stillness of the snowy night, she prayed.

"Thank you, Lord, for Frankie Self. If it be Thy will, please allow us to be together."

She fell asleep with a smile on her face—the same sweet, gentle smile that Frankie, way up on Mount Airy again, was picturing at that moment.

Game 10: The Blowout

Christmas vacation had arrived, and Rex Wells felt he could finally relax for a day or two. He let the team take a few days off before Christmas, but they would resume practice on December 26. Their next game was January 3, down in Corydon, and the coach wanted his team to be sharp for this first game of the second half of the schedule. Corydon was about the farthest the team had to travel during the regular season.

The Hawks hadn't lost anything over Christmas break. In fact, they looked better than ever. They embarrassed the Corydon Panthers, whipping them 85-47. Pruett and McCracken alone outscored the Panthers by two points; Marv totaled 26 and Bob garnered 23. Radcliff and Schmutzler hit double figures with 13 and 12 points respectively.

Frankie hit one of three and a free throw. Defense was his strong suit, and he always got the ball to the hot-handed players. He understood his role, and his intelligent style of play truly reflected both his humility and cleverness.

Each player's personality, in fact, was reflected in how he played the game. Frankie was reserved and quiet but confidently went about his business on the court. Marvin was a more outgoing and confident teen, whose approach to the game was a "Give me the ball, I'll score" attitude. Bob, aka the Enforcer, was the blue-collar, no-nonsense, hard worker under the boards. Butch was the flashy "girl magnet" type. His abilities came naturally and he made his contributions look easy.

Paul was the smartest, the only A+ student on the team, and the sophomore class president. He was consistent, the rudder steadying the ship, and offered his best on and off the court. His passing game was his specialty. This inclination to give the ball to the other players fit him perfectly. "Give and it shall be given unto you" was a Bible verse constantly on Paul's mind, and he lived what he believed.

The other boys did indeed sense a certain spirit about Paul. His surety in his faith, in who he was in Christ, gave the other boys hope and strength. Some people are just that way, able to speak freely about what is in their heart. Paul had plenty in his heart to share, and he did every time he was given the chance, always in a loving and confident way.

In this first game of the new year, the Corydon Panthers had been no match for the undefeated Black Hawks team, every one of whom scored in this game. Second team players contributed too: Mike Watson got a bucket, Jim Conrad sank a pair of free throws, and Belcher hit two hook shots—left-handed. The Hawks' second string could play with the best of them.

Now, the teams that already had faced Springs Valley once this season were dreading the second meeting with the hungry Hawks. For Paoli and Orleans, it was a sort of déjà vu, but this time it was worse for both. Each lost by even greater margins than in their first meeting with Springs Valley. The Hawks outscored Paoli by 18 points. The Valley Boys played their usual strong defense, with Frankie leading the way with three steals. Pruett's hot hand, knocking down 24 points, was complemented by Butch's 16, Paul's 10, and Bob's 9, as the meat of their scoring.

The sizzling Black Hawks then racked up 85 points against Orleans' 59. The boys in black and white with gold trim were really on a roll. They were 12-0.

Marvin put in 38 of those 85 points himself by the end of the third quarter. Coach Wells took him out of the game. Marvin was not happy. He had wanted to achieve a record that would be hard to beat. But Rex wasn't concerned about records. He wanted only for his team to play their best—and he didn't like running up the score on any team. Orleans lost to the Black Hawks by 26 points. The Hawks' main scorers did their job again in this game with four of the starters scoring in double figures, which pleased Coach Wells a good deal.

The Hawks were getting a lot of publicity now in all the newspapers south of Bloomington, Indiana. Winning 12 games in a row draws attention. The Springs Valley Black Hawks were beginning to make a name for themselves as a basketball team, and many locals were beginning to put these boys on pedestals.

When team members went into the corner drug store for a milk shake and a burger, Mr. Deremiah always said, "It's on the house. Keep up the excellent work out there on the court. We're all so proud of you boys." The other popular restaurant, the Chatterbox (which Marvin had dubbed "the Choke and Puke") did the same. In fact, when the Valley Boys walked into their favorite burger joint, they were royalty and were being treated as such by the eating establishments, the local citizenry, and their fellow students.

The local barber, Bill Andrew, offered anyone on the team a free haircut. Fortunately for him, they all had crew cuts, which meant the cuts didn't take long. The Bible-believing barber always made sure to invite the boys to his little country church as well, and he let them know that the congregation was keeping them in their prayers.

The entire town was becoming euphoric about this team. The Black Hawks train had only a few passengers early in the season. Now it had filled and was chugging along at full steam. Everyone was glad to be on this wild ride with Rex Wells and the boys from the Valley.

Another Tragedy Visits the Valley

Butch's dad, Ben Schmutzler, was an avid fisherman. He always enjoyed taking his boat and getting away for a couple days in between his funeral duties. It wasn't unusual for him to take a few days off when things were slow and go down to the east fork of the White River "to drown some worms" at Hindostan Falls. Once the site of a thriving town, the Falls had been given its exotic name by an immigrant who'd served with the British East India Company. The community had been plagued by insects that thrived in the flood plain, and disease and economic woes had destroyed the town in the early 19th century.

On an unusually warm January day, Ben decided he'd get up early and drive down to the Falls to get some fishing in. His wife saw him drive off that morning, but she never saw him again. He simply disappeared—much as the town of Hindostan Falls had.

The local authorities labeled it an accidental drowning, since all they could find was his small boat. An air of mystery persisted for a long time, as some people in town made claims of having seen Ben outside of French Lick even months after his disappearance. However, many years later, Ben's remains were finally discovered. He had in fact drowned, his body trapped under sunken trees for decades.

Butch, of course, took his dad's death as hard as any teenage boy would at losing his father. He no longer joked around after this traumatic event. But on the ball court, he seemed to play like a man possessed—as if he channeled all his hurt and misery into the games. He played his best ball from that point on. Each time he'd go to the foul line, the boys could see him whisper something to himself and look upward toward the ceiling.

Everyone figured he was having a "father and son" talk. Frankie seemed to take this tragedy the hardest among the other team members; he knew what it was like to lose a father.

"Anytime you wanna talk to someone about it, I'm here. I understand what you're goin' through," Frankie assured Butch.

The reality of human mortality now had reared its ugly head twice during this basketball season and hissed at the newly formed team and community. These grim reminders seemed to be reminding all the players and the town's young and old alike that the game of basketball was just that—a game.

But, as Rex observed, so many analogies to life could be drawn from that game. Dream big, work hard, and do your best, and many times remarkable things can happen. Other times, it's simply that bad things can happen to good people. You win some. You lose some. It's just life. It's just basketball.

But this team didn't yet know what it was like to lose a game.

"The shadow of death" had visited the Valley. But being continually buoyed by the team's success, everyone simultaneously felt that fresh infusion of life that much more.

"Go Hawks, go!"

• CHAPTER 10 •

ALL FOR ONE AND ONE FOR ALL

Grover Reeder was the greatest Black Hawks fan in town. No one could argue this point. He was also the smallest adult male in town—the size person that folks in the '50s referred to as a "midget," though they meant no disrespect.

In fact, Grover was known as "Shorty" to everyone in West Baden and French Lick. He didn't mind; after all, he knew local fellas who'd acquired odd and even startling monikers, such as "Fats," "Chubby," "Boob," "Booger Man," and "Stovepipe." Shorty seemed to relish this nickname and his position as one of the local business owners.

Grover loved basketball and this new team so much that he even attended every single team practice—and every game—except one.

He bore a resemblance to the mayor of Munchkinland from *The Wizard of Oz*. Shorty kind of waddled as he walked about town, and he'd become a pleasant and unique part of the landscape, endearing himself to everyone. Everybody loved Shorty. Back when he was in school, he would have trouble navigating the stairs to the second floor. Two boys would sit him in a chair, lift from the sides, and carry him up to his classes. After high school, he'd attended college and now had his own accounting business. He was a smart businessman.

When his father died, he left Shorty the family business—the pool hall in West Baden. Not only did the two towns contain the two historic hotels; they also each had to have their own pool hall. Mick Marshall's Billiards was in French Lick, and Shorty's was in West Baden. Shorty was quite popular with the patrons of his more-or-less respectable establishment, and he always seemed happy to see his friends and acquaintances. He was always giving the West Baden boys rides to places they needed to go, and they went in style: a '57 two-tone Nash Metropolitan in turquoise and white.

One day, earlier in the season, Coach Wells turned to Grover and said, "Hey Shorty, you see and hear a lot of what is going around town. I'd like you to help me out."

"Sure Coach. What can I do for you?"

"Listen, you know how boys will be boys, and we have a pretty tough schedule this year," Rex said. "I would like you to be my second set of eyes and ears. You know, let me know what you hear about or what you see going on with the boys. I know Marvin, Bob, and Frankie come into your pool hall sometimes. Just let me know if you hear of anything that I should know about. I don't want anyone on the team breaking training rules."

"Sure, coach," Shorty responded. "I'd be glad to help you out."

Although Shorty was the owner of two businesses, this informal assignment now became his top priority. He felt he was an assistant coach. After all, he did spend every afternoon at the gym, watching the Hawks practice. It just made sense that he would be the one to keep an eye on things for the coach—outside the gymnasium.

The team members, who had returned to some normalcy with their practices after the week of Butch's dad's funeral, all tried to spend as much time with their starting forward and co-captain as they could.

But Butch was caught with a case of beer in his car trunk. There also were rumors around school that he had been seen in Paoli, drinking in his car.

Coach Wells knew that Butch was the only boy with his own car and therefore may have appeared older than the others. He also knew young men are given to experimenting. Then, too, Butch may have been indulging his sorrows over his father's and Mickie's deaths. Coach Wells put some "feelers" out to find out if the rumors were indeed true, and the coach's "second set of eyes," Shorty Reeder, confirmed the rumor. He had seen Butch drinking a beer up at the Southfork drive-in.

Butch had grown up in a German family home. In many ways, the senior was more mature than the other boys. He dressed like a grownup. He drove a car that any adult would be proud to own and he spoke and presented himself well. Drinking beer for the Schmutzlers was as normal as an Italian family enjoying wine during dinner. To Butch, it was no big deal. He just liked beer, and his dad had begun allowing him to have one at home since Butch was 13 years old.

Nevertheless, Butch was under age, and drinking was against team rules. When the news of Butch's drinking was confirmed to the coach, he began the next practice in an unusual way.

"Billy, put the balls in the rack. We're not going to play basketball today," Rex Wells said sternly. The team knew something was really bothering him; they had never seen him like this. He sat the team down and spoke.

"Boys, something has been brought to my attention," he began. "It's an infraction that I won't put up with, but I do understand that anyone can make a mistake in judgment—especially when one is under certain duress or depression. As all of you are aware, one of your teammates was caught with alcoholic beverages in his car.

"Butch and I have discussed this in private and I have his word that this will never happen again. If it does, he'll be off the team—no matter how many points a game he scores."

The coach had the boys' full attention. He went on.

"Now, I learned something in the military, and none of you will like this one bit. We're going to just exercise tonight, starting with 100 laps due to Butch's poor judgment, and Billy will keep tally of each lap."

A quiet groan went through the group of boys standing around the coach. Rex continued.

"I know you don't think this is fair, but I'm doing this because, just like a chain, we are only as strong as the weakest link. What one does affects us all. Now, start running."

The coach was being more than a coach. He was teaching them about something more important than plays on the court.

When they had completed 100 laps, Rex called out, "Okay, we're going to run some drills. Start with the three-man weave. Now go!"

After a full hour and a half of continuous drills, Coach hollered, "Now, more laps! Get going."

The boys began running their second set of laps, all of them thinking about wringing Butch's neck. Marvin ran up next to Butch.

"Hey buddy, thanks a lot. Crap! Man, this is a hell of a thing to do to us."

Butch felt terrible for bringing this punishment upon his teammates, especially since the rest of the team gave Butch the stink eye as they passed near him during the extra laps that Coach Wells ordered.

When they had run laps for another hour, the coach told Billy to stop counting laps. "Just let them run a little bit more," he said.

This "practice" went on for five hours—the longest they'd ever had. Doc called the parents and informed them that practice would run long that night because there were some special plays the coach was working out with them. The boys didn't get home until 11 p.m.

Rex had taught them all a lesson. They were a team of one, and their coach would treat them that way. They all learned this the hard way.

The reason for this "special practice" never got out. This secret was kept among the team and their coaches. If word had spread, it may have created a lot of distraction, and the coach knew this would not be good for the rest of the season. The next day, Marvin, Bob, Frankie, and Paul held their own meeting with Butch.

"We never want to have a practice like that again," they all told their starting forward. Butch promised he would never let this happen again.

It seemed as if the team came together even more after this event. They all realized they were truly one. And their coach had driven home that lesson in a remarkable way: during that grueling practice, he had run the laps and done the drills with his team.

When he said they were all one, he meant it.

The Lucky Game: #13

The Hawks were on the road this week to play the North Central Tigers in Ramsey, Indiana, on January 28. Perhaps a bit of overconfidence came into play but the boys were now starting to feel the pressure from all the news coverage, and this game nearly saw the end of the winning streak. Looking back, some of the boys determined that the reason for this tough game was exhaustion from the five-hour practice session.

Rex Wells never boasted or made predictions about the next game—even though the townsfolk who once had been on the fence were beginning to mention an undefeated season quite often. Folks like to talk and dream big, and the Springs Valley citizenry were dreaming big dreams by now. "We're unbeatable" was being heard just about everywhere in town. An enthusiastic press perhaps placed too much of the twin cities' image and newfound fame on the backs of these boys.

One writer included in his column part of a letter he'd been sent.

This note was received by a resident from John W. Daley of Indianapolis in which he said, 'From all of the headlines I see in the paper, the Springs Valley team is the best advertising the towns there have had in a long time. I saw them play twice and they looked good.

This type of praise gives the boys a 'pat on the back' for their accomplishments. It does not add additional pressure. It reminds us that we should only 'crow' AFTER the games. It is not hard to understand the feeling of the enthusiastic crowd, for most everyone is certainly 'hungry' for a winner. We noticed in the Indianapolis Star *a letter sent in by a fan, who covered a lot of territory in the note. These brags only put additional pressure on the boys who are doing a wonderful job for our school and the community. We are all guilty, so let us remember, the school is for the good of the children. We are just sideliners.'*

Nevertheless, the pressure was there. How could it not be, when so many articles were being written about them by sports columnists across the state? The boys appeared calm, but each was beginning to feel the weight of his new role. They were all goodwill ambassadors, and part of the greatest marketing campaign the Valley had ever seen.

🏀 🏀 🏀

It was no surprise that the 13th game of the season proved to be the toughest so far. Consistency is a tricky thing to maintain game after game. On this night, the Valley Boys had hit the wall. They just weren't playing their game, and it was as if they were sleepwalking throughout the first half. The Hawks made the first two points but from there were behind the rest of the game until the final stanza.

Early in the game, Bob was under the basket and going up with the ball when a North Central player elbowed him on the top of his head. He started bleeding, and badly enough that he had to come out. The team managers put some gauze on his head and taped it as well as they could. Bob went back in the game, but his injury kept him from being as effective as usual. Later, he told Marvin, "Man, I was seein' stars most of the game!"

Bob still put in 10 points, going two for 11 from the field and six of 10 from the charity stripe. After the game, Doc Sugarman had to stitch him up—again. Bob seemed to be a good candidate for the award for most stitches received in one season. But he was tough in every way. Doc Sugarman even told Coach Wells, "That boy has the toughest skin I've ever come across. I could hardly get the needle through that scalp!"

North Central was a much larger school, five times the size of Springs Valley, and had put together a very strong team. By the end of the second quarter the Hawks were down 7 points, 25-18. This had not happened before during this season. At the halftime break the locker room was unusually quiet. It seemed that every player was wondering if this "team of destiny," as the local paper had dubbed the Hawks, had finally met its match.

Coach Wells sensed the boys were nervous and playing tight. After a few minutes of silence, he spoke up.

"Boys, do you recall what I said that afternoon before our very first game?"

Frankie responded, "All things are possible."

"Yes," the coach answered. "And tonight our 13th win is more than possible. You all know your role. You have confidence in each other. I have confidence in you. Just play your game better and you'll be fine. All you have to do is play better."

It wasn't a complicated piece of advice, but Rex knew how well his guys could play this game. They weren't playing up to their abilities. So, "Just play better" was all he needed to say.

Rex, who enjoyed reading and memorizing poetry—particularly of the inspirational variety—now decided to share one that he had put to memory some years back.

"Boys, you may think this is corny, but I want to convey a message to you through a poem that I memorized a long time ago when I was playing ball at Hanover. Here goes.

> "The thing that makes a champion
> is quite obvious enough
> It isn't any mystic or supernatural stuff
> It's nothing more than giving

to whatever be your chore
Of all the power within you, and just a little more.

It isn't any wizardry, it's not a magic gift
It's merely lifting honestly the load you have to lift
And in the game you're playing
It's giving all your store
of grit and nerve and energy and just a little more!

The thing that makes a champion,
It's simple, plain and clear
It isn't being almost, just about, or pretty near
It's summoning the utmost of your spirit's inner store
And giving every bit of it and just a little more!"

This was the first of several poems that the coach would share with the team. They were a bit surprised but listened attentively. The boys came to like it when the coach would share one of the poems he'd memorized. They didn't need someone yelling at them. Nor did they need someone always telling them what they were doing wrong.

Most of the time, the boys knew what the problem was and could diagnose it on their own. The coach would simply ask them, "What's wrong out there?" They'd all put in their two cents worth about the problems on the court. Then Rex would ask, "Then how do we fix it?" They'd pool their knowledge. The coach then took their suggestions and tried to draw some conclusions, and he'd usually come up with the answer. And they would go out on the court and fix the problem. It was a level of mutual respect that is quite rare between a team and its coach.

Marvin had been in a bit of a "shooter's slump" in the first half and had not been hitting most of his jump shots, hitting only three of nine from the floor. It just wasn't his night. The boys were even missing free throws. Valley trailed throughout most of this contest and even got down by as many as 12 points in the third quarter. By the end of the third canto, the Hawks were still behind by five. The Valley Boys had just eight minutes to turn this game around.

During this two-minute break between quarters, the coach asked, "Does anyone think we can't win this game?" Butch, who was not having his best game answered, "I don't think so." "Okay, you sit on the bench the rest of the game," the always-teaching coach said without hesitation. He knew he was benching one of his best players, but he could not have any team member thinking negatively.

On the first possession of the fourth quarter, Bob dropped in two points underneath. The next time the Hawks got the ball, Frankie threw it in to Marvin.

"Sink it, Marvin," the junior guard said to himself. Then just the opposite happened: Marvin immediately tossed the ball back to Frankie. Frankie passed the ball back to Marvin. This continued as if the two boys were playing pitch and catch. Four times Frankie sent the ball to Marvin. Four times he got it back. Frankie kept thinking, "Dang, Marvin shoot the darn ball!"

Finally, Marvin took another jump shot. It hit the rim and went high in the air, then took a friendly bounce and dropped through the net. Was the momentum changing? The Tigers now led, 40-39.

But North Central took the ball out quickly after Marvin's jumper. *"They caught the Hawks sleeping, as they were not quick on getting back in transition,"* the radio play-by-play announcer was heard yelling into his microphone. The North Central player took the ball out and threw a full-court pass as if he were a football quarterback. He found his target in one of their guards, who had sprinted back as soon as Marvin's shot went through the net.

Frankie tried to get back on his man to block the ball from behind, but he was too late. The North Central player hit his easy lay-up and was fouled by Frankie to boot. But he missed the free throw. The Tigers were up by three. The Hawks came back and scored again.

The teams traded baskets like this for the next few minutes. It was starting to look like the winner of this contest may be the last team with possession of the ball. Finally, North Central's Tigers "clawed their way," as the sportswriter naturally put it, to a two-point lead, 51-49, with under four minutes left in the contest.

Coach Wells called a timeout.

"Now look, boys, this game is yours if you want it bad enough. I know it's tough with Bob's injury, but I know you can overcome this challenge. Marvin, don't worry about your shot. You have the best darned jump shot in Indiana. Shake off the nerves, son."

Coach Wells caught himself as he spoke the word, "son." He realized that a couple of his players were only six years younger than he. Yet the boys huddled around the coach, looking at the hand-held chalkboard most coaches used to explain the next play. But Rex rarely drew up plays, and this time was no different. The coach held the chalkboard to his side, using it every now and then only as a pointer.

"Marvin, it's time to step back up to the plate. We need a 'home run' from you. Frankie, bring the ball down court as fast as you can. Swing it over to Paul's side, coming up the lane to set the screen for Marvin. You get the ball to Marvin at the top of the key. Marvin, I know you'll sink this one. We need to put this game on ice. Now get out there and take this game!"

The coach didn't just want them to tie the game. He wanted them to go out there with every intention of winning.

The boys ran the play just as the coach had explained it to them. Marvin came up the right side to the top of the key, around Paul's screen, and got the ball from Frankie. This time they didn't play catch. The dead-eye shooter turned and fired his trademark shot, one knee hiked in the air as he released his one-handed jumper. It arched high and floated to the basket. *Swish!* Tie game: 51 all.

Sometimes a shooter just knows when the ball is going in. Marvin was already backing up for defense as the ball was making its way toward the basket.

The boys knew it was time to put this one away, as they had done so often before. Paul stole a pass, took it down for a lay-up, and was fouled. The free throw made it a three-point play, giving Valley a 54-51 lead. Valley's 6'1" center could be heard as the team ran back on defense.

"Thank you, Lord, thank you," Paul said.

In scrimmages and games that weren't so perilously close, Marvin would joke, "Paul, you spend half the game prayin' or praisin' the Lord!" Paul would smile and point his finger upward.

The next two possessions for the Tigers didn't go well. They threw the ball out of bounds on a bad pass. The Hawks came down the court and Frankie dished the ball to Bob, who drove by his man and hit a floater from the lane. Springs Valley finally was building a lead. Then both Marvin and Butch were fouled when taking their last shots of the game. They both sank their free throws, putting the Hawks comfortably ahead when the gun went off, 57-51.

When the boys showered after the game, they all noticed the many welts on their bodies. They had toughed out a very physical game.

Coach Wells had been hoping that his team would face a strong challenge. They had been coasting in most games, always holding leads throughout the fourth quarter. He got his wish; the Tigers pushed Valley to the wire. It was the kind of workout the coach knew his team needed to face. He was sure there would be tougher teams ahead, and this would be great preparation.

Rex had told them to simply play their game—to "just play better." They did, but not before some nail-biting moments.

This night served as a teachable moment for the team. It was a kind of wake-up call and would prove to be a foreshadowing of things to come.

"Boys, this one proves that you can think out there on the court and get the things done that need to be done. You played a very good team tonight on their home court. You outsmarted them. You played tough. They played tough. But you guys played smarter. You deserved this win—at least the way you played in the fourth quarter. Remember this night. A heck of a lot can happen in only eight minutes of a game.

The next day's sports column headline read: "S.V.'s Record Nearly Scratched; 'Cause We Count Our Chicks Before They're Hatched." The "We" in the headline surely wasn't meant to refer to the boys on the team, nor their coaches. That was one thing the Black Hawks didn't do. Presumably Jim Ballard, sportswriter for the *Herald*, must have been referring to himself and some others around the Valley. No game is ever a sure thing, and the Valley Boys and their coach knew it.

🌐 🌐 🌐

Four days later, the Hawks played a home game against Bloomfield. They won by 25 points. Things were back to normal, and there was a collective sigh of relief around the Valley—and at the desk of the *Herald*'s sportswriter.

But for this game, Bloomfield High School had changed the venue because of the demand for tickets, and they moved the game to the larger Swiss City gymnasium to accommodate the many fans. Springs Valley was boosting ticket sales at every school they played.

Pruett, Schmutzler, and McCracken were averaging double figures a game for the season, and the team was looking more and more as if it were unbeatable, just as some of the local fans had been saying. Even a few sportswriters up in Indianapolis and down in Louisville were starting to take note of the small-town basketball phenomenon and speculating, "Can these boys go all the way?"

There was one very popular Indianapolis sports columnist, Bob Collins, who wasn't a believer. He continued to dismiss the Hawks as some sort of anomaly, or just a little hick school who played other little hick schools, and not worthy of the ink in his typewriter. He refused to write about the Black Hawks, even though he was receiving post cards in the mail from fans attempting to get his attention for this new team that was "setting the woods on fire" down in the Hoosier National Forest, where French Lick and West Baden nestled.

One of those post cards had read: "*Just a note to let you know Springs Valley can beat any team south of Highway 40. Now I know you hear a lot of bragging and boasting from over the state, but never have you heard those words from French Lick, home of the consolidated school.*

"The Hawks are among the undefeated teams and they are hindered by a schedule that is not among the toughest in the state. But remember, Milan didn't get much mention the first year it came your way to the finals. Watch us take Huntingburg out in the Sectional and then go a long way. If you are looking for a dark horse to get on and ride, maybe you'll saddle up the new Springs Valley Blackhawks."

Coach Wells told the boys to ignore such prophesying from fans, but that was like telling a kid to ignore his birthday cake. It simply couldn't be done.

Five more games remained in the regular season, but the coach continued to counsel his players, "Take one game at a time. Don't think past your next opponent, and most of all, remember who you are, and how you have always played this game—with passion and fun. But most importantly, remember you are a team where everyone contributes.

"I know we've had some great tragedies in this past month, but you boys have proven that you can overcome just about any adversity. You have a great competitive spirit, but there is not an ounce of meanness in you.

I'm proud to be your coach, mainly because I can see the joy that playing this game brings you. In fact, I think that folks who are coming to the games are picking up on this same spirit—a spirit of competition with a smile—and some laughs."

Coach Wells went on.

"Everything that is supposed to happen will, and what is not supposed to happen won't. The Good Book tells us that our days here on earth are numbered and that life is a vapor, and we'll all be old men before we know it.

"I do believe with all my heart that this season will be one of your most treasured memories in life. As we've seen this past month, life can be taken away in the blink of an eye. Just remember that life is a great gift, so we've gotta make every day count, living it like it may be our last. Make the most of your lives. Make the most of this incredible opportunity we've all been given. I believe in you fellas 100 percent.

"Just know: I love you guys."

The relationship between the young coach and his first-year team was very special, and they all knew it at the time. Life was truly a gift, and playing for the Black Hawks was one of the greatest blessings they would ever know. Life was good for these 10 boys, the coaches and team managers who called the woefully tiny French Lick gym home.

This was the greatest life to be living—no matter the size of their gymnasium. No matter the size of their hometowns.

The preseason team photo. Front to back, left side: Mike Watson, Jerry Breedlove, Bob McCracken, Paul Radcliff, Marvin Pruett. Middle, front to back: Billy Rose, manager, Robert Trueblood, manager, Coach Wells. Front to back, right side: Frankie Self, Jim Conrad, George Lagenour, Butch Schmutzler, Jack Belcher. Photo: Freedly Rose, Courtesy of the Springs Valley Herald.

The postseason team picture. Photo: Freedly Rose, Courtesy of the Springs Valley Herald.
Front row, Left to right: Billy Rose, George Harrison, Jim Conrad, Bob McCracken, Frankie Self, Mike Watson, Bob Trueblood
Back row, Left to right: Jerry Breedlove, Marvin Pruett, Paul Radcliff, Coach
Rex Wells, Jack Belcher, George Lagenour, Butch Schmutzler

Our Lady of the Springs Catholic Church.

*West Baden Baptist Church—"The Mt. Zion Church of the
Tabernacle Saints." Photo courtesy of Don Clements.*

West Baden High School (1940s photo).

French Lick High School (1940s or '50s photo).

West Baden Springs Resort, 2017. Photo courtesy of Jerry Copas, Images Aloft Ballooning.

French Lick Springs Resort (2017).

Star Store building (2017 photo)

West Baden Springs Hotel. Postcard by the Curteich Chicago Co., 1946.

The French Lick Springs Hotel (1940s). Postcard by the Curteich Chicago Co.

West Baden Jesuit College (formerly West Baden Springs Hotel). Postcard printed by the Curteich Chicago Co., 1949.

The French Lick Sheraton (1950s). Postcard by the Curteich Chicago Co.

Frankie shooting, with Paul, Marvin, and Bob under the bucket.
Photo: Freedly Rose, Courtesy of the Springs Valley Herald.

Bob cuts down the net after a
tournament win. Photo: Freedly Rose,
Courtesy of the Springs Valley Herald.

"The Enforcer," Bob McCracken,
grabs a rebound. Photo: Freedly Rose,
Courtesy of the Springs Valley Herald.

Butch lays it in at a home game. Photo: Freedly Rose, Courtesy of the Springs Valley Herald.

Marvin shooting, Frankie following. Photo: Freedly Rose, Courtesy of the Springs Valley Herald.

Marvin shooting beyond the arc against Vincennes. Photo: Freedly Rose, Courtesy of the Springs Valley Herald.

Frankie's winning shot in the last 11 seconds against Vincennes. Photo: Freedly Rose, Courtesy of the Springs Valley Herald.

SELF SATISFIES — With 10 seconds left in the overtime period, Frank Self, 5' 7", goes goal high to plop in the lay-up and give the Blackhawks a victory over the Vincennes Alices. After his steal, it was just Frankie and the referee who made it downfloor ahead of the pack.

Frankie's dream comes true. Photo: Freedly Rose, Courtesy of the Springs Valley Herald.

McCracken adds two points from the side. Photo: Freedly Rose, Courtesy of the Springs Valley Herald.

Marvin Pruett at the free throw line.

Marvin from the side in the semifinals.
Photo: Freedly Rose, Courtesy
of the Springs Valley Herald.

Butch shoots a jumper from the corner at
Butler Field House. Photo: Freedly Rose,
Courtesy of the Springs Valley Herald.

McCracken fights for a rebound against the Ft. Wayne Archers' "bigs":
Mike McCoy (#45), Danny Howe (#55), and Carl Stavretti (#35).
Photo: Freedly Rose, Courtesy of the Springs Valley Herald.

The old swimmin' hole.

An ad for Pluto Water, the "health elixir."

The 25-year-old Coach Rex Wells.

"The Big V," early-season team picture. Photo: Freedly Rose, Courtesy of the Springs Valley Herald.

The boys (eating oranges) after a hard-fought game.
Photo: Freedly Rose, courtesy of Rose Photography.

The boys celebrate winning the semistate at Roberts Municipal Stadium
in Evansville, Indiana. Unadulterated joy! Photo: Freedly Rose.

Frankie, Coach, Jerry, and Jim on the bench during the semistate finals.

Coach Rex Wells, 1958 Indiana High School Coach of the Year.
Photo: Freedly Rose, courtesy of Rose Photography.

*Profile of the Black Hawk,
by student artist Phil Beaver.*

*The original Black Hawk mascot,
created by a Walt Disney artist.*

*The Black Hawk sculpture, modeled after the first mascot
drawing by a Disney artist. Courtesy of Rex Wells.*

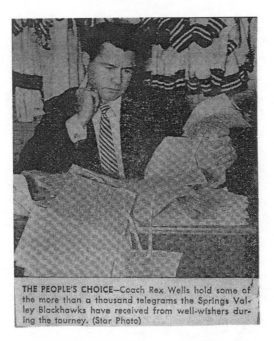

THE PEOPLE'S CHOICE—Coach Rex Wells hold some of the more than a thousand telegrams the Springs Valley Blackhawks have received from well-wishers during the tourney. (Star Photo)

Rex reads one of a thousand telegrams sent from fans across the Hoosier state, rooting for the Hawks to win the state championship.

Barbara Love, drum majorette, and Marvin's sweetheart.

Cheerleaders (left to right) Billy Jo Harris, Joe Ellis, and Beverly Runyon.

Bob McCracken and Patsy Zeedyk.

Marvin and Barbara.

Rex and Margaret during the week of the Final Four. Photo:
Freedly Rose, Courtesy of the Springs Valley Herald.

Frankie and Thelma. Courtesy of Thelma Self.

Frankie and Thelma heading out on a date. Courtesy of Thelma Self.

Cheerleaders Billie Jo Harris and Beverly Runyon watch as the green stripe is painted on Maple Street for some St. Patrick's Day luck.

Team Names:

Front, L to R: Jerry Breedlove, Marvin Pruett, Butch Schmutzler, Paul Radcliff, Frankie Self, Robert Trueblood

Back, L to R: Reserve Team student mgr, John Breeden, Warren "Doc" Keyser, Billy Rose, Jack Belcher, Jim Conrad, George Lagenour, Mike Watson, Bob MCracken, Coach Rex Wells

Butch Schmutzler

Grover "Shorty" Reeder

• CHAPTER 11 •
PROVIDENCE

During Frankie's homeroom period on the following Wednesday before the Providence game, he received a note from the office.

"Uh oh, I hope I'm not in hot water," he thought. He read the note.

"Frankie Self, you have a letter waiting for you in the principal's office."

What could it be? he wondered. Was it from his mom? Then he noticed the post office location stamped on the envelope: "Clarksville, Ind." He ripped open the letter and began reading.

"Hey Self, you'd better have your best game when you come to play on our court. I plan on embarrassing you by outscoring you and keeping you from making one basket. The Black Hawks haven't met their match yet, but you will this Friday night. Can't wait to see all your faces when we put you guys in your place. Signed, Johnny Ford."

Frankie had received a letter from the starting guard on the Providence Pioneers team. Frankie gave the letter to Coach Wells, who read it to the entire team. But it failed to intimidate Frankie or the rest of the team. They had 14 wins under their belt now, and they couldn't wait to play the next contest.

Away games always felt a bit different from home games. This trip to Clarksville brought that same sense of anticipation and nervousness the team usually felt when traveling to another town. Even though the Hawks had plenty of their own fans at their road games, they were still playing on another team's court, where that team had practiced every day of the week and become a family. The familiarity of your own gymnasium, along with the support of the local fans, made for friendly surroundings that encouraged a home team to do its best.

Just the term "home team" makes the *visitors* feel less than welcome in the other school's "house." Not many high school or even college players adapt enough to overcome the odds against them when playing on another team's court. Even the pro teams do not perform as well on other teams' home court at times.

The Providence gym was even smaller than the French Lick gym. The prior day's newspaper article warned, "If you fans expect to see the game tomorrow night, you'd better skip your second cup of coffee. The gym only seats 1,000."

The fact that Springs Valley had won all its games, including their away contests, had most opposing fans waiting for the other sneaker to drop on this fledgling team.

On the team bus on the way to Providence, Frankie looked over to his best friend, Marvin, and asked, "Ya think they'll be very tough?"

Marvin replied with his standard phrase. "You gotta be shittin' me. Sure, they'll be tough. They're Catholics, aren't they?" Marvin reminded Frankie. Then he added, "But we'll win. We're gonna win 'em all!"

Marvin winked at his buddy.

"I'm feeling like I've got my shot back. I'm going to shoot their lights out tonight!"

Frankie smiled.

"Leave some of the lights on so we won't be playing in the dark, okay?"

Bob McCracken was listening in on their conversation and piped up.

"Hey, it's divine providence that we beat Providence."

Paul, sensing an opening for a theological discussion, quickly added, "It's all in the Lord's hands."

"Yeah," Marvin exclaimed, "but it's our hands that's gotta make the baskets!" Paul ignored his buddy and continued.

"Frankie, do you remember when you asked me to pray for the team's name and colors to not be 'Grasshoppers' and green?"

Frankie nodded.

"Well, I've been praying every night and day since then about this team," he said. "My mom and dad and our entire church have also been praying for our team's success—that we'd play to the best of our ability in each game."

Marvin overheard this.

"Okay, preacher, what about the other teams we're playing against who are praying to win the same games?"

Paul had no answer, but Frankie just said, "Hey, it's working, it's working. Paul, keep up the prayers. Tell your mom and dad and your church 'thanks.'"

Frankie didn't want his comment to alienate Marvin.

"I think God helps those who help themselves. I don't know if the Bible says this or not, but it makes sense to me that God has a lot bigger things to deal with than the outcome of basketball games in Southern Indiana. If He's really up there, and listenin' to our prayers, it sure can't hurt to ask for His help every once in a while. I really believe that the team who wins is the team who has worked the hardest and who has the best team players that have the greatest desire to win games. And I think that team is the Hawks!"

"Thank you, Mr. Billy Graham," Bob dryly chimed in.

"Hey, you guys."

Coach Wells had overheard the conversation and decided it was time to enter it. The busload of boys got very quiet. The Coach stood up in the middle of the aisle, figuring it was as good a time as any to have a serious talk with his team.

"Boys, we all come from different but somewhat similar backgrounds. Not every one of us believes exactly like the other person, and that's all right. I don't think God expects us to all think just alike. That's what makes life interesting.

But, I'll tell you one thing: there's something special going on with this team. I think we all know it too. Up to this point, I haven't said much about being an undefeated team, but now it's time we have this little talk.

"There are a lot of folks out there who are watching this team now. I've even had a couple of requests for interviews with reporters from the Louisville *Courier Journal* and the *Indianapolis Star.* It seems our little consolidated school and this team has gotten attention from around the state.

"It's true, basketball is just a game, but we all know how important these games become to the people around us. Just imagine if there were no fans at the games. It would be just us and the other team competing against each other—kind of like a friendly scrimmage on a Sunday afternoon at the park. That's about all it would amount to if no one else cared. But a heck of a lot of folks do care and want to see this team win. It is something for them to attach themselves to and feel a part of—their hometown team."

Rex had their attention,

"We are a part of them, all of those people who've gone before us. And they are part of us. We're all in this together, and it seems to me that with every game we win, this team is becoming more and more important to the folks coming to watch us. And the reason for that is because you have given our two towns something very special, something they've both needed for a long while now: pride. A much-needed sense of pride.

"You as a team have brought French Lick and West Baden together as one. You have given some life back to our community, accomplishing something that I don't believe anything else outside of this game of basketball could do. You have breathed some new life back into French Lick and West Baden, and that is something you can take considerable pride in—because you are only being yourselves.

"Just keep being honest and true to who you know you are."

The young coach paused to think of how to tie together everything he was saying to his team. He had started his remarks with one particular thought, but now he had begun to think aloud. He certainly didn't want to put undue pressure on his team and make them feel as if they *had* to continue undefeated, but at the same time, he wanted them to appreciate just how much they meant to their towns—former foes—which, with each win, were melding more tightly into one community.

This team and its undefeated season had taken on a life of its own. The Springs Valley citizens were with them now, even though it took the first four games to get everyone on board. There was a lot riding on this team's back, and the coach was well aware of the pressure. Did his team feel it?

Finally, he addressed what, he later learned, had secretly been on every player's mind.

"Guys, don't worry about what happens if we lose a game. That's the wrong focus. You've done a fantastic job playing basketball so far. We only have five more games left in the regular season and all you need to do is think about one game at a time.

"Do what you've been doing from the get-go. Just go out there each game and give it your best. That's all Doc and I expect of you. And that's all anyone should expect. That's really all any of us can do—our best. And like Paul says, 'It's truly in the Lord's hands.'"

Coach Wells sat down, wondering if what he'd just said had made any sense to the boys. Who knows, maybe they hadn't even worried at all about losing. Maybe these boys just loved to play basketball so much that, in their young minds, each game was about that only—playing hard to win that game.

Once again, he considered how they had put together a team of players who'd formerly been the greatest of rivals. They got along well and everyone seemed to understand their individual role—even the team managers. Marvin, the former West Baden high scorer and Butch, the French Lick star, both got along famously, and never allowed their "star status" to come between them.

Every single one of these guys, Rex thought, relished the idea of being on a team and contributing. It seemed that they were the mature ones in this whole situation. The older fans, who were supposed to be imparting wisdom to their offspring, were really the ones in desperate need of learning something important. These high school boys were teaching the people of these two small towns a very big lesson.

"Thank you, Lord, for this team," Rex silently prayed as the team bus pulled into Providence's parking lot. "Thank you for allowing me to coach this kind of a team. These are good boys. I know this is special and I'll always be thankful, no matter what the rest of the season brings."

The coach's prayer went up as the players, Doc, and he got off the bus. Doc looked at the tiny gymnasium and whistled through his teeth. Billy Rose, one of the team managers, reminded the players, "Big things can come in small packages."

Rex leaned over to Doc as they walked along.

"What if we really are a team of destiny?"

Doc answered, "So, you do believe in divine providence, eh?"

The Game of Providence

The normal warm-up time was given to the road team before the home team came out on the floor. Valley got its shoot-around in and left the floor. For some reason, there wasn't the usual joking around with each other. Perhaps it was the conversation on the bus about God's hand in all of this, but the boys were really in a pensive mood before this contest.

I wonder if this will be the game that ends our winning streak? This was on the minds of all the players and the coaches. But no one dared speak the thought aloud.

As the boys dressed for the game, Coach Wells came in to the locker room.

"I'm so proud of you guys. A coach couldn't ask for a better bunch of guys to play for him," he began. "Uh, whatever happens tonight, I just want you guys to know that you've blessed my life more than you'll ever know. Even if we lost the rest of the season's games, I'd still consider this a very good season. No, it's been the greatest season ever . . . and . . . "—Rex began to get a little choked up, and he swallowed hard.

"You know how I feel about you guys. Go out there and have some fun playing this team. And remember one thing. These boys put their basketball trunks on the same way you do—one leg at a time. Now let's go play some Hawks basketball!"

The boys ran out onto the court and gathered around the jump circle, feeling a bit of angst. Just the suddenness of the blast from the pistol signaling the start of the game was enough to make a shiver run up and down their backs.

The gymnasium was packed. Just as most Springs Valley games had been this season, this one had been oversold. That meant too many spectators, which would mean more chaos and heat in the Providence gymnasium on this frigid winter night.

The Hawks got the tip-off, went down the court, and put up the first shot. Marvin's jumper missed by a mile.

"Geez Louise! What the hell was that all about?" Pruett scolded himself running back on defense. Providence got the rebound and pushed the play up the court quickly—a Springs Valley signature. Their center caught a bullet pass from their guard for an easy bank shot under the basket. Two to zip.

Frankie brought the ball back to Valley's side of the court, dribbling past the time line. He passed to his fellow guard, Marvin, who sent the ball to Paul under the basket. Paul put up a clunker that just lay on the back of the rim before it rolled off. The Providence center grabbed the rebound.

"Crap," Paul muttered under his breath. "Sorry, Lord," he said aloud as he ran back on defense.

Providence scored for the third time in three possessions. It was 6-0.

This was not the way Rex wanted to see the game begin. The bad run continued during the next Valley possession. Butch let loose a long jump shot that missed everything completely. Paul pulled the ball in as if it were a pass. The Providence fans really began to whoop it up at the shot that didn't reach the goal. The player guarding Butch had grazed his arm during the release of the shot, causing the uncharacteristic result. This was the one foul of the night that the refs didn't call.

"Good grief, what's going on?" one of the team managers, Robert Trueblood, asked the boys watching from the bench. No one answered the rhetorical question, but all were beginning to wonder the same thing. This wasn't how the Black Hawks played ball—ever.

Marvin was pissed off about all the talk about God on the bus trip to the game. "A lot of good He's doing for us right now," he thought.

Paul faked his man, as if going up with the ball, then put up his rebound of Butch's missed shot. The ball rolled around the rim and finally dropped through, mercifully cutting short the "air ball" chant.

At last, they had scored. It was 6-2—only two buckets down. Maybe that's all they needed to get back into playing their game.

But the missed shots kept coming—even from Marvin Pruett. Yet the reality was that their shots were missing because they were being fouled on each possession. It was as if the Pioneers were making sure Valley couldn't even get a decent shot off, and Marvin was their special target. The highest scorer on the team was hacked on his next jump shot and got to the foul line for two shots. He made one of two.

He was cussing so much the other team was blushing. He made sure the refs couldn't hear him, though; he wanted to stay in the game. "Maybe I'll find my shot before halftime," he thought.

Both teams were being called for fouls, and fortunately, the Hawks started hitting their free throws—lots of free throws. The first quarter ended with Valley taking the lead, 18-14, with most of their points from the charity stripe.

But having only a four-point advantage and hitting just four of 10 field goals in the quarter—with Bob McCracken hitting three of his shots and Marvin only one field goal—was not a good sign for the Hawks continuing their winning streak. And the second quarter didn't get better. In fact, things got much worse. Valley left the court at halftime eight points behind. Things were not looking good for the visiting team.

When they all got in the locker room for the 15-minute break, Rex gathered the team around him. He tossed his clipboard aside on the bench and looked every boy in the eye as he gazed from player to player in a circle around him.

"Look, guys. This isn't the best team you've ever played. I know you'll face bigger challenges than this team."

He needed to harness the players' attention and get their heads back into the game. It was time for them to begin playing like they had been so capable of doing up to now.

"Now listen to me. There's only one guy on their team who would've made our team. I cut guys in October who are better than these guys. I want you to run the plays you've practiced—and listen to me if I call out a play.

"Calm down. There's no pressure on you except what you are placing on yourselves. Just play your game. Relax and just play better. Think about what it's like when you guys are back in town playing at the park or over at the college. Never forget about the fun of playing this game. Picture yourselves there at that outdoor court on a Sunday afternoon."

Rex recalled his secret visits to the outdoor court they played on at the Jesuit college.

"I would drive by and see you fellas playing on many a Sunday last summer," Rex said. "I was amazed at the good ball movement and the plays you would run—just playing by instinct. Let those same instincts take over now. You don't have to try so hard to make something happen.

"It's all about performing those fundamentals that you all know. Passing the ball to the open man, finding the best shot on each possession. And defense! Keep the other team from scoring.

"You know I believe in you guys. You've already made believers out of everybody in Southern Indiana. You have nothing to prove to anyone! Just go out there, play hard, play defense like you're possessed . . . and most of all start having fun, like I know you do when you play your game.

"Now get out there and show them what the Black Hawks are all about!"

There was a knock on the locker room door and in came Clayton

Conrad, Jim's father. Clayton had been the superintendent at West Baden, and after the merger of the two schools, he was now the West Baden junior high principal and coach of its basketball team.

"Boys, I don't normally do this, but I'm seeing just how hostile this game is becoming. I think someone has instructed the refs to just keep calling fouls to keep this game under control. But it's backfiring, I'm afraid. Just calm down, and play your game and you'll be all right."

Just then, Doc came in the locker room.

"Coach, we've got a big problem out there. Some of our fans just about got into fisticuffs with some Providence fans—in the middle of the court!"

"What?!" Rex couldn't believe his ears. Doc told him that the Providence principal and their coach wanted to see him. Rex learned that both some Valley fans and some locals who had been drinking were just about to have it out.

"And Coach, you won't believe this, but one of the men on the court exchanging unpleasantries happens to be the sportswriter for the *Springs Valley Herald*!" Doc exclaimed. "It's getting ugly out there."

Maybe it was the fact that 43 fouls had been called in the first half alone that had led to the hostility in the gymnasium. The fans were mad at the refs. It didn't take too many choice words and name calling by the rowdies before the fans were ready to do battle.

This was serious, and Rex knew it. If the game were called because of fan violence, the Hawks would have to forfeit the game, spoiling their undefeated record. Even worse, their entire season might be over if the Black Hawks were suspended for bad conduct.

Rex assured the Providence coach and principal that things would calm down during the second half. The presence of Clarksville's finest, the local sheriff and two policemen, had broken up the fan frenzy on the court. A couple of the most inebriated were escorted out the door.

The home team collected itself during the 15-minute intermission and came out playing as they had in the first quarter. The Pioneers' coach had let his boys know in no uncertain terms just what he thought of their poor play, which was leading to the Hawks' many free throw opportunities. This coach had done his homework. He was aware of how the boys from Springs Valley tended to take over games, often in the final quarter. He realized he'd better do something drastic to get his team on track to whip the Hawks.

"You're throwing this game away," he had shouted in the locker room. He did not mince words. He hollered, screamed, kicked over wastebaskets, and slammed his fist into locker doors. He had his team's attention, and the boys were scared.

"I hope you don't let these hilljacks come into your house and make you look like a bunch of fools," he raved. "Because that is exactly what is happening out there. Now stop acting like a bunch of numb-nuts and start playing like I've coached you.

"My gosh, you're on your own court. Start playing like it! If you guys lose this one tonight, there's gonna be a lot of laps run around this gym—TONIGHT!"

His players came out as if someone had lit a fire under their behinds. They so desperately did not want to run laps after the game, and they knew how hard practice would be on Monday if they let this game slip away.

But the Valley players, who up until this moment seemed to be in a trance of sorts, also stepped it up in the third quarter, and came back looking like a different team. They would now demonstrate their true style of play. The coach's words had gotten through.

During the first two minutes, the Hawks displayed strong defense and began to narrow the score. Providence couldn't get a decent shot off on their first three possessions, and the refs kept calling fouls on both teams.

Marvin sank one more jump shot. He hollered to Frankie, "I told you I was going to knock their socks off tonight."

"Keep knockin' 'em down, Marvin!" Frankie hollered back to his fellow guard. But he was thinking, *I'm glad he didn't wait much longer to start knocking the Pioneers' socks off!*

The Black Hawks' defense was unmerciful, as were the referees in calling fouls. Providence couldn't do anything with the ball. Frankie smothered his man, swatted at the ball, and picked up his fifth foul, even though he hadn't even touched the player—it had been "all ball." The playmaker and defensive star was out of the game.

The coach put Jim Conrad in for Frankie. Jim had done well in previous games, and Rex thought this would give his sophomore some experience. Jim was guarding the best player on the Pioneers, Johnny Ford—the boy who had sent the letter to Frankie. On the next Providence possession, Johnny Ford took it to Jim. He had a double-fake move Jim Conrad wasn't ready for. Ford scored, leaving Jim standing as if his feet were glued to the floor.

Mike Watson went in for Jim. The sophomore would have to gain experience on another night.

Marvin had hit three free throws, but this and his one field goal would be all he would contribute in this third quarter. There was a good reason Marvin was having trouble; one of the Pioneers players would pull on the elastic band around his shorts to distract him. Rex could see that something unusual was occurring on the court. He called time out.

"Coach, that guy guarding me keeps tryin' to pull down my shorts!" Marvin complained.

"Okay, I know how to take care of that." Rex immediately turned to Bob. "McCracken, when you guys go under the basket, give that guy who's buggin' Marvin a good elbow and let him know why."

Rex never promoted dirty play with his boys, but he knew this had to stop. The Hawks were smart, but they could be as tough as anybody—especially when Bob McCracken was in the game.

The team called Bob "the Enforcer" for a good reason. He could always be counted on to follow orders and come through. On the next battle for a rebound underneath, he gave that troublemaker a little more than a nudge: he delivered a big elbow to his side, putting his entire 170 pounds of muscle into the boy's rib cage. He crumpled to the floor.

"No foul?" Bob suggested hopefully to the referee. But the rattled Pioneer was sent to the line for his one-and-one free throw opportunity. His ribs were aching so much that his shot fell short. The message had been received. The player stopped harassing Marvin.

During the next timeout, Coach Wells took Bob aside.

"I said to rough him up a bit, not knock him out!"

As the boys went back on the floor, Marvin noticed Bob chuckling.

"What's so funny?" Marvin asked. Bob shook his head.

"I just remembered something. You remember that rim that the West Baden janitor, Mr. Spoonmore, gave to me? Well, I fastened it to the wall in our hayloft. One winter we were playing ball up there. The hayloft doors were open and I knocked my brother clean out of that barn."

"I can believe that," Marvin replied.

This evening was the Enforcer's night. Bob was taking care of business on both ends of the court. He was being fouled almost every time he touched the ball, but he was hitting from the foul line—the one thing that was keeping the Hawks in the game. But the Pioneers also had a player on fire. Johnny Ford had 20 points by the end of the third session, which had the Pioneers up 59-53.

For the Hawks, it was time for a gut check.

The players on both teams were tired by this time after playing such intense defense. Paul, the Valley's starting center, fouled out on the second Pioneers possession of the fourth quarter. It was becoming more of a free throw contest than a game of running plays and hitting baskets. The two teams seemed to be trading foul shots on almost every possession.

George Lagenour, the second-string center, came in the game for Paul.

"Stay between your man and the basket, George," Paul reminded him as George ran to the scorer's bench to enter the contest.

There were so many fouls being called against each team that Rex hoped this would give his team the edge in the final minutes. They had a pretty decent foul shot percentage. Three minutes into the fourth quarter, and two Valley starters had fouled out; Frankie and Paul were now on the bench. This was not good for the Hawks, now short one of their best scorers and ball handlers. All those starters could do now was cheer on the teammates who had gone in the game for them.

Butch, Marvin, and Bob, meanwhile, were all playing with four fouls. These three, along with Jack Belcher and Mike Watson, were now going to have to get the job done somehow. The strongest aspect of the Valley team throughout the season had been its depth; when one player wasn't having his best night, another player would step up. This had happened in every game, it seemed.

By now, the star player for Providence had also fouled out of the game, and their best rebounder had four fouls. The Providence coach was about ready to blow a gasket. He had been complaining to the referee about the "ticky-tack" fouls that had been called on his team. The refs in fact had not been lenient whenever a player barely touched another man on the court. It was hard for the fans and coaches to believe that any game could have so many fouls called—and against both teams.

Both squads were playing their hardest, and with so very much on the line. The Valley Boys were back in their own mode of playing—team ball. They were moving the ball quickly up the court, passing to the open man, and getting off shots that Providence could only foul to stop. This only caused more frustration for the Pioneers—the kiss of death for any team. Still, their sharp-shooting guard had kept them in the game, scoring more than half of their second-half points. It really hurt their team when he left the game with five fouls.

The time clock wound down to just over three minutes and the scoring margin had remained consistent for most of the second half. It was 67-59, with the Pioneers leading. Valley fans were getting nervous. Here was another game where the Hawks would have to come from behind.

Another foul was called on Providence's starting forward. Butch had received a pass from Mike and was going up with the ball when it just left his hands and went out of bounds, as if it were some sort of magic trick that had caused the ball to levitate on its own. There had been no real contact, but the referee who had made the call was on the back side of Butch and it appeared as if the Providence player had hacked the Valley's star forward.

Their coach came off the bench like a tiger ready to pounce upon his prey and charged out onto the court. He just couldn't take it any longer. He had already thought that the refs had called a bad game, and this last call, which was truly a mistake, was the spark that set off the ensuing explosion. This call had taken his best rebounder out with his fifth infraction.

"What the hell are you talking about? He didn't even touch him! Are you kidding me? How about *seeing* the play before you make a piece of crap call like that?!?"

The ref knew he hadn't seen the play clearly and that he may have blown the call, so he let the coach let off some steam. Still, he couldn't reverse the call. He would try to give Providence a makeup call on the other end of the court against Valley.

But the Providence coach had one more expletive loaded up, and he just had to release it. He was halfway to the lane and badgering the referee, who was nearing the end of his patience.

"You blind son of a bi . . . uh . . . biscuit eater! Why don't you get your eyeglasses prescription refilled?" Everyone in the gym could see what was coming. The ref's whistle blew.

"You're outta here!" the official bellowed as he dramatically pointed toward the locker rooms. The Providence fans booed, screamed, and shouted curses at the referee, and nearly as loudly as the coach had. But the coach was gone. Only a couple of minutes remained in the game.

It may have been a calculated move on the coach's part, as it put the hometown crowd—already testy—in a mean-spirited mood. A few soda cups hit the floor. The principal got on the PA and asked the crowd to calm down or Providence would be the team having to forfeit the game. In a few minutes, the game resumed—without the home team's coach, and minus a couple of fans who had to be escorted out of the building after physically threatening the referees.

The last three minutes of this game would be long for everyone involved, the teams as well as their loyal fans. This game was important for Providence, regardless of the threatened punishment laps if they lost. Springs Valley's reputation had reached everywhere in this part of Indiana, and the Pioneers wanted to be the team to finally knock the Hawks out of the sky.

When the air cleared after the Providence coach had turned it blue, Butch was finally able to take his two free throws. He sank them both. The Pioneers still held a six-point lead.

Providence got the ball in-bounds even though the Hawks were all over them "like a wet blanket," as Doc put it. He was shouting, "Stay on your man!" as the Valley fans chanted at the top of their voices, "Defense, defense!"

Providence players were trying to hear instructions from their assistant coach as they advanced the ball up the court, but it was nearly impossible to compete with the roar of the crowd.

The Providence center received a tipped pass from his guard and he immediately went up for a shot. Butch fouled him as he reached in, trying for a steal. He became the third Hawk to foul out of the game and joined Frankie and Paul on the bench.

Three of the top Springs Valley players were now out of the game. The Valley fans were wondering: Could the Hawks pull this one out without them on the court? The next 120 seconds would tell.

The Providence boys were playing as if their lives depended on the outcome. Both teams were playing close defense, which meant the foul calls continued. More than halfway through the final quarter, the Hawks found themselves still down, 67-61.

Jim Conrad came back off the bench to pump in a couple of points during the fourth period. And now, with the three starters out, Bob McCracken took over the game. The number of fouls being called in the game turned in Valley's favor, with Bob hitting four free throws and a shot underneath to tie the score with only one minute left in the game.

Finally, and for the fourth time, the Hawks had knotted the score again. It was 67-67. Valley got the rebound after a Pioneer player took a bad shot, but a quick double-team trap caused Mike Watson to stop and try to pass to an open Hawk. He jumped as high as he could just after crossing the half court line and heaved the ball toward Marvin, who was coming out to help. A quick-thinking Pioneer player intercepted the ball, and slowly dribbled toward the Pioneers basket, waiting for his teammates to set up a last shot that could break the tie for the fifth time to win the game.

"Don't foul. Don't foul!" Coach Wells kept yelling from the sideline.

Jackie Belcher's man was taking the shot. Jackie's reflexes won out over the coach's instructions. And Jackie fouled his man.

These two free throws could end Valley's winning streak.

Things got desperately quiet on the Pioneers' side of the gym. The hometown fans were all holding their breath as the first of two free throws clanged off the rim. The player's anguish was apparent to all. He knew he had just lost the chance to take the lead. The poor free throw shooter knew that another miss would give Valley the ball, and possibly the game.

Instead of trying to make the free throw, he sent the ball to the basket as hard as he could, hoping his team could get the rebound and put up another shot.

The ball hit the front of the rim. The Pioneers' second-string center came in over top of Bob and brought the ball down. The timer's clock was ticking: 24 seconds, 23 seconds, 22 seconds.

The boy jumped up straight, all 6'3" of him, five feet away from the goal. His long arms extended above the rest of the players, and he let go his shot just to the side of the basket, putting up a bank shot.

The ball hit the glass too high, and it came back down to the front of the rim, bounced back up, and, for what seemed like five more precious seconds, bounced twice on the unforgiving rim. Then it spurted off to the side.

Jim Conrad, who had come in the game for Butch, grabbed the rebound and tossed it to Mike Watson, who brought it down the court. Mike fired the ball into Marvin, praying their sharp shooter had one more of his sweet jumpers in him.

Mike's man made a move toward Marvin, knowing that he would probably put up an outside-the-perimeter jump shot. The assumption was right—but Marvin, having an uncharacteristically off night, missed the shot. He followed his release, however, and quickly grabbed his own rebound.

With just 15 seconds remaining, Marvin fed the ball to Mike, who was cutting to the basket for a perfectly timed pass that the 5'7" guard didn't have to put on the floor. He caught the pass, took two steps to the hoop, and softly laid it in, high off the glass.

He made the layup just as he did in pre-game drills. But this basket initiated a roar from the visiting crowd in this small gymnasium that could've registered as seismic activity.

Valley had taken the lead, 69-67. Mike Watson, a player who had made three baskets up to this point in the season, had given them the lead. It was Mike who had scored the very first two points in Springs Valley basketball history, but this basket was even more important. Just as before, when Mike had hit those first two points, his dad could be heard above the din of the Valley crowd.

"That a way to go, Mikey! That's my boy!"

The scoreboard clock read five seconds. Providence took the ball out as the Hawks pressed them down the court. They got the ball to their guard, who took a long jump shot from some 20 feet out.

It was so close. But the ball went in and out, speeding around the rim once and squirting off to the side. Bob McCracken grabbed the arching rebound.

The Pioneer fans let out an "Oh!" like the air whooshing out of a tire punctured by a railroad spike, as the Pioneers' last shot defied their collective prayer. The pistol fired off just a moment later, as the timekeeper from Providence just couldn't bear to pull the trigger, firing the blank cartridge to signal the end of the game. Their boys had come closer than anyone to beating the Black Hawks.

But the clock read 00:00. The game was over, and Mike had hit the winning shot on a perfectly timed pass from Marvin. The boys from the Valley had demonstrated well how to play team basketball.

Coach Wells, along with the Hawks on the bench, ran out to meet the five remaining players as they headed toward their bench to celebrate the win. The Providence gymnasium, which also served as an auditorium, had a stage on the end where the visitors' bench was located, and just as the gun fired, ending the game, an elated Hawks fan jumped off the stage. The 200-pound boy landed on Doc Keiser, nearly breaking the assistant coach's back.

The visitors ran off the floor. Bags of popcorn, soda cups (some partially filled), and roster brochures came showering down on the Springs Valley team. The Hawks dodged the objects thrown as they ran to the locker room. They wanted out of the bedlam that the outcome of this game brought on.

The boys had learned a lot about hanging tough in a hard-fought contest. In the rebounding column, Paul Radcliff had pulled down 17, and Bob, Butch, and Jackie all had 13. This had given the Black Hawks more chances to score. Despite their size, they were a great rebounding team. They didn't do too badly from the free throw line, either, hitting 35 of 48. Butch had once complained that he wasn't getting enough shots. Bob, never one to mince words, told his co-captain, "If you get more rebounds, you'll get more shots!" Butch took the advice.

This had been their closest game yet. Still, they had the "W," and it felt good to come back after being down 10 in the first quarter. One more away game and then two home games were left in the regular season.

The sportswriters in the next day's papers called this game a "foul fest" with 61 fouls being called during the contest—43 in the first half alone. As it turned out, the Hawks had made 35 free throws, while scoring just 34 points from the field. The Hawks had nearly as many fouls called on them as the Pioneers did, but Coach Wells always told the boys not to argue with a referee. He didn't either. He knew that refs can make mistakes, but it's an even bigger mistake to get on a ref's bad side during a game.

This was the only game where Frankie, Paul, and Butch had fouled out, and they'd left the bench players to finish the task of defeating the Pioneers on their home floor. It was clear the boys understood that it takes every man doing his job to pull out a win.

For Mike Watson, hitting the winning basket was a sort of "poetic justice," as he had lost his starting position to Frankie. Still, there were never any angry words of jealousy spoken by the senior guard, who had been relegated to the bench by a junior. There was mutual respect, and Mike had demonstrated his maturity in the situation. There was a very good reason that he was the senior class president and a member of the Student Council. He understood diplomacy and patience in leadership.

The Black Hawks fans all formed a line with their cars, all honking, ready for the trip home behind the team bus. The love fest for their team was continuing. The state cop from French Lick, Wayne Stalcup, turned on his lights and escorted the team back home. Wayne gave the team this special escort to every away game they played. The town was behind this team, and whatever folks could do to help, they did.

Doc sat down on the bus next to Rex. "How's the back, coach?" Rex asked.

"Aw, it'll heal. I took a couple of Bayer. I think the fans are becoming so caught up in these Hawks' games, they're beginning to believe they can fly!"

Doc sighed. He was truly hurting, but the joy of this win was easing much of the pain. The assistant coach looked at Rex and reminded the head coach of his remark on their way into the Providence gym earlier that evening.

"I think you may be right. This is a team of destiny."

Rex smiled and said, "Did I say that? I know one thing. I never want to play a game like that again!"

Both coaches laughed. They knew they were experiencing a once-in-a-lifetime season. And they were loving every second of it.

The next day's sports page headline read, "The Finest Team Around We Know; Their Record Stands, Fifteen & 0." The article described how Bob McCracken took over the game with 22 points, hitting four from the field and 14 of 22 free throws. The team had an uncanny way of one player or another stepping up when most needed. Marvin had had an off night, hitting two of 16 field goal attempts. Butch scored 13 points and Paul scored 16 points before each fouled out.

The Providence game had been a very close call in more ways than one. Things were so tense that this game could have been stopped to avoid further skirmishes. The subhead of the article had read; "John Barleycorn – Biggest Problem."

"We are forced to call to the attention of the fans," the writer said, "the importance of holding your tempers. We noticed a few who had over-indulged in the jug. We are going to speak plainly here just what may have happened. We were all pretty hot at the officials, but if one swing had been made at any one of the irate fans gathered at halftime, the result could've been thus. Springs Valley would've been reported for bad conduct and no doubt, we would've been suspended for the remainder of the season."

But as the dust settled after the game, more and more of the townsfolk in Springs Valley were asking themselves, and each other, "Could this team go all the way and have an undefeated season . . . and then go far in the tourney?"

It was beginning to look possible, even probable.

The "Old Rebounder," who had been prognosticating this team as going undefeated, was already pecking out his next column for the school paper. He was now assuring his classmates that the Hawks would not only go undefeated, but would win their sectional as well.

An event of that magnitude had not occurred since the 1946 sectional win, and the thought of this happening again kept the entire town floating on air—reminiscent of the hawks that soared high above the Valley.

• CHAPTER 12 •

TOWNS (AND A TEAM) TURNED ON THEIR HEADS

By now, almost every basketball fan around was on board with the Black Hawks. In fact, the train was packed, and no seats were left. Even Noble Katter, the school principal, had jumped aboard, and was decked out in a black and white outfit with a gold bow tie to the games.

Because of the demand for tickets to each game, a system had been implemented. "A" tickets and "B" tickets were distributed to indicate which games folks could attend. The principal wrote an explanation regarding the game ticket shortage. It seemed that all had gotten aboard who were getting aboard—but not everyone had a ticket!

An Open Letter to Springs Valley Fans

I would like to explain the distribution of tickets to the Shawswick game. We sent only 268 tickets to Shawswick and got 148 in return. Yes, this is only about 1/3 of what we could have used. The tickets were distributed as following: 25 players, managers and coaches. (players bench)

201 to students of both schools. 3 yell leaders. 3 bus drivers (two fan bus, 1 player bus) 27 parents of *the ball players. 9 to 1/3 of school employees . . . I do not have tickets and have 10 students that had season tickets on the waiting list. The sectional tickets will sell for $2.75. We cannot sell single session tickets here. They may be purchased at the door for seventy-five cents. At this time, I wish to thank everyone for their cooperation and understanding of our crowded situation this winter.*

P.S. Whether we win or whether we lose, let's have the ability to pass out congratulations with a sober breath. When boys play as hard as they have they need a stimulant, not a depressant. Since some of the fans are playing the game as hard as the players, let's heed the coaches' advice: ALCOHOL AND BASKETBALL DOES NOT MIX.

The wild game at Providence down in Clarksville had really gotten out of control, and the principal had to make a plea to fans to prevent the mayhem from happening again. It would be unimaginable to have to forfeit a game for bad fan behavior at this point in an undefeated season.

Towns in Love

The next game of the season would be on Valentine's Day, February 14. Marvin was wondering what he could give Barbara, his special Valentine.

"How about the 16th win in a row," his girlfriend suggested. Marvin was walking his girlfriend home from school before practice. This had become a regular thing, as their relationship had grown more and more serious. The couple liked to walk up past the drug store and across the street past Caldwell's Jewelry store. Barbara always commented on a certain necklace with a heart-shaped locket that sat in the display window.

Everywhere they'd go together, people would stop Marvin and

ask him the usual question about what he thought of the team's next opponent. Then they'd say something like, "Keep those jumpers going in," and inform the high-scoring guard that they were behind the team 100 percent and that they'd be at the next game, cheering them on. Marvin was getting used to the fans' adulation and he always smiled and thanked them, but the novelty had worn off; he heard the same comments over and over.

The entire town was crazy with Black Hawks Fever. You couldn't drive past one storefront, gas station, or barbershop without seeing a poster of the team mascot in the window with whitewash lettering that said, "GO HAWKS!" Nearly every business establishment had the team's schedule, which included the team photo, taped in very visible places, as if anyone needed a reminder of the team's next game.

It seemed as if nothing else in the world existed. The only news anyone could discuss was about this ball team and their season. Men in the barbershop were now talking about the team's chances for winning the sectional and possibly the regional tournament games this season. It was as if there had never been conversations way back in October about the coach who was "too young and wet behind the ears," or about the unruly kids who were protesting the proposed team name and colors.

No one was complaining now about how rock 'n' roll was taking the younger generation down the wrong path. In fact, the older folks in town were beginning to envy these once-unruly students. Some folks now in their thirties and forties were recalling the last time they'd had a winning team playing in the French Lick gymnasium, back in 1943 and 1946. They were quite nostalgic, remembering the vitality of their younger, carefree days. A 17-year-old, after all, believes that anything is possible—with so much of life ahead, and many dreams that are to be lived and made into memories.

The town barber would hear the men reminiscing about their days of playing basketball and sharing their fondest memories of their high school days. "I suppose that the business of life is making memories," he would often say. "Because in the end, that's all you have." The citizens of the Valley were certainly making memories—some of the greatest ones they would ever have.

Everyone felt rejuvenated by the team's success and were feeling even younger. The possibilities were beginning to be discussed openly almost everywhere in town. No one wanted to jinx the Hawks, but it was impossible not to imagine what may lie ahead for the team that was representing the community better than any team had in the past. Everyone on both sides of the tracks in West Baden and French Lick was proud to announce that they were a part of Springs Valley.

The Ladies Aid committee at French Lick Christian Church decided to make earrings in the shape of the Black Hawk head, using black felt and sequins, and women all over both towns were sporting them. Solidarity now existed among all the Valley residents—no matter their church denomination, job description, or lifestyle. Springs Valley was now one community.

This was a new feeling because nothing like it had happened before. People from both towns were laughing together, slapping each other on the back, shaking hands, hugging, and crying tears of joy after games as they shouted in unison, "GO HAWKS, GO!" It was an amazing thing to behold. No church meeting, revival, Fourth of July fireworks display, or Christmas pageant had ever had this kind of effect on these people's spirits in the past.

The Black Hawks were a goodwill machine. The older citizens, who remembered the days of the grand resort hotels and the shared sense of pride they created in the two towns, had a renewed insight into human nature: We're all so similar, and the differences are very few. We all want the same things in life, but sometimes we focus on ourselves so much that we begin to believe that our desires, hopes, and dreams are unique. We look at other people as being different. Then we separate.

The Valley population was now climbing a mountain together, and, from atop this peak, they were seeing things more clearly than they ever had before. They were seeing themselves in each other, and now were realizing, after so many years, that they were much more alike than they realized.

Back to Shawswick

There was so much anticipation for the next game. Sportswriters were calling this "the Big One." The Shawswick Farmers had not been defeated since their very first game of the season—against the Valley Boys. They had one thing on their minds: "to harvest some revenge," as the writers might put it. The Black Hawks had won their first 15 games—quite a feat for any team, anywhere, on any level. But the Farmers were enjoying their own winning streak of 16 games. The hype before the game guaranteed a sell-out.

Marvin Pruett was very good at any sport that required directing a ball to its desired destination. The sharp-shooting junior had put in a good amount of time at one other location besides the basketball court. Marvin could shoot a mean game of pool.

There were even a few times when he may have won a little bit of money, when an older fellow judged he could take advantage of a kid. He and Frankie would patronize Shorty's Pool Hall any time they could, spending some winter Saturdays there and shooting billiards all day. They played for free because both boys put their time in working for Shorty, cleaning and racking up balls.

They had heard a rumor at school about something Shorty was up to, and they thought they would stop by the pool hall to investigate. Marvin and Frankie, in other words, were going to be eyeing the guy who was supposed to be keeping his eye on them.

The pool hall sat right off the main drag going through West Baden, just at the end of the Homestead Hotel. It was the local hangout for many males of the species—including high school boys. Entering through these doors was somewhat of a rite of passage into the male world—where the things that men do and say were quickly learned. Marvin had learned some of his most choice words from Shorty himself, in fact.

The pool hall was a "shotgun" building, holding only three tables of play. The blinds usually were pulled down, with only the lighting that hung over each table to dimly illuminate the room. A blue haze of smoke from cigars and unfiltered Camel and Pall Mall cigarettes hung in the air, creating an otherworldly atmosphere. The smell of stale beer was ever present, and a few empties always sat on the window ledge.

Yep, this was a grown-up haunt to be sure, and the boys from West Baden always enjoyed going to Shorty's.

"Hey Shorty, how's it goin'?" Marvin called out as he and Frankie entered.

"Oh, oh . . . uh, just keepin' the lights on, ya know," Shorty answered awkwardly. There were a bunch of fellas standing around him as the boys came through the door, and he was shoving something into his pocket.

"Pretty tough getting tickets to the Shawswick game?" Frankie asked one of Shorty's customers.

"Oh yeah. 'Bout impossible," one man said, holding a pool cue in one hand, his other hand in his bib overalls pocket.

Marvin piped up.

"Yeah, I heard you might be able to get a ticket here."

"Not here. I think they're all sold out, aren't they?" Shorty blurted out.

The boys hung around for a few minutes, then took off.

"Something's going on here," Marvin told his buddy.

"Yeah, somethin's mighty fishy all right," Frankie lamented. Then he laughed. "Hey, I think we just did our best imitation of the Hardy Boys!"

Marvin laughed as well. "Yeah, you were Joe and I was Frank."

"No, buddy. I'm Frank!" the little guard shot back.

Marvin and Frankie left the pool hall, shaking their heads, having guessed what Shorty was probably up to.

"I hope he doesn't get in trouble for this stunt," Frankie lamented.

"I bet it's true. He's gotten his hands on some tickets somewhere, and he's making a lot more friends this week," Marvin said.

The boys had guessed right. Shorty had acquired his own printing press somewhere and had decided that he would print some "extra" tickets for this sold-out game. He created his own "Admit One" tickets that looked like those used at most venues, such as the local movie house and the carnival that always came to town. He was passing out the tickets and telling everyone that he gave one to, "Make sure you get there when the doors first open."

The actual tickets for the game, meanwhile, had sold very fast, so the coaches from both schools tried to acquire the larger gymnasium in Bedford, which seated 4,600. Unfortunately, there was a charity event scheduled for that same night: a wheelchair basketball game. So, the 1,800 ticket holders had to be crammed into the Shawswick gymnasium for another sold-out-plus game. The boys from the Valley were doing even more than bringing their community together; they were helping the schools they played add to their athletic department's coffers.

Game night came, and a whole bunch of Hawks fans showed up with the phony tickets just as the doors opened, as Shorty had counseled. The ticket taker didn't notice the color of the fake tickets and let them all in. When the Shawswick fans got to the game, there were a whole lot of Springs Valley fans taking up too many of the bleacher seats. This was the one game where Shorty himself had chosen to stay home, fearful of what he might run into.

The ticket shortage sparked a ruckus but the school leaders came up with a solution, more or less: they filled every single open space, and lined the entire court, with folding chairs. There was not a foot of open space at either end of the court; the chairs were set right outside the baselines. Where there weren't chairs, people stood, just inches from the court. The players couldn't take a shot from the corners without hitting a spectator.

Shawswick proved to be more than just farmers this time around. Like the Valley's players, these country boys had spent a good deal of time putting the ball through a hoop on the side of a barn. Those "agri-fellas"—as one sportswriter actually referred to them—played the game of their lives as they sought to keep their own streak alive.

The Black Hawks did their best as well, blocking out their forwards and their center, who had a distinct height and weight

184

advantage. Farming develops a lot of muscle—baling hay, slopping hogs, feeding and milking cows, bringing in the corn harvest, and a thousand other demanding tasks. These Farmers were as tough as could be expected.

And they played tough—a little too tough. The 6'4" center guarding Paul, for example, elbowed him throughout the game.

"Bob, you know what to do. Get that kid's attention, will you?" Coach Wells suggested.

Bob complied. On the next Farmers possession, the trouble-making player went down at the foul line—and hard. Bob had delivered a message once more by way of a well-placed elbow. Fortunately, the refs didn't see it, and the intervention strategy worked. The Farmers' center stopped elbowing Paul. (Even during the Black Hawks' practices, Coach Wells would tell whoever was guarding Bob to just give him a path to the basket, if he was going to the hoop. "Just let him through," the coach told them. Rex didn't want any of his players to be hurt in practice scrimmages.)

This game started off as well as any Hawks game had to date. Frankie hit the first shot from the top of the key. On the next two possessions, Marvin drained jumpers that didn't make a sound as they slipped through the net. The Valley fans made plenty of sound, however. Paul was the next to score, knocking down a 15-footer, then Frankie hit a free throw, putting Valley ahead, 9-2. The Farmers finally scored, but a high-arching shot from Bob and a free throw from Butch doubled the score in the Hawks' favor, 12-6. The Farmers then got serious, closing out the quarter to make it 18-14.

Not long afterward, the Hawks once again found themselves behind going into the second half of play. The teams traded the lead until the end, when the Hawks had a two-point lead at 68-66. The Farmers' star player put up a prayer at the end of the fourth quarter, and it took a high bounce off the rim. He grabbed his own rebound and drained it at the gun. Tie game, 68-68.

Overtime.

The many lead changes and the game going to overtime meant

the game was living up to all the hype. It was just what the sports prognosticators predicted: "The Big One."

Bob was fouled on the first play in overtime, and he hit the free throw. The Hawks were holding the ball with a razor-thin one-point lead. Bob was fouled three more times and put in three more points. Butch was also fouled four times and hit all of his free throws. Butch, it seemed, always came through in the clutch. He was the most consistent player, tallying 12 to 18 points a game. He brought his same game on this much-needed night in Shawswick, scoring 12 points in the contest.

The Farmers were not going down without a fight. In overtime, Valley controlled the time playing "slow down" ball, as there was no time limit for each possession. (Bobby Plump had held the ball for nearly five minutes in the last game of the 1954 Final Four before he took the final shot to win that game.) Three of the Farmers fouled out in their attempt to steal the ball. Coach Wells, who always made the boys put in plenty of time at the foul line at each practice, was now seeing this diligence pay off. The Hawks hit 27 of 34 free throws in regulation, and seven of nine in the extra minutes.

The Hawks dodged still another bullet in this game, taking control in overtime. In the extra minutes, they hit free throws and one field goal, winning 77-72. The winning streak continued, and there were only two more games to play in the regular season.

The Springs Valley Black Hawks were now one of only three teams in Indiana still undefeated. Sportswriters in newspapers from Indianapolis and Louisville were really taking notice. As one writer put it, "The two towns of West Baden and French Lick—longtime bitter rivals—have come together to cheer on their one team."

Truer words were never written.

Soon, these towns' names would be familiar to many more in sports media throughout Indiana. Sportswriters across Hoosierland were starting to explore the history of these two towns. More than a few would be sitting at their typewriters late into the night, trying to meet the next day's deadline—hammering out their articles, tiredly exhaling, as the names "French Lick" and "West Baden" crossed their lips for the first time.

A Tired Team

As great as the winning streak appeared to everyone outside of the Hawks organization, the pressure of being expected to win the next game was beginning to take its toll on all the boys.

Clayton Conrad, the Junior High School principal, chatted with his son after the difficult game at Shawswick.

"Jim, why do you think the first game of the season against the Farmers was so much easier?" he asked him.

Jim paused, thought a few seconds, and blurted out, "We're just tired of basketball."

Now this was an eye-opener for his dad. But the team had truly hit a wall in that last game. The pressure, along with the intense schedule of so many games within only a couple of days, was wearing the Hawks down.

Yes, simply put, they were tired—emotionally and physically.

Clayton Conrad called Coach Wells.

"Rex, I think I've discovered why these past few games have been so tough," he told him. "Jimmy just shared something with me I think you should know."

"Go ahead, I'm all ears," the coach replied.

"Well, I think the boys are simply worn out. When I asked Jim this evening what he thought the problem was, he just said, "We're tired of basketball."

"Hmmm . . . I guess that makes sense," Rex said. "They have put in a lot of time on the court—both practices and games. And that five-hour practice probably didn't help them recuperate too much.

"Okay," Rex said. "I think I have an idea." He hung up the phone after thanking Conrad for the insight.

At the next day's practice, Rex told Billy to put the basketballs on the rack.

"Oh, oh, not again," Marvin whispered to Bob.

"Yeah, I wonder who goofed up this time," Bob answered. But the coach surprised them.

"We're not going to do anything today that has to do with basketball," Rex told the boys as the team managers stretched the volleyball net across the gym floor. "We're just going to have fun today."

For the next few practices, the undefeated basketball team was going to play volleyball, dodge ball, or inside baseball. Rex was going to let their minds and bodies relax, getting away from the stress of what this unique season had brought upon them all.

So, for a time, the Springs Valley Black Hawks played volleyball, laughed, and joked around again—if not more than ever. They were just kids again, playing and having fun—the way playing basketball had always been for them.

"Marvin, Marvin, Marvin's in Love"
(with apologies to "Tammy")

Marvin had helped deliver Barbara's Valentine's Day gift of the 16th straight win, but he didn't stop there. He walked up to her after the game just before he got on the team bus. He handed her a small, fuzzy black, hinged case. Barbara's mouth opened in amazement.

"Could it be?" she wondered. She popped it open. There before her eyes was the heart-shaped locket the couple had been looking at in the window case at Caldwell's Jewelry store.

"Oh, Marvin, I love it. I love it so much!" She exclaimed while jumping up and down. He helped her fasten it around her neck.

"Look, you can put something inside the heart," Marvin reminded her as he opened the pendant, his hands just under her chin. He could smell Barbara's perfume, hair spray, and some mysterious scent that always reminded him of vanilla Cokes. He couldn't wait to hold her in his arms again, just like the night after the Christmas concert in his mom's car.

Marvin loved everything about Barbara: her looks, her walk, the tone of her voice, and her Southern Indiana accent. He felt he could see Barbara's soul when looking in her eyes—could see her love for him. He wondered sometimes if someday, they would be married.

"I Only Have a Nose for You"

The next night, Marvin and Barbara drove up to Orleans to the theater there to see the Debbie Reynolds movie *Tammy and the Bachelor.* Although Marvin wasn't looking as forward to seeing this film as he had been to see *The Blob,* he was making good on his word. He'd promised to take Barbara a few weeks back when they had double dated with Frankie and Thelma to see *The Seven Voyages of Sinbad* at the Springs Valley theater.

Barbara was glad to at last be going to this "girl movie." The second Marvin drove into her driveway, Barbara ran out to the '48 Plymouth. Marvin's mom had driven it up to Bloomington a few weeks back and got the infamous $50 Earl Scheib paint job—in olive green. It now resembled an Army tank.

"You should make that boy come to the door," her mom called out to Barbara as she bolted out of the house. She couldn't wait that long. She was looking so forward to their date—away from French Lick and West Baden.

The couple couldn't go anywhere in the twin cities without spending half the time talking to some avid Hawks fan. Since the night of the autograph hounds at the hotel's Christmas program, Marvin and Barbara had been driving up to Bedford and getting a pizza pie from Grecco's—just as Frankie and Thelma had. This quaint establishment had become the place for both couples to go, both on double dates and alone. Not a soul recognized them there, and this was just the way these new hometown celebrities wanted it. But the last time they'd gone to Grecco's, lo and behold, there were Coach Wells and his wife, Margaret. Marvin guessed that the coach was there for the same reason—to be alone. And to grab some of that great pizza.

Marvin kissed Barbara lightly on the cheek as she hopped in his car. He noticed the silver heart locket. "Can I look inside?" he asked, already opening it.

He popped open the half-heart shaped lid and saw something odd; it resembled an Egyptian pyramid, with two tunnels at the bottom. But it was hard to see in the dim light of dusk.

He squinted. "What in the world is that?" he asked.

"It's your nose. I didn't have a small-enough picture of you," Barbara said, "so I folded the only one I had—your school picture."

Marvin burst out laughing.

"MY NOSE?!" He kept repeating it and shaking his head, continuing to laugh as they drove away.

"I'll cut my head out of the team photo," he promised. "It'll be small enough, I think."

"Good idea," Barbara agreed.

Marvin began humming a familiar tune and then began improvising new lyrics. The 1953 Sinatra hit "I Only Have Eyes For You" had become "I only have a nose for you." They laughed all the way to Bedford. Life was good. Could it get any better than this? They wondered.

Marvin was curious where he and Barbara would wind up in the next few weeks—the next few years. They arrived at the movie ticket window. "Two for *Tammy and the Bachelor*, please," Marvin said to the lady in the window.

Tammy wasn't the only one falling in love. Barbara and Marvin were meant for each other.

Marvin felt as if he were on a ride that had begun when he was much younger, learning this game of basketball and honing his skills as a shooter and ball handler.

The Valley Boys, when they were in sixth grade, had once had the honor of being invited up to the Castle Knoll Farm. This grand farm was just a few miles up State Road 56 heading toward Paoli, and there was a basketball goal inside the biggest barn. The high school boys on the 1951 Sprudel team had played there during the colder months when they weren't in a high school game. All the boys from West Baden had grown up watching the Sprudels teams of the late '40s to early '50s. They had all tried to imitate their star player, Frosty Hamilton. Marvin had seen that boy's shot go in time after time, and he copied Frosty's jump shot to a T.

Frosty, Keith Wininger, Ward Elliot, and Rex Wells had served as fine role models for the Springs Valley team of the future, and the Valley Boys had learned from the best in the West Baden team of '51. Basketball in the Valley was more than a tradition. It was more like family heritage being passed from one generation to the next. The Valley Boys had honored that heritage, and Marvin had become the latest Frosty Hamilton.

His preparation had been long and consistent. His mom, like so many West Baden and French Lick residents, had to find work out of town. She drove each day to her factory job in Orleans, leaving the house at 6 a.m., and would drop Marvin off at the school. Mr. Durant, the janitor, would open the gym for Marvin so he could practice—even on Sundays. This boy had lived, eaten, and slept basketball, and it showed in his play. He could hit the outside shot, but he knew how to drive to the hoop as well.

When Marvin was in eighth grade, he scored 40 points in one game against Loogootee. The Lions coach had said, "That is the greatest jump shot I've ever seen from an eighth grader." Marvin made the varsity team his freshman year at West Baden. Now, two years later, he found himself the leading scorer, averaging nearly 20 points per game. Many sportswriters simply labeled him "rugged."

This unbelievable season, he felt he was continuing this ride, accelerating, heading toward a destination of something great, apparently, that was seemingly predestined. One thing he was certain of: there was a whirlwind surrounding him, and so much happening all at once. He just knew that he was going to hold on for the ride of his life to wherever this school year was taking him.

Marvin, as the leading scorer in most games, did indeed feel more pressure than the other players. He wondered where the team would end up this season.

And he wondered if the things Paul talked about regarding his faith were true. He wondered if he could ever know God. Paul said he had a relationship with Jesus. Could a guy like him be saved?

He wondered.

Game 17: Dubois

Tuesday night's game would have the team taking the bus southward to play against the Fighting Jeeps of Dubois. The pronunciation of the town's name had long ago lost any trace of the original French and had become "DEW-boys." Anyone heard using the French pronunciation would instantly be recognizable as someone who "ain't from around these here parts."

The town was justly famous for one very special thing: broasted chicken. Hoosiers from miles around would make the drive to Dubois to savor this culinary delight, and the boys all asked if they could stop and get some for their team meal prior to the game. This sounded like a great idea to Rex and Doc, as their team surely deserved to be treated and fed well. The team bus left an hour earlier than usual to have time to partake of this Southern Indiana delicacy.

At one time, a town council member had gone so far as to suggest naming the team "the Fighting Chickens," but the consensus from nearly everyone in Dubois had been that "Jeeps" was certainly more intimidating. No doubt the fans were imagining the fun the sportswriters would have after each game. The columnists would always be attempting to incorporate the team name in painful headlines: "The Hometown Chickens laid an egg last night—in their own nest!" Or, "The Chickens were fried as they attempted to peck their way back into this game." On and on it would go.

So the name Jeeps was welcomed by all—except, perhaps, the folks who owned the broasted chicken establishment. And the sportswriters, of course.

"What the Heck is a Jeep?"

Webster explains what a jeep is: "a small, sturdy vehicle, normally used by the military," and the name derived from pronouncing the acronym "GP," for "general purpose." But there was another "Jeep"—a fictitious animal that began to appear in the "Popeye the Sailor Man" cartoons in the mid-1930s.

Someone, somewhere, perhaps, was as fond of the Popeye cartoons as Principal Katter was of his grasshoppers, and had made this decision for his community. And if you've ever seen this mean-looking little animal that appeared to be a combination of a dog, cat, and mouse, with its clown nose, you can picture the team's cartoon mascot quite well. It was obvious; this Jeep had more fight in it than might be expected from a chicken. Still, out of all the animals on the planet, the folks in Dubois had named their team "the Fighting Jeeps."

This next-to-last game of the season was another sell-out. The small Dubois gym was so packed that when the players took the ball out of bounds on the sidelines, it was impossible not to step on the feet of the fans.

The Dubois Jeeps had a record of 13 wins and 6 losses, and this was an extremely tough game. As was true of most teams that the Valley Boys played, these boys were much bigger than the Hawks.

The Jeeps had a set of identical twins on their team, Teddy and Freddy Hill, who were known for pulling the stunt of trading places just as many twins have done—whether it was on dates or the classroom. It was rumored throughout the basketball season that they would also exchange jerseys if the better player of the two got in foul trouble in the first half. (The twins were so close in looks, they had the ability to fool even folks who knew them well.)

They were both 6'4" and weighed around 220 pounds. One of the twins was the better player of the two. At the start of the second half, Bob believed he was guarding the same twin as he had been guarding during the first half—but he began noticing that this boy suddenly had a slightly bigger nose and ears than his *nearly i*dentical brother. Bob called him out in true McCracken fashion.

"Hey, you're not the same guy I was guarding in the first half!" he accused him. "You changed jerseys with your brother! You're Freddy, not Teddy!"

"No, I didn't," the player retorted. I tell ya, I'm the same guy you guarded in the first half."

"No, I can tell—your voice is different too! I'm going to bring this to the ref's attention," Bob said angrily.

"McCracken, let's just meet after the game and settle this outside. I'm going to kick your ass," the twin suggested. Bob couldn't wait.

It wasn't clear whether the Valley Boys were fortified or weighed down with the chicken, mashed potatoes and gravy, rolls, and pecan pie they ate before the game. But they still notched up one more win against the bigger Dubois "Jeeps." The final score was 54-46.

While it appeared that a fight would soon be ensuing outside the gym, things began heating up inside as well. Just as during the Providence game, the fans from Dubois and Springs Valley were meeting on the court, exchanging unpleasantries. It was nearing an all-out brawl. Attempting to calm the crowd, the local self-appointed constable, Ralph Brown, made his way through the ruckus with his badge held high above his head in a Barney Fife manner, shouting, "I'm the law! I'm the law! The party's over. Now break it up and y'all go home!"

The two Fighting Jeeps twins decided that neither had much fight left in them and they chose not to "kick Bob's ass" after the game.

Bob was waiting, willing and able to take on the twins. Then, as happens with boys when certain threats are made earlier in the heat of the moment, they exercised better judgement, and didn't follow through with their threat. The boys all knew where the "true fight" belonged; in a 32-minute contest on the hardwood—not with fists, outside the gymnasium. These two teams would meet again soon.

The Valley Boys had won by a relatively comfortable margin, and Marvin had his shot back. The team seemed to be back in early season form. Their play looked as if it were an athletic ballet as they smoothly moved the ball with sharp, clean passes, got rotation on their half-court play, and found the open man cutting to the basket. Playing volleyball and thinking about something other than basketball for a couple of practices seemed to have done the trick. The boys were playing Black Hawks basketball once again.

One more home game remained on the regular season schedule, and a Black Hawks win would mean an undefeated season. They all knew it was now very possible, if not probable, that this is how their regular season would look: 18 wins and 0 losses. *Oh, that would look so good in a scrapbook someday,* was the thought on many minds.

Still, Coach Wells insisted: no counting your chickens before they hatch! Just eat them—but maybe not before a big game.

• CHAPTER 13 •

THE PERFECT SEASON

"Sugar in the morning, sugar in the evening, sugar at suppertime. Be my little sugar and love me all the time."

Careening down the stairs to grab a piece of toast before running out the door to get to school, Frankie could hear the McGuire Sisters on the radio. Thoughts of Thelma raced through his mind. It seemed that every song he heard reminded him of his girl. Tab Hunter's "Young Love, True Love" came on next as he gobbled down the quick breakfast of toast and Hershey's cocoa that his aunt made for him every winter morning.

Frankie grabbed his letter jacket and ran out the door to meet Thelma and walk her to school. He'd never felt as awake in the mornings as when he'd leave early enough to meet her on their two-mile treks to school.

At 7:30 on the dot, they met halfway, near the lumber company at College Street and Adams, so they could have a long, leisurely stroll to school. As they walked along, Thelma asked Frankie, "How do you feel about tonight's game with Salem?"

Frankie paused for a moment, thinking about his response. He finally answered, "Oh, just about like all the rest, although it does seem like every game is gettin' tougher," he confided to her. "Every team we play now has something to prove. They all want to be the team that ends our winning streak.

"All I know is that we have squeaked out a few of our games that could've gone the other way," he went on. "Just a few different plays or baskets scored by the other team, and we would have lost a few of those games."

"I guess this is the reason for the article I read by Jim Ballard in the *Herald*," Thelma answered. "It was about whether it'd be a good thing to lose a game before tourney time. He said, 'This would be a question with a lot of 'pros and cons.''"

"Imagine that: someone thinkin' it might be a good thing to lose a game," Frankie said incredulously. "What would be the 'pro' side of losin' a game?"

Thelma just listened politely. She knew there was so much on her boyfriend's mind.

"No one would've ever guessed at the beginning of the school year that we'd be in this position. I just want to go out there and do our best each game—even a game on a Tuesday night," Frankie said. "Who makes up these schedules anyway? We've had more games on weeknights this season than ever before."

"Uh huh." Thelma understood that Frankie was thinking aloud, and it was better not to interrupt him.

"I like playin' on Friday nights the best," he continued. "It just feels better to be buildin' up to the last school day of the week."

But the last two games of the season would fall in the same week: the 17th game with Dubois was on Tuesday and the 18th and final game was tonight, Friday. Frankie was eager for the tip off.

It was rather cold on this Monday in February. Frankie could see Thelma's breath as they walked along and could even smell her Wrigley's Spearmint gum. He even loved the way she chewed her gum. He recalled the taste of their first kiss, and just how her wonderful spearmint breath had filled his senses. Frankie also loved seeing Thelma in her buttoned up sweater. He and she were color coordinated, with Frankie in his black cotton letter jacket with the leather sleeves and Thelma in her black sweater with the big "T" on the right pocket.

Frankie felt as if having Thelma at each game was a sort of good luck charm. Every time he glanced over at her, she was so full of life and energy, cheering him and the rest of team on with the rest of the student body.

Frankie and Thelma were as in love as any high school couple could be. If there was a better feeling in the world, Frankie hadn't experienced it yet.

"Y'know something, Thelma?" Frankie asked. "There's somethin' that every athlete who's ever played sports has thought of at one time or another. It's wonderin' what it's like to be the guy scorin' the go-ahead touchdown in the last seconds of the fourth quarter. Or hitting that home run that wins the game in the bottom of the ninth inning.

"It's somethin' that only happens maybe once in a lifetime—if you're lucky, really lucky," Frankie said. "To experience that feelin'— it must be like some sort of answer to a lifelong prayer."

"What are you trying to say?" his blonde beauty asked him as they walked along. "Tell me, Frankie."

"Well, I've been thinkin' a lot about this. I keep havin' this same dream."

"Uh huh. Go ahead," Thelma prodded him.

"I've been seein' myself in a dream," Frankie said. "The best dream I've ever had—I mean the best dream outside of the dream I've had of you and me together.

"The team is down during the last quarter of the game. We finally catch up in the last few seconds or so. It's either a steal or an outlet pass to me for a fast break." He grew more animated.

"Then I'm off to the races, all alone, dribblin' down the court. I score the winnin' basket, and it's the greatest feelin' in the whole wide world!"

"Oh Frankie, I wish that could happen in real life!" Thelma exclaimed.

"Oh, it's just a dream," Frankie admitted sheepishly. "But there is one other great part of the dream each time."

"Yes, go on," she prodded him. Frankie's greatest cheerleader was hoping to hear what in fact her boyfriend went on to say.

"I, uh . . . I always look over to you there in the bleachers as the final buzzer goes off," he said shyly. "When the last second ticks off the clock, you're jumpin' and runnin' to me." By now he'd almost forgotten where he was.

"You jump into my arms, and the rest of the team picks you and me up onto their shoulders and they carry us off the court as we're holdin' hands, laughin' and cryin' for joy."

"Oh Frankie, that's a wonderful dream." Thelma was blushing. "I'm so glad I'm a part of it. Sometimes I wake up in the middle of the night and think about everything that has happened during this school year, all the wins and meeting you, and . . . well, you know, becoming a couple. Sometimes it seems like I've been dreaming, then I become truly awake, and realize that it's not a dream, but something very real."

She sighed deeply. "I don't think there will ever be another time in my life when things will be this exciting."

"Yeah. I know what you mean," Frankie agreed.

As they navigated the stairs on their way into the school, their thoughts remained far, far away.

The past three months had indeed seemed like a dream to Frankie. He wondered yet again as he reached his locker: *Gosh, could the Hawks really go all the way this year?* He didn't dare speak his thought and quickly put away the notion for fear of thinking too far ahead. He remembered what the coach had told the team at the beginning of the year: "Take one game at a time." And that's what he was trying to do.

But by now, it was nearly impossible to stop thinking what most of the town folk had been talking about since the 10th win in a row. How could anyone *not* now be thinking about having an undefeated season? All the Black Hawks were pondering this same question, but none of them had ever voiced it.

Frankie's early morning reverie was finally interrupted when someone came up from behind and pushed him in the back.

"Hey, Frankie, are ya all fired up for tonight's game?" Mike Watson had snuck up behind him.

"Yeah, I think we can get another 'W' tonight. I don't think Salem is all that tough this year," Frankie responded, assuring his teammate.

Mike had on his letter jacket too. And as they walked through the entrance doors, so many students were wearing black and white that Mike yelled, "Hey, it looks like a bunch of penguins!"

Frankie whispered to Thelma, "I think it looks like some other kind of bird. Black Hawks!"

Inside the school, the air seemed charged. Frankie could almost feel the energy being generated by all the students who were now slamming their locker doors and running late to the first class of the day. The mood throughout the halls was one of elation on game days, and the teachers seemed to be more lenient with the students' tardiness.

This deep into the undefeated season, the beginning of each class always seemed to be a discussion about the last game played or the next game coming up. The teachers were as caught up in the hysteria as the students. Principal Katter was a complete convert: he now wore a black suit, white shirt, and black tie on most days—with a "GO HAWKS!" button pinned to his lapel. By now, even he had nearly forgotten all about his Grasshoppers idea.

But the school was hardly the only place where the feverish support was evident. This was now Black Hawk country, and every store and shop window displayed the pride the entire town felt for their hometown team. Most storefronts had banners with a painting of the head of the Black Hawks mascot, or the original drawing that the Disney cartoonist had created, with whitewash letters reading, "GO HAWKS, GO! WE'RE BEHIND YOU ALL THE WAY!" Albright's Market had its windows so filled with team photos and newspaper clippings that it was impossible to see inside the store from the sidewalk.

It was truly amazing just how much the two towns had transformed in only four months' time. Now, there was no division whatsoever between the former archrivals. The "Hatfields and McCoys, Southern Indiana edition" had at last reached a truce. They all got along now as if there had never been a feud for the past 50 years.

Springs Valley was now more than just a name. It was a reality: one community, cheering on its team, dreaming the same dream. There was a constant feeling of goodwill and an ever-present current of excitement in the air that all could feel. The buzz in town was palpable, from the youngest first grader to the oldest citizen. The euphoria revealed itself in how people carried themselves and talked to each other.

The old men who gathered at the barbershop couldn't stop talking about their team and its chances in the tourney, now fast approaching. Kids in grade school were drawing their version of the Black Hawk mascot for their art classes. Preachers were now using the team to illustrate their Biblical teachings: how individual strands of cord woven together make one strong rope, or how two logs burn brighter together than one alone.

It seemed as if every single person in the twin towns was on the same page.

Young Guns

The last game of the season against Salem was a home game. It was standing-room-only in the woefully tiny gymnasium. Those folks who couldn't squeeze into a bleacher seat stood packed around the entrances.

There hadn't been enough tickets to meet the demand since the team's last game before Christmas break. Not only were the hometowners attending the games, but also basketball fans from all over Southern Indiana. Everyone wanted a seat at these games to see this upstart team take on its next rival, which was always playing its hardest to be the one team to take down the undefeated Hawks.

It was an unprecedented time in Southern Indiana basketball. Miniscule Milan hadn't been undefeated in 1954, though they did boast an outstanding 19-2 record before going on to win the state title—and everyone wanted in on the action. WSEZ radio was selling ad time for these games as never before.

The Salem Lions made the 28-mile drive west on highway 56 to the Valley. They knew that playing the Black Hawks in their own gym with their undefeated season on the line would be a challenge, to say the least. But they weren't going to just lie down for the Hawks. As the sportswriters later wrote, "The Lions came out roaring, scratching and clawing."

The game was like several others that the Hawks had played. Valley trailed the entire game, and was down nine points halfway through the third quarter.

There were a few people at the Sheraton Hotel who were feeling anxious as they listened breathlessly to the play-by-play on the radio. An ice sculpture had been created with numbers three feet high: 18-0. But the sculptor was standing by with his hammer and chisel, ready to transform that sculpture into a 17-1 commemoration if things went badly.

Coach Rex Wells, however, was not one to panic. He had seen his team come back from deficits before—in five of the last six games, in fact.

"Providence had us down by 11," the 25-year old coach told a Louisville *Courier Journal* sportswriter. "Winslow had a 13-point lead, and we were down by eight with Shawswick and seven points behind Dubois.

"We always find a way to come back."

This game with Salem was no different. The Hawks finally caught up when Paul nailed two free throws to knot it up at 54 all with 10 seconds left in the third. Then at the beginning of the final session, Paul sank an outside set shot. Bob followed up with a layup that saw Valley taking the lead in the fourth quarter. The Hawks played "slow down" possession ball during the last three minutes. The ice sculptor could relax. The final opponent of the regular season went down like the rest, 68-62.

They had done it.

The Springs Valley Black Hawks, a school in its first year, had won every regular season game, which no Indiana school had done before. History had been made, and they had sealed the deal in a home game in front of their own rabid fans. Hollywood could not have produced a better scenario.

As the gun fired to signal the end of game and a perfect season, the tiny, antiquated gym, filled well beyond its 1,100-seat capacity, seemed to explode as the students and fans poured down onto the court. In their jubilant celebration with the team, they hoisted the players and coach onto their shoulders and carried them off the court.

The ladders appeared, the nets were cut, and the celebration was on.

"There won't be any nets replacing these until next season," Rex exclaimed to Doc. "We'll be practicing in bigger gyms to get ready for the tournament. Huntingburg is three times the size of this gym!"

Going undefeated for the season was a mighty big deal, and a one-night celebration was simply not enough. The next night, Saturday, a bonfire and pitch-in dinner continued the celebration. Then the party moved to the Sheraton hotel for another sock hop.

As Marvin and Barbara were dancing, he made sure to pass close by Bob McCracken.

"Hey Bob, don't get too near that fire, okay?" Marvin was reminding him about what had happened at the bonfire after the first win of the season. Bob smiled. As if he'd forgotten.

But he was a little distracted. He had stepped up in the game once again, leading the scoring with 22 points, making a huge contribution in this last game of the undefeated regular season. But one play in particular stood out for him. He had driven to the basket, and one-handed the ball softly off the glass for a lay-in. As he was running in a wide turn toward the side of the court, he looked back in time to see his shot going in.

But in the process, he nearly bowled over the head cheerleader, Billie Jo Harris, standing on the sideline. He stopped her from falling, and he looked at Billie Joe to apologize. Suddenly his eye caught a girl's face in the Springs Valley booster section.

Time seemed to stand still. "Who is that girl?" he asked Billie Jo. "Tell her she's the most beautiful girl in French Lick."

Billy Jo later gave her the message and gave Bob her name: Patsy

Zeedyk. That was the beginning of another courtship and lifelong love to emerge from this unpredictable season. They were a couple for the rest of their high school days and beyond.

In this heady atmosphere of excitement and success, romances were blooming, and hearts and games were being won simultaneously. Many memories were made in 1958—and many choices with lovely, lifelong implications.

Hot Rod Hawks

The boys were feeling their oats. Bob had recently bought a '49 Custom Ford convertible with money he'd saved working part-time at Brownie's filling station. It was candy-apple red with whitewall tires. The dual carburetors and tail pipes were a teenage boy's dream. His dad had matched Bob's savings so that he could afford it, and now Bob was driving his very first car.

This was a grand event, worthy of celebration. Bob called up his buddy.

"Hey Marvin, ya wanna take a spin in my new set of wheels?"

"Are you shittin' me? You got a car?"

"Sure, I do."

"Come and pick me up," Marvin answered. Bob was calling from Brownie's, having washed his new prize possession and gassed it up.

Bob picked up Marvin and they went to the Chatterbox to hang out a while, showing off the "cherry" Chevy. When they'd downed their burgers and sodas, Bob took off out of the parking lot—a bit too quickly.

"Hey, are ya tryin' to imitate Butch?" Marvin jabbed his friend.

"Naw, I just wanna see what this baby can do," Bob replied—just as he noticed the state cop, Wayne Stalcup, following him out of the parking lot and down State Road 56. Bob made a quick turn at the road that went up to the dump, with Stalcup not far behind.

The Valley's winding roads and hills are not conducive to speed, but Bob didn't want to get a ticket, and he believed he could outrun the cop. Bob made it up to the dump turnoff. But he approached the very next corner at 60 miles an hour. He couldn't slow down enough—and the car went flying off the road, bouncing down a steep hill and toward a pond before going airborne. After flying some 50 feet, it came down hard and stopped just short of the pond.

Cows were scattering. Ducks were flying. And Bob's car was dying. The landing demolished the undercarriage and axles, blew out all four tires, and bent the entire frame. The radiator spewed steam.

Bob, who'd sustained so many wounds through the basketball season, of course hit the windshield with his head and had to get stitches. But by some miracle, Marvin held on tight, and hadn't been injured in the least. All Marvin could say was, "You gotta be shitting me! You just wrecked your car, you knucklehead!"

"Yeah, but I outran the cop, didn't I?" is all Bob could think of to say. But he was sick at what he had just done. He knew it would be a long while before he could save up enough money to replace his car.

Later that week, Bob was back at the Chatterbox. On foot. When he met Officer Stalcup's eyes, the cop motioned for Bob to come over to his table.

"Bob, I saw you boys gettin' out of your wrecked car down by that pond where you ended up the other day. I saw that you were okay, so I just thought I'd let you stew in your own juices after that dumb thing you did.

"I could've given you a lot more than just a ticket. You were running from me. You do know that is against the law, right?"

"Yes sir, Bob answered. The "Enforcer" braced himself to encounter some enforcement himself.

The cop looked Bob in the eye and said, "I was only going to give you a warning. You sure didn't have to take off like a bat out of Hades. Do one thing for me, please. Promise me you'll never do anything like that again, okay?"

"I promise sir. I promise," and he meant it. He did keep his promise and never sped away from a cop again.

And that was the end of it. Wayne Stalcup figured the boy had been punished enough already by demolishing his new car. Plus, Wayne was well acquainted with the team by now since he gave the

Hawks an escort to each away game. The last thing he wanted to do was spoil the momentum for the star forward during this historic season. An arrest and the inevitable bad publicity would surely change the "win 'em all" attitude that permeated the towns.

• CHAPTER 14 •
THE SECTIONAL

On the day of the sectional tournament, the team and coaches had started the day at Rex's Aunt Harriet's house for a late breakfast before boarding the bus to Huntingburg. (This woman was a godsend, Rex would always tell the world.) The team would play that evening in the first game of the 16-team tournament. Springs Valley had drawn the bye, so they would be playing only three games.

As the bus rumbled along, Frankie walked up to the front, where the coaches always sat.

"Coach, I'd like to talk to you."

"Okay, Frankie, what is it?" Wells was curious about what his little defensive demon had to say.

"Well, coach, I been a-thinkin'. We're gettin' ready to play against some teams with size—that have much taller fellas, who have three Indiana All Stars on their teams. I think it'd be a good idea to put Jackie in for me during these games, since he's four inches taller."

Coach Wells listened, thinking again about how selfless Frankie Self truly was. Frankie had started every game since the third game of the season, and always did an outstanding job as a defensive player. But Rex thought that he just might have a valid point—an indication of just how confident Coach Wells was in his substitute players.

Rex also realized just how mature and perceptive this 16-year-old boy was. He was truly a leader. Coach Wells thought about his suggestion for a few seconds and answered, "Okay, Frankie, that might be a good thing to try. I'll start Belcher in the next game, and put Butch at guard." Jackie Belcher was 6'1" and had stepped up in several of the games this season. The coach had to agree with Frankie; the Hawks could use some more height in these upcoming games. Frankie smiled as he returned to his seat.

"Hey Self, what were you talkin' to the coach about?" Marvin asked.

"Aw, I was just askin' him what hotel we were stayin' in when we get to Huntingburg."

Frankie would never let on about what he did for fear of appearing as if he were patting himself on the back. That wasn't Frankie's style in the least.

"Boys, we've gone the whole regular season undefeated and that's no small feat—for any team—in any sport at any level. It's not a common thing at all, I promise you. Do you realize that you are the only high school team in the state that has never lost a game—in the history of their school?"

Coach Wells was sharing these thoughts with his gifted team in the locker room before the first afternoon game of the Sectional at Huntingburg, about 30 miles away from French Lick in the southwest corner of Dubois County. Huntingburg was another small town, but bigger than Springs Valley. As was the case everywhere in small-town Indiana, high school basketball games were the highlight of each school year for most folks, and this fact was usually reflected in their "hoops arenas." Huntingburg's was the biggest gymnasium around and could accommodate the great crowds that showed up at tourney time.

This is where the teams of West Baden and French Lick had traveled to for years to play when March rolled around each year. Even the name of this town had always sounded intimidating to most boys from the Valley. Just walking into "Huntingburg's house," which was more than four times the size of the gym in French Lick, was daunting. This is the town that the teams from both Jasper and Huntingburg had owned in years past during the sectional and regional tournaments. But this would be the very first time for the consolidated Springs Valley team to play there.

Cat and Mouse

The Hawks were scheduled to play Dubois again in the first game of the tourney, and Bob was looking forward to his reunion with the Hill twins. Valley had beaten the Jeeps by eight points just two weeks ago, yet everyone was still expecting a very close and competitive game. This time, however, Coach Wells had decided they would not fill up on broasted chicken and mashed potatoes prior to the game. The fans of both teams all remembered well how many of them had met on the hardwood after the game in Dubois. There was no love lost between these two schools.

Mr. Ellis had to keep the Star Store grocery open on this Saturday even though most of the town was in Huntingburg for the game. He was quite proud of his stock boy, so he turned on WITZ, the Jasper radio station covering the games. He always enjoyed hearing the play-by-play announcer saying Frankie's name. But, being alone at the store without his helper, Mr. Ellis had gotten busy with a couple of deliveries and had not been able to catch the first three quarters of the game.

When he had finished unloading boxes of produce and restocking his bread shelves, he switched on his Philco radio, which still sat at the back of the store behind the meat counter. He heard the familiar announcer.

> *"If the Black Hawks pull this one out, they'll be the only undefeated team in Indiana. They're the only school that has never lost a game—this being their very first year as a school. I guess that's how you're supposed to put that—anyway, they've never been beaten. . . . And Valley has the ball. Pruett goes underneath to try to get a shot and he is fouled by Freddy Hill. That is foul number one on Hill."*

Then, as he finally sat down to listen to the last quarter of the game, Mr. Ellis realized something very unusual must be happening on the court. He was hearing screaming—girls screaming. But they weren't exactly like the screams he would hear from girls seeing Frank Sinatra or Elvis Presley.

"Gosh, I know Marvin Pruett is a good-looking boy, but I never thought girls at ball games would start screaming over a player," the grocery store owner pondered.

The announcer began an unusual play-by-play of the action going on at the Huntingburg gym.

> *"Hey, it's a mouse on the floor. There it goes . . . and Pruett stepped on it and the girls are screaming as he tossed it off to the side."*

The announcer couldn't contain himself any longer while describing what he was witnessing, and he burst out laughing.

> *"I cannot believe what I am seeing! Well, now there's some comic relief in the middle of a tight game. A mouse comes out on the floor—and it was really cuttin' across."*

The color commentator interjected, *"He missed it the first time."* The play-by-play announcer offered a recap.

> *"Marvin Pruett, the 6'1" guard for the Black Hawks— saw the mouse, he took a swipe at it, missed it, then he squished it good. Then he just picked it up by the tail and threw it off the floor. The girls screamed and everyone else laughed. But now, we're back to basketball as Pruett goes to the charity stripe."*

Marvin had picked up the mouse and disposed of it casually, tossing it aside just as he might lob a wad of paper in the trash. After tossing the varmint aside, he went to the foul line for his two shots.

Then, as was his habit, he licked his fingers before shooting his free throw. The crowd reacted with disgust, and the girls got one more shriek at the thought of Marvin Pruett licking mouse germs off his shooting hand.

The Hawks had added one more peculiar incident to their list of unusual events this season—things that had never occurred in any basketball team's history. One player, Jack Belcher, had been shot with the timer's gun during their first game of the season. They had been showered with sodas and popcorn after the game plagued by the 93 foul shots taken at Providence. Fistfights between fans had nearly broken out at two of their games. And now, Marvin Pruett had stomped on a mouse on the court in the middle of a game.

For some inexplicable reason, these types of things seemed almost commonplace by now for this unique team during this unique season. Of course, the sportswriters had a heyday with this. One wrote:

> *"Among those who failed to squeak through the sectional tourney at Huntingburg was a mouse that wandered out onto the floor yesterday afternoon during the Dubois-Springs Valley game. One of the players, Marvin Pruett, of the Valley team squashed 'Mickey's cousin' underfoot and is shown in the above photo wiping away the remains with his feet and towel."*

Another article, headlined *"Valley Good at Playing Cat & Mouse,"* said, *"Marvin Pruett, sharp shooting guard for Valley, averted a possible panic by the female fans in the 6,200-seat gym with some exterminating footwork."*

The Dubois Jeeps wanted revenge for the loss they'd incurred at the hands of the Hawks only two weeks prior. They proved again to be a very worthy opponent.

The first quarter had the Hawks behind by two points, but by halftime they had pulled ahead, 36-32. Although the Hawks maintained a five- to seven-point lead throughout the second half, the Jeeps came back in the final minutes.

With only 60 seconds to go in the contest, they had shaved Valley's lead down to only two points. With 50 seconds left in the game, Bob McCracken, the usual deadeye from the foul line, missed the front end of a 1-and-1.

The Jeeps then knotted the game at 59-59 when their star player, Freddy Hill, sank two free throws.

The excitement and tension in the packed gymnasium was palpable as the Black Hawks' season hung in the balance. Valley took the ball down the court slowly, setting up a last-second shot. Mike dribbled the ball down the court and passed it to Marvin. Bob, who knew Marvin quite well after having played for six years alongside the jump-shooting marvel, coasted back on offense. He knew that with only 20 seconds left, Marvin would hold the ball.

"No rush to get back for a play," was the Enforcer's thought. He knew Marvin would take the last-second shot, and it would probably be his well-known, much-appreciated, high-in-the-air jump shot—if he could get open.

In fact, every member of the Hawks team had become somewhat of a spectator, all watching what their star player would do. No one set a screen for Marvin. He couldn't seem to get around his man to get a decent shot off. Nineteen seconds, 18, 17, 16, 15—five precious seconds ticked off the clock as Marvin dribbled the ball, knowing he had to sink this one to take the game.

Everyone in the gym, including the players of both teams, *knew* that Marvin would take the jumper. But Marvin, going to the left side of the lane, turned his back on the man guarding him, switched dribbling hands, then reversed himself to come to the right side around the foul ring, where Paul set a pick for him. The player famous for his "last-second shot from outside" heroics surprised everyone: he drove down the lane unimpeded for a layup on the right side for his 23rd point of the night.

Valley was up two with 10 seconds left in the game.

On Dubois' last possession, they missed a rushed shot. Butch pulled down the rebound and threw the ball to the fast-breaking Paul, who was fouled with one second left on the clock.

It was over. He sank both free throws, giving the Black Hawks a victory in the first game in the sectional and their 19th win, 63-59. Springs Valley had lived to play another game—undefeated.

Spuds

In their second game of the sectional, the "matinee" game on Saturday afternoon, the Valley Boys would be playing the Spuds of Ireland, Indiana.

A team named after a vegetable. Why not name the team "the Fighting Irish" as Notre Dame had? Or perhaps "the Wild Irish Roses," "the Danny Boys," or "the Smilin' Irish Eyes"? Anything but a vegetable—especially one that evoked the history of the great Irish potato famine.

The Hawks had already taken the floor as the Spuds ran out onto the court. Mike Watson hollered at his teammates, "Hey, look you guys, that could've been our school colors!" as the Ireland cagers, in predictable green, entered the playing arena.

Looking back from this point in the season, it seemed like years ago that the four starters from West Baden had been diving and splashing at their favorite swimmin' hole just last August, discussing the odd name being proposed for their team. They almost felt sorry for the team they were getting ready to play. Almost. The Hawks felt that Spuds was not even a good name for a bowling team.

To the Springs Valley players, it seemed as if they had been Black Hawks forever, and the thought of being a team of any other name just seemed impossible. Their name fit the winning team so very well. The latest posters taped up in storefront windows in town depicted a hawk in the attack position, its legs and talons extended, descending and ready to pounce on its prey.

The players loved their team's image. The towns loved their team. The Hawks were a perfect fusion of player talent, coaching talent, school spirit, and enthusiastic backing from an entire community that seemed without equal.

Ireland played a strong first half and was down only six points at halftime. But as the third quarter began, the Hawks switched into that last gear they had that always seemed to put the game away. They put a defensive whammy on the Spuds, holding them to only two of 24 shooting in that period.

Butch was continuing the one-man tear he'd been on since the time of his dad's death, playing with passion and leading the team with seven of 13 field goals and four of five free throws for a total of 18 points, helping down the Spuds 67-48.

At this point, Coach Wells put in his second team and let Butch stay in the game to lead the way. Rex didn't like teams to run up the score, believing it was unsportsmanlike.

The Spuds didn't have too much fight in the second half. And yes, the sportswriters left no pun unturned in describing the Spuds loss. *"The Spuds were half-baked in yesterday's match-up."* And *"Spuds Roasted."* And lines like, *"See ya later, taters!"* and *"The boys from French Lick French Fried the Spuds."*

"Pride Cometh Before the Fall"

The Valley Boys were one win away from seizing the sectional championship. The night game would pit them against the much larger Huntingburg team—on the Happy Hunters' home court, no less. Springs Valley had not faced this team yet during the season because of the vast difference in the sizes of each school. Most Huntingburg fans thought that Springs Valley had simply been lucky throughout their season, and had not yet met a very strong team. The local sportswriters were giving the edge to Huntingburg.

A former Evansville basketball star who was covering the game for the Louisville *Courier Journal* wrote:

> *"I thought that Springs Valley's performance against Dubois was mediocre, and I didn't see much improvement in their second game against Ireland. I can't see them having any chance against the much bigger home team, Huntingburg Hunters, who've only lost two games this season, playing against much bigger schools than Valley."*

Butch Schmutzler came into the locker room where the team was putting on their uniforms for the night game. He was carrying a fresh afternoon copy of the *Courier Journal* in his hands.

"Look at this bull," he told his teammates, waving the sports page in the air. The writer had essentially written off the Hawks. It seemed obvious that this commentator had not done his homework.

> *"Sure, these young fellas have formed a pretty good team, winning games against other small teams, but they've not played the likes of these big boys here in Huntingburg. Their tallest player is only 6'1" and they should be no match for our Hunters."*

Frankie just smiled that grin of his.

"Let's just show this guy how we can play against his boys," he said. "Let's send them happy hunters home—unhappy, without a trophy."

Marvin, of course, could manage only one response. "You've gotta be shittin' me!"

Paul quietly reminded everyone suiting up for the game.

"'Pride comes before the fall,'" he quoted, "'and a haughty spirit before destruction.'"

Bob, once again, said quietly, "Let's just play some ball."

Butch wadded up the newspaper.

"Okay fellas, let's go out there and outshoot those Hunters!"

And they did just that. Thirty-two minutes could not have gone by any more slowly for the hometown team hosts. Valley took the lead early in the first quarter and held it. The Hawks played their kind of game—holding the ball, controlling the pace of the game, running deliberate plays, making the extra pass, and finding the open man for the best shot.

By the end of the third quarter they had a 30-point lead. It was an embarrassment to the hometown crowd. They just wanted this game to be over. The Hunters, meanwhile, didn't know what had hit them. On this night, they were certainly not happy hunters. They had waltzed onto their home court expecting a rout, but instead, they walked into a buzz saw—a well-oiled machine that, despite a height disadvantage, cut the "giant-sized" Hunters down to "midgets," as one article described it afterward.

During a 20-second timeout called by the Huntingburg coach, Bob said, "Fellas, I think we're givin' them fellers a good whippin'."

"Yeah, I think they forgot their ammo today," Marvin quipped.

"Boys, this game ain't over yet! Keep your head in this. I don't care how big your lead is, concentrate on playing ball—not seeing who can be the next Jerry Lewis," the coach, told them in his quiet, stern demeanor.

The boys in black and white put the Hunters away easily, winning by 25 points. As the Hawks cut down the nets, the Huntingburg fans were leaving the building in shock.

"Who are these guys?" one Hunters fan was heard saying. All of Huntingburg's fans were walking out, gazing downward and shaking their heads in disbelief as they slowly and sadly left the building. Meanwhile, the *Springs Valley Herald* photographer snapped the winning team, apparently a team of destiny, and captured a look that said, loud and clear, "We Are Winners!"

The smiles and expressions on their young faces said it all. A French Lick team had not won a sectional since 1946, though West Baden had come eight points shy of taking that title just last year with four of the five starting players from this newly formed team.

Perhaps that naysaying sportswriter might have looked up West Baden's championship-caliber team record from last season—15 and 7. Maybe he should've talked to some of the teams that Frankie, Bob, Marvin, and Paul had faced the season before. Or better yet, he could've interviewed those 25-year-old Jesuit priests these boys had honed their skills against every summer since their seventh-grade year!

The Hawks remained undefeated at 21 and 0—the streak intact. Next week they'd return to Huntingburg for the regionals. Most sportswriters were now putting everyone on notice. This team was one to be reckoned with.

Rex talked to his team in the locker room after the ceremonies.

"Boys, I heard you complaining about some sportswriter's column, where you thought you were slighted a bit. I understand how you feel. I like to get respect too, but let me tell you something. That's a good thing, when you are underestimated by your opponent. Do you think they came out to play you hard when they thought that you'd be a pushover? No! These kinds of players are never championship material. They think they can just show up and win. These are the teams that beat themselves by being overconfident and not preparing seriously for their opponent."

The coach went on. "That poor excuse of a sportswriter did you guys a big favor when he wrote that column. The whole town believed what he wrote, and you guys came in here and cleaned their clocks! I once heard a wise man say, don't ever believe your press, good or bad. That is darn good advice for anyone. When you start allowing the written word to affect you, you're in trouble."

"I know that negative column got you pretty fired up, but you need to have that fire all the time when playing another team," he counseled them. "It must be something that comes from within—not from an outside source. You have proven that you can stand toe to toe with the best teams—and I mean any team in the state. Right now, you are the only team that has gone unbeaten.

"Whaddya say we come back here next week and have a repeat performance?"

217

The entire team hooted and hollered with as much glee as 10 boys could muster. Tonight, they were celebrating, cutting down the nets, and rejoicing. But next week would be still another hurdle.

By now, most folks in Orange County were openly talking about getting to the state finals. After all, this team had a spotless record for the season and were now being ranked in the top 10 teams in Indiana. But for the moment, the team had only the next game in mind.

"Regional, regional, regional!" they shouted while walking out to the bus. The state cop who always accompanied them on their road games turned on his patrol car lights, escorting the boys back home.

The ride back to Springs Valley was filled with conversations about the game, the sportswriter who dismissed them, and next week's game with the bigger teams coming their way. The Hawks could not have been more fired up. The bus rolling back home was full of boys who could hardly contain their feelings. The winning streak and the euphoria were intact for one more week.

At the front of the bus, Coach Wells and Doc just sat back and listened to the sounds of a genuine joy ride.

• CHAPTER 15 •

REGIONAL, HERE WE COME

"Thelma!" Frankie nearly shouted into the phone. "We're in the top 10 teams in Indiana! We're ranked at #10, Vincennes is ranked #9, and Ft. Wayne South is #1! Can you believe this?"

Thelma didn't respond immediately, but when Frankie took a breath, she just said, "Oh, I bet you're better than number 10."

"Thelma, there are 736 high schools in the state, and our little old Springs Valley is #10! Can you believe it?" Frankie exclaimed.

"I'm so proud of you and our team, Frankie. I love this . . . what is happening with you and me and what is going on in our town . . . I mean towns," she said. "I remember you telling me about your mom and dad, when they were dating in high school, how they would break up after a French Lick/West Baden game. I just feel like I'm walking on air most of the time. I wish this would never end."

Thelma abruptly stopped talking as if she were far away, her daydream carrying her off.

"Maybe it never needs to stop," Frankie replied. He hung up the phone after they had said goodbye and "I love you" to each other. Frankie had alluded to the two of them having a future together, and he meant it. He wanted to marry this girl as soon as he graduated. But this was a bit further down the road.

If the citizens of two neighboring towns could be experiencing a surreal moment simultaneously, French Lick and West Baden surely were. They were all living a dream that would never be repeated in this community's history. Ideally, when a once-in-a-lifetime thing happens, people realize when they are living in that time. Every Springs Valley resident was soaking this up, knowing that this was it, and that the chances of this ever repeating itself were inexpressibly remote.

That is, every resident but the high school sports columnist. The Old Rebounder was already writing articles that included the word "dynasty" and such phrases as "the next few years." Frankie and Marvin were only juniors, and Paul and Jim Conrad only sophomores, so naturally those four would be returning next season. So why not assume another undefeated season was possible?

When Coach Wells was interviewed by the Old Rebounder, he was quoted saying once again, "Never count your chickens before they hatch."

Coach Wells never looked beyond the next game, much less the next season.

Rex's Wisdom

"We're strictly a second half ball club," the 25-year-old Hanover grad told Jeb Cadou Jr., the sports editor for the *Indianapolis Star.*

Just prior to the sectional games, Cadou wrote, "His Black Hawks had just won their 18th consecutive game to finish the season, beating Salem, to finish the season unbeaten and preserve Springs Valley's record of being the only high school in Indiana that has never lost a basketball game—quite the feat for such a young coach and a newly formed team by two schools consolidating."

The journalist asked how the coach kept his poise and didn't get frantic when his team was down by nine points in the third quarter. Wells said he had the boys call a time out and they quietly talked things over.

"I ask, 'What's wrong?' They immediately tell me, then I ask them, 'How do we correct the problem?' They share their ideas. The kids pool their knowledge and I just try to draw some general conclusion from what they tell me—and then, they go out and do it."

A typically humble response from Rex, giving the boys so much credit, but this was truly a team built on the familiarity of the players with one another and with their coach. After all, they had literally grown up together and Rex had coached them in their seventh and eighth grade years. He was only a few years older than his seniors.

"Some people expected the pressure of being undefeated would get to us," he told another reporter. "I don't believe the pressure has bothered us one iota." Requests for interviews were coming in from all the bigger newspapers across the state. Even telegrams were being delivered from well-wishing fans around the Hoosier state.

"Could this be another Milan?" a few columnists were asking. Could this truly be the making of the next "David vs. Goliath" meeting at the famed Butler Fieldhouse at Butler University in Indianapolis? This question was starting to appear in many sports pages, and, as could be expected, was the talk of the two towns being introduced to the rest of Indiana in the columns. The sportswriters had more to write about, pointing out the positive aspects of what a consolidation of two schools can do for a team.

Rex Wells, however, wasn't taking the bait. He would always answer the writer's question about getting to the State Finals and repeating the "Milan Miracle" the same way.

"We take our games one at a time, and our next game is against Dugger, then Vincennes if we're fortunate enough to win in Huntingburg. If we win the afternoon game, we'll go on to the next one . . . and think no further ahead."

The Gift that Keeps on Giving

The afternoon game of the regional at Huntingburg was rather anticlimactic. It was like one of their earlier regular season games or the Huntingburg "upset," where Valley led by 10 to 12 points all the way. The final score was Black Hawks 63, Dugger 54. But the night game was another story altogether.

That evening, back at the 6,200-seat hoops hall, Rex made his pre-game talk.

"Guys, we all know that Vincennes is ranked 9th in the top 10 in the state, just next to you guys at #10. I don't want you to dwell on their ranking or yours. You're a ranked team too, but forget about all the stuff that these sports writers decide. The number you are ranked doesn't make you shoot better, pass better, or rebound any better.

"The only thing that matters is how you go out and play each game. The only thing you need to think about is playing this game the way you have always played: with a great desire to win, by just doing what you've been taught—the fundamentals of this game. Hustle, but always be thinking ahead.

"I have great confidence in you boys because I know what kind of fellas you are," he went on, "and that has as much to do with winning as anything. Sure, it takes talent, and you boys have plenty of that, but there's a couple of other ingredients that only champions possess. Passion and heart.

"You always run back to the bench when I call a timeout. Don't think I haven't noticed this about you. This action alone says so much about you guys. Your eagerness to hear what I say to you signals your great desire to win a game. You've demonstrated that as well as any team could possibly do this year.

"We've had some close ones, yes, but you are still undefeated, and that is something very few teams have ever accomplished."

The coach went on with one more bit of advice and encouragement.

"You guys are the greatest winners to have ever come out of this part of Indiana. Don't forget that. Don't panic if they get a lead. You guys understand how to finish the game. You've shown me many times in the regular season."

Rex knew that his boys' inspiration simply came from the love of playing this game. It showed every time they walked out onto the court. He ended his pre-game talk.

"Just know how proud I am to be your coach. Now go out there and play your hearts out. And whatever the outcome, just know that I . . . well, you know how I feel about you guys. I have the greatest respect for you and you'll never know the joy you have brought to me."

The team loved their coach and they always appreciated his pre-game talk. Coach Wells had a calming effect on his team that always put them in the right mood to go out on the court and play with a sort of determined relaxed pace, yet they would out-hustle so many other taller players and bigger teams. Sometimes it's the bigger heart that has more to do with winning than physical size and strength, and the Valley Boys had a lot of heart.

Sixth man Jack Belcher, who had contributed much in the last couple of games, raised his hand.

"Yes, Jackie?"

Never one to be too serious, Jackie asked, "Coach, why does this team call themselves 'the Alices?'"

The coach paused, scratched his head, and rubbed his chin, then answered. "I don't know. I really don't know."

"Okay, thanks, Coach," Jackie replied. The boys all laughed. Some of the pregame tension was eased once again by the boys just being themselves— another reason, perhaps, that this team handled pressure so well. They simply didn't take this next big game more seriously than all their others.

The boys took the floor for their warm-ups. As Frankie dribbled toward the sideline, where Thelma was seated only a couple of rows up in the Booster Club section, he looked her way. She winked, and Frankie's heart was overwhelmed for a moment. He could hardly believe that his team was playing for the regional championship title, and that his sweetheart was there, watching the game. He was proud of his girlfriend, as she was proud of him.

"Hey Frankie, I think the pep band is going to play, 'All I Have to Do Is Dream,'" Marvin said, laughing as he dribbled by his teammate. Frankie realized sheepishly that he'd just been standing there with the basketball under his arm, staring at Thelma.

Marvin's quip snapped the guard out of his daydream. Frankie just smiled at Marvin and yelled, "Okay, I'm back now!"

"Let's get this game won," Bob chimed in. "Let's just do it!"

"Yeah, let's do it," echoed Mike Watson, standing beneath the basket, as he heard the conversation going on at the foul line.

The Valley Boys were just a little nervous, as their banter was revealing. Even with all their previous wins, and their typical nonchalant attitude, the Valley Boys did realize just how gigantic this game was—for them, for their hometowns, for Springs Valley.

No team from either French Lick or West Baden had ever made it this far in the tournament that rolled around every March. Most of the Valley residents had made the trip across State Road 56 and down 231 to Huntingburg to cheer on their team. These tournament games were anticipated more than Christmas with all its suspense at what opening the next present might bring. Right now, the Hawks had given their citizens 22 wins in a row, just about the best present a fan could hope for. For the last four months, the Hawks were the gift that kept on giving.

But the next four quarters would be the Hawks' greatest test to date.

The Alices of Vincennes

Tip-off time was 7:30. The game started a few minutes late, as so many fans had descended upon Huntingburg. All the local restaurants had filled with hungry guests from out of town between the afternoon and evening games, and the fans created a traffic jam on the one road going in and out of town. That meant fans were arriving to the Huntingburg gymnasium a few minutes late.

Some of the fans of the losing team from the afternoon game had sold their tickets, but most wanted to see the outcome of the Valley vs. Vincennes game. The gym again was standing room only. There were simply not enough tickets for all the people who just had to see this game tonight between the Black Hawks and the Alices of Vincennes.

The Alice name shows up in various places throughout Vincennes as part of an historical legend. In 1779, during the Revolutionary War, the French had retaken Fort Vincennes from the British. The story goes that the French soldiers rescued Alice, an Anglo-American girl who had been kidnapped by Indians. She was adopted by a prominent French family who brought her back to a life among English-speaking Protestants.

This story became a very popular novel, *Alice of Old Vincennes*, written in 1900, and became a well-known Broadway play in 1901–02. Taking advantage of a cultural phenomenon, the town became full of "Alice" references, including an Alice Park, an Alice Hotel, an Alice Soda Shop, and an Alice Movie Theater.

The name finally came to rest with the high school sports teams. Why not? It had been used for everything else, including the logo for a canned tomato company. Still, the Alices' name didn't sound very manly to the Hawks.

🌐 🌐 🌐

The local newspaper sports writer believed that Springs Valley had gone as far as it could go. The team was now competing with a team of a new caliber. It was thought by most that Vincennes would teach this team from the hills of Orange County a lesson or two about playing out of their league.

The teams got through their warm-ups and ran to the sidelines. The players could feel the high energy and exuberance of the fans. "David vs. Goliath," the sports columnist headline had read. The expression had been so overused since the Milan Indians Final Four upset back in 1954, but it was still a fitting description since Vincennes had boys much taller than the tallest Black Hawks player.

The columnist, apparently an Alices fan, wrote:

> *"The Hawks, who have left quite a wake by winning all of their games this year, will have a chance to show the entire state where they truly rank. Are they really in the top 10 teams, right next to the Alices? No more will the size of Springs Valley's opponents come into play in the assessment of the Hawks' ability.*

Vincennes is the best team they will have played this season, and everyone is hoping for this matchup in the night game."

The column seemed a bit condescending toward the Hawks. But Vincennes got its wish. Ten boys met at the jump circle at center court. This was going to be an electrifying game.

The Alices, their center a full five inches taller than Paul, got the tipoff, and their star guard came down the court and sank a 15-footer. The hometown crowd went crazy.

Valley took the ball out. Butch was still at the guard position when the coach put Jack Belcher in for Frankie because of the Alices' height advantage. Butch brought the ball up the court and passed to Marvin, who came around Paul's pick at the foul line. He was immediately double-teamed and tied up. His pass to Jackie was intercepted, and Vincennes' fast break gave them an easy layup for a 4-0 lead.

On the next Valley possession, Butch brought the ball down the court, and passed to Marvin, who fired it to Paul. He banked in an easy two points. Coach Wells shouted, "Press, press," and Valley put a full-court press on the Alices, but they passed out of it to an open man under the basket for another Vincennes score. It was 6-2.

Then Vincennes returned the favor and put on a full-court press that trapped Butch at mid-court. He called a smart timeout rather than lose the ball with a wild pass.

"Guys, you gotta relax out there and start playing your game," Rex counseled them. "You're letting them dictate the tempo so far. Stop thinking about how big this team is. Sure, they're bigger, they're strong, but you guys know how to play smarter!

"Now, get out there and start outsmarting them!"

The coach's instruction seemed to go unheeded on the next play. The Hawks inbounded the ball and Butch passed it to Marvin, who took it down court for his patented one-handed jump shot. The ball went in and out, spinning around the rim once and spurting out into a Vincennes player's hands.

Marvin, in his frustration, let go a "DAMN IT!" as he ran back down on defense. Butch looked up at the scoreboard the next time he had the ball. It was now 8-2. *Boy, this is a tough team, he thought to himself. Maybe those sportswriters were right. Maybe we have met our match . . . and then some.*

Butch swung a quick pass to Paul, who touch-passed it to Marvin, who hit his jumper. Swish. It hit only the bottom of the net! 8-4. The fouls then began to get called against Valley. The heavy whistle-blowing that followed made it seem the refs were not going to let even a touch get by them without calling a foul on the Hawks.

Coach called a time out. This time he didn't ask his usual calm question, "What's wrong and how do we fix it?" He simply said to the boys, "Everybody, just remain quiet for one minute," and the boys just huddled there together with their coach.

Only their breathing could be heard within the circle, with Coach Wells kneeling in the middle. No doubt the crowd thought Rex was giving his boys instructions on how to guard or rebound against these taller players, but only silence was needed to calm his players down. Not a word was spoken during the timeout.

It worked.

The Hawks came out of the silent huddle playing a stifling defense the Alices had never encountered. They held Vincennes to only one more point with two minutes left in the first quarter, and caught up, tying them, 9-9. But Vincennes was not going to roll over. They scored three more buckets to Valley's one to wrest a 15-11 lead at the quarter's end.

Valley was back to playing its game of calm, collected, but determined basketball. Marvin turned on the juice and hit five jump shots in a row to begin the second eight minutes of play. Marvin's mom could be heard as usual by everyone around her: "That's my boy!"

Marvin's shooting brought Rex up off the bench, cheering his boys on. Oh, how a coach loves to see those outside shots go down. As was usual, the rest of the starting five contributed as well, with Paul hitting a shot underneath and Bob making two of his free throws. At the halfway mark, the score was tied, 26-26. The Hawks were holding their own. The Vincennes fans and players were more than surprised.

No talk was needed in the locker room. The coach had said his piece prior to the game, and realized that quiet and calm was all his players needed during the break. By now, they knew how to win games, and tonight was just one more game. They had the great desire to win, and they knew what they had to do in the second half. The little mascot's dad, Harold "Hoober" Agan, brought oranges from his grocery store for the boys to eat at halftime. Only the sound of 10 boys downing some vitamin C could be heard.

When the game resumed, Coach Wells looked at Frankie and said, "Go back in for Jackie. We need your quick hands."

Frankie had not been starting since the beginning of the sectional games, when Jack Belcher was put in the games for his height under the boards. They had won those games, but this one was so very close, Rex determined he needed his "defensive player of the year" back in the game.

Jim Conrad, on the bench, whispered worriedly to Jerry Breedlove. "Man, now we're goin' *smaller*? We're already smaller than Vincennes!"

At the start of the third quarter, Vincennes began pulling ahead, earning a nine-point lead. The Hawks' fans were getting very tense; this was the largest lead the Alices had had in the contest. Now was the time for Valley to change the momentum.

Frankie was playing his usual great defense, tying up his man and making it difficult for the Vincennes guard to get any shots off. He got to the line for three free throws and made them. Paul hit three of his shots from his forward position—10-foot jump shots or hook shots from just beyond the lane line. Marvin sank one more jump shot in that period.

Still, they found themselves down by seven points at the beginning of the fourth quarter, and to the Hawks' fans' dismay, the scoreboard read 46-39. They hoped fervently that their Hawks would again find a way back in the late minutes of the game, as they had so many times before.

After six minutes of play in the fourth period, the Alices held an eight-point lead. But Coach Wells was not worried. He had confidence in his boys, because he had seen how they reacted to pressure again and again. And they had remained as cool and calm as their coach.

With only two minutes left in the game, Coach called timeout.

"Boys, this game isn't over yet." He noticed that Paul now had tears in his eyes, thinking that eight points with so little time left on the clock was insurmountable.

"Hey, it's only four baskets. Give me the ball," Marvin said confidently. "Just give me the ball."

During this game, in fact, he had been hitting most of his outside shots, from 15 to 20 feet out.

It was the Hawks' ball, and Marvin kicked into high gear. Frankie brought the ball down with Marvin trailing. Frankie penetrated, then passed the ball back to Marvin. He nailed his next five shots in a row, racking up a quick 10 points. One writer dubbed him "the long-range sniper." He was on fire, finding the range for his shot. By now his mom was losing her voice.

The Black Hawks' fans were now on their feet on every possession. Frankie tossed in another bucket and a couple of free throws. Bob McCracken threw in four more points. But Vincennes would always answer with their own scoring, and the score was tied with only 46 seconds remaining. It was the Hawks' possession, and Springs Valley held the ball for a final shot. They got it to Marvin.

In and out.

The final buzzer sounded on a tie game, 54-54. Overtime!

The tension, anxiety, and apprehension the Springs Valley fans endured going into extra minutes was excruciating.

Both teams played a slower game in the overtime period, holding the ball longer on each possession. Marvin hit another shot from beyond the arc, but the Alices came back with their own outside shooter, who drilled the basket. Valley failed to score the next time they held the ball, but the Alices didn't miss their next opportunity to score as Butch fouled out of the game, and they hit the ensuing free throw.

Jackie was back in the game for Butch. Valley didn't score again on its next turn with the ball. The Alices' star player, Larry Wright, was fouled during his shot on the next play, sending him to the free throw line again. He hit both to give Vincennes a three-point edge, 59-56, with only 34 ticks left on the clock! The Alices believed they had this one in the bag.

The Hawks were perilously close to having their season end at last. Their defeat looked imminent. But they could never be counted out until those last seconds were off the clock. This would be the "highlight reel" game of the year.

Frankie's Dream

The following day, one sports column read:

> *"The caliber the two teams showed in the overtime period was impressive. There was no scurrying around. It was a methodical business operation. The teams played somewhat cautious but determined. This game truly seemed as if the last team with possession of the ball would win. After nearly 5 minutes of cautious play, and low scoring, the Vincennes Alices were up on the Hawks, 59 – 56."*

The writer then continued, in apparent disbelief.

> *"From here on the* New Republican *newspaper cannot vouch for the accuracy of its report. Six points and a three-point victory for Orange County's first regional champions was almost too much for this paper's weak-hearted reporters. With less than 34 seconds left, the Blackhawks were down one point after Jack Belcher grabbed a rebound and put it back in. Vincennes was going to hold the ball till the final seconds when Frankie Self stole the ball from their*

*careless guard, streaked down the court alone and
laid in two points, putting the Blackhawks in the lead,
60-59."*

☻ ☻ ☻

As Alices guard Frank Landy had brought the ball toward their
basket, he made a pass to his fellow guard, Roger Benson. Roger
was planning on just holding the ball as he stood in the center circle,
letting the seconds tick off the clock. Frankie, reading the pass,
grabbed the ball from Roger the second it hit his hands. Frankie was
like a cobra striking. He grabbed the ball so fast that the astonished
Vincennes guard just stood there as Frankie raced toward the Hawks'
basket. The Alices' fans were even more astonished.

The radio announcer screamed, "Frankie Self intercepted the
pass!" but Frankie simply took the ball out of Benson's hands before
the Alices guard had complete control. He raced down court and laid
the ball in to give Valley a one-point edge. The Hawks had not had a
lead for the entire game until now.

The "little guard that could" had saved the game with 10 ticks
of the timer's clock remaining, but the Hawks had to defend to keep
Vincennes from going up on them by a point with one final basket.

It was bedlam in the gymnasium. The Alices brought the ball
down the court with 10 seconds remaining to take the shot to win the
game. In too much of a hurry, they got a shot off but missed it, and
the rebound came to Frankie, who was immediately fouled.

With only three seconds left, the 5'7" guard sank his two free
throws, putting the game on ice. The scoreboard read 62-59. The
Black Hawks had won another game that they weren't supposed to.
But in the minds of the Springs Valley fans and students, the outcome
was exactly as they had envisioned.

Regional champions.

Frankie hugged Thelma courtside as soon as he could get to her
while the Hawks' fans flooded the court.

"Your dream . . . your dream, Frankie. It just came true. It just came true!" Thelma shouted above the sounds of jubilation. Frankie's steal and two points, plus his two free throws, had won the game. He now knew what it felt like to hit the winning shot in a game.

Frankie, only now realizing this, just replied, "Yeah, yeah, it did. Wow! I guess it did!"

The cheerleaders for the Alices were lying on the floor crying, and the Vincennes fans were sitting in the bleachers, stunned at what they had just witnessed. How could this have happened? No one seemed to be able to comprehend what had just transpired before their eyes.

The next morning's sports column headline read: "Self's Winning Basket Quite a Thrill; Sends Blackhawks on to Evansville." The article included: "It took an All-American performance by substitute Frank Self to protect that victory string."

It couldn't have happened to a nicer guy.

The Hawks were going to the semi-state in Evansville. This simply was not to be, according to most prognosticators in the sports world—but it was happening. It was really happening. One sportswriter spoke for many when he wrote, "This may be another Milan Indians story that occurred as the greatest upset in Indiana State Finals basketball just four years ago."

The boys from the Valley were in the semi-finals. History was being made before everyone's eyes.

Triumphant at Home

The local barbershop brigade back in French Lick, having been rather negative back in September about the upcoming basketball season, were now singing a very different tune. Men who had derided the young coach and his choice of players were now proclaiming the virtues of the coach and pontificating about how the consolidation of the two schools was the greatest thing to happen since the two iconic hotels had been built at the turn of the century.

One old fella sprawled in a chair in the waiting area.

"I knew somethin' unusual was a-goin' on back last fall when I saw them kids carryin' them signs with that ol' hawk painted on 'em. I just had a hunch that we were enterin' into a new time.

"I reckon change is good," he added at the end of his barbershop speech, as if proclaiming his prophetic skills.

No one challenged the prophet, even though the barber, at least, distinctly recalled this same man complaining that his son didn't make the team last October. They were all simply too happy now to argue about anything.

Everywhere one went, folks were smiling and being more polite than usual. There was no other topic being spoken of. No one cared that Elvis was now in the Army or that Sputnik, the Russian spacecraft, had orbited the earth. World news didn't matter—only what was happening locally, where everyone was expecting things to get much bigger in these next two weeks.

The boys were heading to Evansville. They were playing in the semi-state finals! They were in the Sweet Sixteen for the very first time for any team from either French Lick or West Baden.

It was something the team hadn't even slightly considered back in September. This basketball squad was living a dream. Not one of the 10 players and two coaches ever wanted to wake up.

"Drea-ee-ee-ee-eam, dream, dream, dream . . ."

Sweet Sixteen

It was not a dream. The Hawks were in the Sweet Sixteen. They were one of only 16 remaining teams in the entire state, and the next two games would determine whether they would be one of the last four teams standing.

As the practices and scrimmages went on during the week preceding the games in Evansville, the boys seemed more and more relaxed. Of course, none of the boys nor their coach ever verbalized anything that would sound like they were overconfident. The boys didn't try to psychoanalyze or buy into any of the hoopla. They just knew they loved to play and tried their hardest to win games.

Winning was much more fun than losing, so why not win 'em all?

The Hawks realized they had done something no other high school team had ever done. Theirs was a brand-new school, and it had never had a team loss. Yet it somehow felt natural to them, as if they had planned it years before in the days of playing on those asphalt and concrete outdoor courts.

Everyone felt there was a specific destination they had begun throttling toward five months earlier at the start of the season. It was more than just earning one more win. A sense of purpose beyond the basketball court had attached itself to these hoopsters.

Not many people in life ever get to live their dream. Frankie, Marvin, Paul, Bob, Butch, Jack, Mike, Jim, Jerry, and George, along with Rex and Doc, were living a dream season. But dreamers all awake sometime. The only question is, "When?"

Redemption

"Keep those prayers going, Paul." Now, Marvin was encouraging his Bible-believing buddy to keep in touch with the omnipotent one.

"I've never stopped," Paul would answer. "And I also pray for you to come to Jesus."

Marvin would pretend he didn't hear this last part, but in his heart the sharpshooter was doing his own bit of praying. This extraordinary season was now giving Marvin reason to consider deeper things. "Why us, God? Why me?" he asked. "Are you there, Lord? If so, please help me and our team play its best. And, uh, sorry for all the cussin'."

Marvin admired Paul and his contentment in life. He ended his prayer with, "Help me be more like Paul . . . uh . . . amen, I guess."

Marvin now felt something inside he'd never felt before. And for the first time in his young life, he had just spoken aloud to the Creator of the universe.

"The Alpha and Omega. The Beginning and the End. The One who holds all things together," as Paul would always remind everyone around him. Marvin was connecting with the One who knows the outcome of all things. He felt that a great weight had been lifted off his shoulders, and he was experiencing a love and contentment he'd never realized before. For the first time, he felt like everything would be okay—no matter what happens on the basketball court. The pressure he had always felt to perform at his peak of 20 or more points per game seemed to disappear. He felt a calmness that matched Coach Wells's outward demeanor.

Marvin wondered to himself, "Is this the 'peace that passes all understanding' that I've heard Paul go on and on about?"

It *was* that "peace," as Marvin would later conclude. He no longer felt the weight that his performance on the court was the only way to measure his worth. He felt love. He was starting to understand Paul, and why he was always so calm and in a good mood. He knew he was part of a team. The outcome wasn't up to only him. He didn't have to make that last-second shot any longer to be Marvin Pruett.

That night while going to bed, he breathed a deep sigh as he fell asleep, resting better than he ever had—not dreaming of upcoming games, but of the past, of playing this game for fun with his buddies.

His last thought as he drifted off: "I love this game, but I love these friends of mine even more. I'm one lucky guy.

"Thank you, God."

• CHAPTER 16 •
MORE THAN A GAME

Full On to Semi-State

On the ride down to Evansville, the mood in the team bus was lighthearted. A bystander might think that these boys were just heading on a field trip to the Evansville Museum of Science and Art. It was as if the reality of what was happening had somehow not sunk in.

They were heading to Evansville, situated on a hairpin curve of the wide Ohio River in the far southwestern corner of Indiana, where the state line looks as if it were scribbled by a child. The Hawks would play two games for the opportunity to be in the Final Four. The venue was Roberts Municipal Stadium, the largest they had played in to date. Its capacity was 12,732—twice the size of the Huntingburg arena—and 10 times the size of their home court.

"Boy, this is going to be a far cry from the French Lick gym," Marvin said quietly to Bob.

Bob just looked at Marvin. *"Everything's* a far cry from our gym," he deadpanned.

By this point, their destination seemed inevitable. The Hawks had put away one team after another, all season long. And now, in the postseason games, they were dispatching the bigger schools' teams quite handily.

The regional win in Huntingburg had earned the respect and attention of every sports columnist in Indiana. And they were now using the term "Blackhawks basketball" to describe a style of play that was deliberate, controlled, and smart.

Ironically, even with the team in the bright spotlight all around the state, Coach Wells was still trying to get the writers to spell their team name correctly, as two words.

The coach usually read the sports pages at home, having been sure to have Margaret cut out and save everything being written about his boys, but today he read as the bus bounced its way to Evansville.

"Hey Doc, Bob Collins had something interesting to say about us in the *Indianapolis Star*," Rex Wells told his assistant coach. He read the first paragraph aloud from the capital city's morning paper.

"Springs Valley, the most delightful outsider to muscle into the big league since Milan went the distance in 1954, provided the hottest regional sparks last Saturday."

"Boy, there's been an awful lot of comparisons to Milan," Doc observed.

"Yeah, I know. The writers are also commenting on the connection with Marvin Wood."

Both Rex and Doc knew that Wood, the famed Milan coach, spent his first years of coaching in French Lick. This was in 1950–52, just before he went to Milan in the fall of '52.

"The idea of the smaller team knocking out the bigger team is very romantic. Even seductive." Rex was waxing philosophical. "It's what keeps this all-state tourney going, I think. If they ever change it, and break it up into divisions according to school size, it will lose its charm entirely, I believe."

Doc agreed. "These games just allow for the best teams to emerge—no matter where they come from or how small or large the school is. It's just what makes this tournament so interesting. Let's hope it never changes."

Some of the boys were keeping track of the daily newspaper's sports pages, too; everyone likes to read wonderful things written about them. Well, almost everyone.

Bob McCracken's family didn't take the newspaper. They lived so far off the main road that a paperboy would probably never find their house anyway. But that's not why Bob didn't read the articles; after all, there were plenty of newspapers floating around school each week. He simply did not care about what people said or wrote about him or about the team.

Sure, he loved a gym packed full of people cheering on his team, but he never paid attention to what was going on off the court—during the games or after. He was focused on one thing and one thing alone: stuffing the ball back in the basket after fighting for rebounds. He used all the muscle in his 5'11', 175-pound frame to block out the other players, just as he had done to Butch during those early scrimmages prior to the start of the season. Jerry Breedlove, the second string forward, always called Bob "Muscles" because of how he felt after guarding Bob in practice scrimmages.

Bob was the kind of guy who didn't take any crap from anyone, and he was the kind of player who always said that he didn't notice the crowd once the game started because he was concentrating so much on what he had to do. (Spotting Patsy Zeedyk, "the most beautiful girl in French Lick," in the crowd was apparently a dramatic exception.)

If he ever noticed a teammate slacking or not doing his job, Bob let him know it in no uncertain terms. And his team needed this kind of personality in a player who never stopped working his hardest to win for the team and never sought glory for himself.

Bob demonstrated his work ethic in every single game. The next two games illustrated this well. In the first regional game against Terre Haute Gerstmeyer, he was the high scorer, meaning that again, the team ignored the script that sportswriters put out every day in their columns.

Terre Haute was such a large school that not many of the writers gave Valley much of a chance. They all learned something after this first afternoon game of the semi-state.

"Valley Boys Slam Door Hard on Hall and Gerstmeyer," the headline read in the next day's column. The writer went on:

"Down at Evansville Saturday with the high society of Indiana high school basketball, Springs Valley's indomitable Blackhawks let it be known in the opening minute of their first appearance that they didn't come along just for the ride. They jumped out front of the Black Cats of Terre Haute Gerstmeyer, and there they stayed until the final gun blasted them into the finals against Princeton."

Another wrote, *"Springs Valley demonstrated a hard-driving, clever ball-handling attack that made the Black Cats stumble over themselves as if they were walking in a gunny sack."*

The same writer singled out the leading scorers, Bob and Marvin. *"McCracken gave the Cats fits with his driving, twisting antics under the boards and he came up with 26 points, with 7 field goals and 12 free throws. Guard Marvin Pruett proved himself an equally efficient workman and wound up with 22 markers."*

The Black Hawks handled the Black Cats with multiple weapons. Pick and roll plays that led to easy layups, Marvin's outside shot accuracy, an excellent team free throw percentage, and the continued ability to control the clock: it was a powerful combination.

They weren't a "run and gun" team with a fast pace, racing down court and taking the first shot. They settled in and ran their plays, making the sharp, quick, extra pass to the open man who usually ended up putting points on the board. The Hawks came to play, and from the starting tip-off, they made this very clear. They took the lead right off the bat and kept a 20-point margin throughout the entire game. The second team players were put in the game with a 21-point lead, and Valley easily won the afternoon game by 11 points, giving the starting five some deserved rest.

George Lagenour came in the game for Paul at center. He soon realized something he'd not known before this game. The sports reporters had been calling the Terre Haute Gerstmeyer center the best in the state. George concluded very quickly that the player he was guarding could not possibly be what the press was claiming.

George knew because he had to guard Paul in their daily practice scrimmages. The second-string center had to convey his discovery to Paul after the game.

"Hey Paul, that guy was much easier to guard than you are," George told him. "I can never control you at practice, but handling this guy was a breeze compared to you." It was a timely compliment for the Valley center, who had gotten into foul trouble early in the game.

The Hawks had been coached quite well by Wells, but there was more at work here. These boys with varying personalities came together to create a single team personality—"cool as cucumbers," as one writer put it.

After witnessing how the Hawks dismantled Gerstmeyer in the afternoon game, Frank Wilson, a leading columnist for the *Evansville News,* made this assessment. It was perhaps the best summary of how this team operated.

"They're not big. They're not fast," he wrote. "They're just good. To watch them is a mystifying pleasure. To see them win games gives one the feeling that there's a little hope left for all of us, particularly the little guy."

Everyone loves an underdog, but the way the Black Hawks were disposing of these teams, some were questioning if any team, big or not, could stop their momentum. By now, the boys from the little valley had become the popular favorite. There's something quite reassuring and inspiring to folks who see the little guy beating the bigger fella. The Valley Boys were making that happen, game after game.

By now, this team hadn't known a loss for 24 contests in a row. A team that wins continually expects to win. Perhaps this accounted for the Hawks' relaxed demeanor, which every fan seemed to notice. No swagger, just a quiet confidence. The boys were a reflection of their coach—displaying this gentle warrior approach to all their contests in the arena while keeping a cool head.

Jeff Agan, the eight-year old who wore the mascot outfit at every single game, was still in action at these tournament games. The team mascot was now a part of the "entire package," and had even become what some referred to as the team's "good luck charm." During the break after the first game against Gerstmeyer, the black hawk mascot outfit was hung in a closet near the locker room. When Jeff's family came back from grabbing a bite of supper before the second game against Princeton, they panicked. They found the top and bottom of the black hawk suit, but the head for the outfit was missing. Someone had swiped it.

At this point in the season, a coach doesn't like anything to change—even the presence of a little boy in a black hawk costume. Call it superstition, but when Rex heard of the missing "head," he announced, "That black hawk head must be returned immediately, or we aren't going out on that court!" He may have been bluffing, but this demand was heard by the right people, because the head to the black hawk outfit was returned within a few minutes.

They played their 25th game against Princeton in the evening contest the same way, as if they were in the most comfortable place they could be. They were playing before at least 11,254 crazed Black Hawks fans in the biggest arena they had ever played in. But the Valley Boys played their game as calmly as if they were back home in their own gym. They simply did as Bob McCracken always emphatically said: "Let's just play ball."

And play ball he did, leading the way in scoring in both games for a total of 49 points, with Marvin knocking in a total of 34 points for both games.

"Springs Valley Machine, But No Monster," the headline read in the Sunday Louisville *Courier Journal*. The writer began quoting one observer:

> *"A methodical machine that simply grinds up its opponents. The 22,508 fans that packed Roberts Memorial Stadium, and watched the smooth working, well coached team by Rex Wells chew up Terre Haute Gerstmeyer and Princeton, are ready to agree. However, it isn't a monster-type machine that would*

> *scare the kiddies. As a matter of fact, it is a thing of beauty created by coach Wells and five boys who don't know how it is to lose. The sell-out crowd at Evansville left shaking their heads in amazement at the satin smoothness two seniors, two juniors and two sophomores showed in the two games."*

The article went on to describe how the Hawks "dismantled" both teams in a "workman-like fashion." The writer also took note of the "heady play" shown by Frankie, coming in the game as a substitute.

> *"After Princeton had rallied from a 12-point deficit to tie the game near the end of the first half, the 5'7" jumping jack, whom Wells describes as the best jumper he has ever seen, hit a field goal and a free throw to push the Blackhawks ahead 25-22. That seemed to take the starch out of Princeton. The Tigers never threatened again and limped off the floor on the short end of a 71-54 score."*

Later, the nets were cut down and the team picture was taken. It displays the exhilaration and happiness beyond measure that the 10 players, team managers and coaches, and even the little Black Hawk mascot were overflowing with.

They had won the semi-state. The "team from nowhere" had done it. They were in the Final Four—a title that very few high school teams can lay claim to.

The black and white glossy photo of the players, coaches, and team managers right after the nets were cut down are indelibly printed on the minds of virtually every Valley citizen of the time. Nearly every family had purchased a copy of the photo of the team that was on the front page of the *Springs Valley Herald*. Young boys were adding this 9" x 11" glossy to their scrapbooks, forever enshrined in sequence among the many articles and sports page photos to help relive this fascinating season one day.

There is a great need in the human spirit to belong to something much bigger than ourselves, and Springs Valley's fans were no different from people everywhere. The need is apparently inexhaustible, and Little League parks, high school and college arenas, professional courts and fields of play, and countless other venues are filled year-round with athletic contests of all kinds. Many of the rabid fans are reliving their own days of glory, and attending these games becomes a sort of ritual for these stars and all athletes of yesteryear.

It seems there is a deep psychological need to feel the thrills and agonies of competitive sports. Like the coaches and players, we become emotionally involved and feel a part of something greater than ourselves. Sharing in the sadness of losing, and the elation of winning. Pulling for *our* team.

"Our team" was captured in this one photo that depicts nothing but pure unadulterated joy.

At the finish of the game, Margaret ran down to her husband and gave him the biggest kiss in public they'd ever had since their wedding day. She was so happy for her man. She just looked at him and said, "You have always been my coach of the year."

Those evenings early at the start of the season, when Rex was dealing with the unsolicited advice from disgruntled parents and the holdouts from yesteryear, were now all but forgotten. He and his team of small-town country boys had made it to the Final Four with their perfect season of 25 games won in a row.

What a ride they were on, with one more stop—Butler Fieldhouse, Indianapolis, Indiana.

• CHAPTER 17 •
THE BIG SHOW

'27 Straight in '58'

The headline read, "27 Straight in '58 Springs Valley Aim." So many Hoosiers were looking to Springs Valley to upset the #1-ranked Ft. Wayne South Archers. The Hawks were the underdog, but the boys and coach didn't mind a bit.

An article in the *Springs Valley Herald* included a quote from a local who summed up the feelings of the Valley residents.

> *"GO BLACK HAWKS GO. The large gold and black banner swayed with a pulsing motion between the entrance to the French Lick Sheraton Hotel and a filling station. One person said, 'It's about time we had something to talk about besides Pluto Water and a hotel.'"*

And talk about this they surely did. It's all anyone could talk about. Each day, the residents of Springs Valley were reading about their team and their towns in the *Indianapolis Star* and Louisville *Courier Journal*.

Their team was in the big show, and headlines like "Hawks Refuse to Lose" and "Springs Valley Set to Pull a Milan Upset in IHSAA's Biggest Show" were raising hopes everywhere. It had happened once, the thinking went, so it could happen again. Sportswriters across the state voted unanimously: the Black Hawks were the sentimental favorite in Hoosierland.

Of the 748 teams that began the state-wide tourney, only four teams were left: the Crawfordsville Athenians, the Muncie Bearcats, the Ft. Wayne South Archers, and the Springs Valley Black Hawks. Could Valley win two more games and make it 27 in a row?

The Black Hawks phenomenon had put French Lick and West Baden back on the map even more prominently than they had been during the heyday of the grand hotel resorts. No fancy buildings—even with one having been deemed a "Wonder of the World"—could compete.

Coach Wells was named Indiana High School Coach of the Year by the Indiana Sportswriters and Broadcasting Association. Articles were written about Rex, with photos of him and Margaret taken at the Sheraton Hotel on one of their days off, just seven months after they were married. Life was changing quickly for the young marrieds. They were eating dinner out more and more, and leaving those TV dinners in the freezer. There was even one photo of Margaret giving Rex that big kiss after the semi-state win that appeared in the Louisville *Courier Journal*. She was as lovely as any fashion model. Rex may have been coach of the year, but she and Rex were couple of the year in most folks' eyes.

This beautiful woman and this handsome man sure made a great-looking couple—as if they had walked out of the Sunday paper's *Parade* magazine. But it was noted by one reporter that the newlyweds might be mistaken for Springs Valley students since Rex was only 25 and his wife only 19.

With all the news coverage promoting the Black Hawks and their coach, the congratulatory telegrams were pouring in. At least 1,000 had been sent to Rex and the team from well-wishers from around the Hoosier state. Rex enjoyed several phone conversations with Marvin Wood, the coach of the famed Milan championship team of 1954. Coach Wood also sent a telegram to the team. It was full of encouragement; he realized that the Hawks were being compared to the other small-town team from Indiana that took the prize just four years earlier.

Coach Wood reminded Rex that the court in the Final Four is the same size as theirs at home and the basket is at the same height. However, it had been a few years since the Milan coach had coached the French Lick Red Devils in 1952. Rex didn't remind him that the French Lick court was actually 16 inches narrower and a foot shorter than regulation courts.

As one reporter noted, "Little Springs Valley, the consolidated school of two towns, has become the favorite of many Hoosiers whose team is no longer in the tournament." Bob Collins, the well-known columnist for the *Indianapolis Star*, had waited until the last week to jump on the Black Hawks train. He wrote, *"If all the people who wanted Springs Valley to win the tournament were asked to stand at once this morning and holler, the state would resound with a roar that would make the hydrogen bomb sound like a cap pistol."*

He ended his column thus: *"For what it's worth, they've finally convinced this unbeliever. Ruefully he now concedes he should have paid closer attention to the steady season-long barrage of mail from French Lick and West Baden."*

Monday was St. Patrick's Day, and a few of the men of Irish descent from the Our Lady of the Springs Catholic Church decided to paint the traffic stripe up and down Maple Street green. It seems that these men thought that St. Patrick needed to be recognized and thanked for the "luck" of the Irish that had been bestowed upon the twin villages this basketball season. One article continued to use the term "Greenhawks" when reporting on the "Irish" fun. For the boys, this recalled the earlier threat of naming the team "Grasshoppers" and using green as the team color. It was not a good reminder.

When Frankie and Marvin saw the green stripe, Marvin just said, "Are you . . . shi . . . uh . . . kidding me?" They walked back to the hotel laughing about what had just happened.

"I think I'll never like green for the rest of my life," Frankie insisted as they returned for another order of hamburgers, sodas, and fries. They sat on the large porch veranda that wraps around the front of the hotel entrance, rocking back and forth in the big wooden rockers. They ordered "room service" from the front porch.

"Man," Marvin sighed. "This is the life of Riley."

Frankie agreed wholeheartedly.

"If they only had a pool table," Marvin added.

Besides being St. Patrick's Day, the Monday after the semi-state win was a day off for the Valley's students and teachers. People were simply worn out after the emotional highs of the previous weekend and the subsequent celebrations. Just as Coach Wells and his wife were getting attention from the press, the boys were being treated as local celebrities as well. All the restaurants in town had signs in their windows reading, "Come on in, team. Everything is free."

The Sheraton Hotel, however, had pulled out all the stops, beginning by inviting the boys to a luncheon. At least one writer found humor in the situation.

"As the waiters were serving other guests *pâté de foie gras*, the kitchen was besieged with orders for hamburgers and french fries," an *Indianapolis News* reporter wrote.

The boys also were invited to take advantage of the many luxuries offered at the hotel. This was some high cotton these boys found themselves in, and they were loving every minute of it. All 10 players hung out at the hotel as much as they could that week, getting rubdowns, taking steam baths, swimming, bowling, and playing games of ping pong. Not to mention ordering lots of hamburgers and fries. The calmest people in town seemed to be the boys at the very center of the maelstrom, just having the time of their lives.

As reporter Bob Collins observed after having visited the Valley to watch them practice, "The boys were 'cucumber calm.'"

When Coach Wells was asked about his boys, he said, "They're not cocky. They're just confident. As far as being overly nervous, no, I think they believe that this is just a chance to play basketball one more week." And it was true. It seemed that the pure joy and love of the game trumped everything else going on around the Valley Boys.

The Ft. Wayne South team was to be more than a worthy opponent this coming Saturday. The smaller Springs Valley team would need to play the best game of their lives to out-shoot these very tall Archers from up north.

While the boys had been taking full advantage of the Sheraton's hospitality, Coach Wells and Doc were together most of that week, going over plays and strategies to combat the "treetop" front line of Ft. Wayne South. Rex was visibly tired. He would lean back in his chair, squint, and rub his eyes. He was emotionally and mentally exhausted. Who wouldn't be, after the whirlwind he and his team had just gone through?

One reporter after another was calling his office to set up interviews.

"Doc, this phone has now become an instrument of torture," Rex said wearily. After countless calls, Doc would answer the phone in a higher register and say, "Mr. Wells is not available at this moment. Can he get back with you?" About that time, there'd be a knock on their office door: another reporter with a photographer behind him, requesting his time.

"Where are the players right now?"

"Where are you practicing?"

"Are you worried about the size of Ft. Wayne South?"

"What is it like—having an undefeated season?"

The questions were all about the same, and Rex grew weary of answering the same ones over and over. Yet he was gracious to all who came to the Valley wanting information about this fledgling team that no one had ever heard of before.

Rex knew a phenomenon had occurred in the Valley, and he tried to accommodate every reporter and photographer's wishes. He would contact the boys and let them know that a certain newspaper wanted to get some "reality shots" of the boys doing things around town. Of course, Rex and the boys acquiesced.

Photos were taken of Marvin and Bob playing miniature golf at the hotel, where they had been spending their time when they weren't heading up to Orleans to practice in the Bulldogs' larger gym. Another photo showed Marvin, tongue sticking out playfully and pretending to break an arrow over his knee—depicting what the Hawks planned to do to the Ft. Wayne South Archers.

Another photographer and reporter took the coach, along with Marvin, Frankie, Bob, Butch, Paul, and Jackie behind the hotel in the courtyard garden, where the Pluto Water well sat ensconced in a marble-tiled, Greek-style gazebo that had stood since in 1901–02, the year both resort hotels in town had been built. The boys acted as if they were taking a drink of this sulphurous spring water, which, lest anyone thought poetry was dead, had recently been dubbed "hiney wine" in tribute to its laxative powers.

Just as it had for decades, a solid glass dipper hung in the gazebo so that anyone could walk up and take a sip. Marvin recalled Jackie's adventures in flatulence in the previous year's French Lick-West Baden game and quipped, "Man, after what I heard about what was coming out of Belcher last year during that game, I don't want to even get near this stuff!"

The photographer laughed and said, "I was wondering what your team's real secret weapon was!"

One photo session with Rex and Margaret had the handsome couple driving a golf cart on the Sheraton grounds. Another photographer even visited the family farm of Jim Conrad, where four of the boys—Jim, Jerry Breedlove, George Lagenour, and Mike Watson—all climbed on the Conrads' tractor. The caption read: "The Springs Valley Boys are no strangers to a tractor. The team consists of both town and farm boys."

The press couldn't get enough of this team that had seemed to come from nowhere. But all these boys knew where they came from: small towns and farms. They were just good kids, reared and grounded in solid, hard-working families, the kind of young men who behaved well and always kept their composure. If they had any negative commentary on a situation, they'd just keep it to themselves. They didn't allow any of the celebrity thrust upon them to turn their heads one little bit.

That week, when the boys were summoned to the gym from their classes to take team pictures, every one of them had forgotten their uniform at home! There had been so many photos taken of them in their street clothes that week that they didn't realize it was an actual team picture in full uniform. Since half of the boys lived outside of town on farms, Rex hopped in his car, racing to every player's house to pick up their uniforms and warm-up jackets for the photos, which would appear in every paper in Indiana.

Coaches from other Southern Indiana teams were offering to help the Black Hawks however they could. Orleans had just built a new subterranean gymnasium, much like Huntingburg's. Their coach offered the use of this facility to Rex, knowing it would help the boys to prepare in a larger space. So the boys began practicing each afternoon in the larger gymnasium some 18 miles north. They would be in Butler Fieldhouse on Saturday—a building that seats 15,000 fans and is known as the "Cathedral of Indiana Basketball." With each advance to the next level of the tourney, it seemed, the arenas doubled in size. The Fieldhouse was the largest basketball arena in the world up until 1950, and those hallowed walls fairly reverberated with history.

Would the boys finally be intimidated? Saturday afternoon would tell.

With only 958 tickets distributed to the twin towns, there would be a lot of folks watching the game on TV, or listening to it on the radio, including Mr. Ellis at the Star Store. He wouldn't miss this game—even if it meant stocking shelves without Frankie there. There wouldn't be many shoppers today anyway.

All radios and TVs would be tuned in for this game. The anticipation was palpable. It was the only thing on the mind of every person in Orange County. Even those teams that Valley had beaten during the regular season would be cheering on their former rival. For now, they had joined forces with the team representing Southern Indiana. They truly wanted the Hawks to win this one—for every little school in the state.

Dream On

The headline read, "Springs Valley Is Sentimental Favorite in 48th IHSAA Shootout." So many Hoosiers were rooting for Valley to go all the way, and many, including sportswriters, believed they might just pull this off. Even one writer was obviously pulling for the boys when he wrote:

> *"They don't believe it's possible for a small school with the shortest team to win the Indiana high school basketball championship . . . for the first time since Milan in 1954. But you throw in a couple of quick baskets in tomorrow afternoon's opening game against skyscraping, top-rated, all powerful South Side's Archers and you'll quickly find out how thunder sounds inside Butler's 14,543-seat fieldhouse.*
>
> *"Keep throwin' them in and your record of 27 consecutive victories with a two-game sweep tomorrow, and you'll have every Hoosier, from the furthermost fieldhouse seat to the furthermost TV set in a positive frenzy of good fellowship. You have a psychological advantage in addition to your innocence. You've never been beaten since 'your parents,' French Lick and West Baden, kissed and made up and decided to consolidate into one high school last year."*

Referring to the Ft. Wayne South team, he left the Valley Boys with one last thought: *"They can't legally play more than five boys at a time, just as you."*

This sportswriter was rooting for the Hawks, but he may have gotten one thing wrong. These boys were not innocent, in the sense of not knowing what a loss felt like. They had played this game just as long as any other player who would be on that court on Saturday. They had known the feeling of loss—just not during this season.

They simply weren't ones to overanalyze things or worry too much about losing.

The problem was that three out of Ft. Wayne South's five starters were six inches to a foot taller than any of the Hawks, and in the game of basketball, height does make a difference. And the great challenge in their 26th game would be figuring out how to handle a big ol' country boy named Mike McCoy. He stood 7' tall—the tallest player, in fact, ever to have played in the IHSAA tournament.

The Hawks' tallest man, meanwhile, was 6'1". McCoy had 11 inches on Paul and more than a foot on Bob McCracken. In addition to the 7' player, two other boys on the front line were 6'5" and 6'4". As strong as Bob was, trying to block out this high school giant to gain position and taking on these other "bigs" would be the challenge of his life.

Higher Cotton

Thursday, the team traveled to Indianapolis and checked into the Sheraton Lincoln downtown. They all ordered room service for their dinners. The high cotton just kept getting taller and taller.

It was hard for the boys not to feel a little nervous when they showed up Friday morning for their introduction and shoot-around at Butler Fieldhouse. Rex recalled what the Milan coach, Marvin Wood, had shared with him, so he, too, took the tape measure and showed the boys that the goal rim was still 10 feet off the floor and the free throw line was still 15 feet away from the basket, just like at home. It was just located in a much, much larger space.

"Let's just pretend we're playing outside," Butch suggested.

"Yeah, this is about as big as all outdoors. That's a good idea, Schmutzler," Marvin shot back.

As much as they tried to be nonchalant, this was just an awfully big step to take from that little gym in their hometown. Even having played so recently at Roberts Municipal Stadium in Evansville could not entirely prepare them for this. Butler's Fieldhouse was more than 15 times the size of their home gym, a fact that can rattle even the best player. They would be playing in the biggest basketball showcase in the world, against a team with the tallest high school center in the world!

During their two-hour shoot-around Friday before the big game, Rex went out to the court and made five shots in a row. He wanted the boys to know he was close by. Rex was nervous in this gigantic place, just as his boys were. Some of the press thought he was just another member of the team, with his crew cut and youthful appearance.

Rex saw that the bleachers closest to the floor were beginning to fill up with people. Lots of people! There were about 200 folks sitting on one side of the arena.

"Hey, these folks need to leave the building while we're practicing," Rex told one of the security people standing nearby. The coach worried that someone from the other team might be taking notes. The security guard just laughed.

"I've been to the last 10 Final Four games here, he informed Rex. "They always let the public in to watch the teams practice. It's part of the mystique of this place. Folks are interested in seeing these teams up close."

It turned out that one of those spectators was Bobby Plump, the Milan hero who had hit the game-winning shot in this same fieldhouse back in 1954. Jeb Cadou Jr., the *Indianapolis Star* columnist, noticed and talked to Plump after practice.

"Among the more favorably impressed of some 200 spectators was a neatly dressed, young six-footer, sporting a crew cut. He came to Butler via Pierceville and Milan and his name is Robert Plump. 'Man, they can hit that basket,' said Plump after watching the Black Hawks swish the net for a half hour or so."

Plump was not seeing things. The Valley Boys were knocking down all their shots. The Milan hero was impressed. The boys did notice one thing about the size of the building's effect on their shooting. The vast space and high ceiling seemed to make that goal appear closer than in a small gym. The vast space played tricks with depth perception—for all ball players.

"It seems like I don't have to arch my shot so much," Marvin observed to Frankie. Sophomore Jim Conrad noticed that the forwards better use the backboard as much as possible.

"Hey Bob, this building can play tricks on you. Better concentrate on that glass more. Plus, you know how tall those Ft. Wayne guys are." But Bob, who had been the second-highest scorer all year, didn't think he would need to change a thing; he thought he'd just play ball as he always had.

After the boys had some time to shoot around, Rex called a short scrimmage—the starters against the second team.

Not long into the practice game, Mike Watson, as usual, was guarding Marvin.

"Hey, I bet I'll keep you from scoring," the 5'7" guard always told his buddy. Mike always got the task of guarding the all-star player, and he knew that Marvin would go up for a jump shot by hiking his knee up first.

"I'm going to block his shot," Mike thought. He waited for it. Marvin hiked his knee to go up for his shot, but Mike hesitated, not wanting to jump too early. As Marvin's knee came down, Mike jumped as high as he could, attempting to change the ball's trajectory. But when Mike came down, he landed on Marvin's foot.

This is how most sprained ankles occur in basketball, and Mike was no exception. But he played through the pain during the rest of the scrimmage. The boys went to see a movie that night, and Mike was even able to go. In the morning, however, his foot was swollen to the size of a grapefruit. He would not be able to play in the first game of the Final Four that afternoon.

"Come on coach, tape me up," Mike pleaded. "I can play, I'm sure."

But Doc and Coach Wells agreed that the sprain was just too bad for him to be running—especially in a Final Four match-up game. George Harrison, the 11th player, was called up from the junior varsity team to suit up for Mike.

The folks listening to the game back home, however, never knew; George Harrison had to wear Mike's #35 jersey, and the announcers apparently didn't get the message.

Another Milan on the Horizon

Coach Wells realized the mighty steep mountain his team would have to climb in this next game. The Hawks' coach had seen his team overcome great odds in the past. In fact, Rex truly believed his boys would be the next state champs. Rex never let on to his team that this game would be different from any they'd ever played—because he didn't believe it would be—no matter the height disadvantage. However, size-wise, the reality was that it was almost like asking a junior high school team to play a college team. Still, the boys, who had not tasted defeat this season, remained confident.

With their style of play, they had proven time and again that they could outsmart the other team, using their well-honed skills in playing true team basketball. It had worked for them all season. Why wouldn't it work again? The team managers continued telling them, as they had long ago at the Shawswick game, "The bigger they are, the harder they fall!"

When the boys got back to their hotel on Friday afternoon, Marvin grabbed a newspaper in the hotel lobby.

"Ooo-whee, those boys are big 'uns!" he remarked, seeing a photo of the 7' center, Mike McCoy, and the two 6'5" forwards.

"Man, those guys are trees!" Bob chimed in, looking over Marvin's shoulder for a glimpse of what lay ahead.

"But remember those games against those Jesuits?" Bob asked. "They were at least this much taller than us—and stronger. We beat them good, didn't we?"

Bob was probably the scrappiest player in Southern Indiana—perhaps in all the Hoosier state. Bob's vertical jump, according to one photo taken during a game with his elbow above the rim, clearly shows it to be three feet. One sportswriter noted that Bob could jump as high as a 6'8" player.

But he had not come up against any player this tall before. And dealing with one giant was one thing, but going against the giant's two "little brothers" as well? Game time would tell, but the boys felt a definite sense of apprehension upon seeing the three front-line players the Hawks would be facing. Still, as the only undefeated team in the state, the Black Hawks never let on that they were even a little bit nervous in facing these Goliaths from Ft. Wayne.

The team was restless just sitting around their hotel in downtown Indianapolis the night before the game, which is why Doc had suggested that they all go see a movie. He thought it might help the boys relax and get their minds off the following afternoon's challenge. Rex agreed. They walked down Meridian Street to the Circle Theater on the city's famous Monument Circle to see *South Pacific*. It was no *Blob* or *Seven Voyages of Sinbad*, but the boys enjoyed getting out of their rooms for the night.

Game Day

Saturday, March 22, came, and the boys were given a big breakfast of bacon and eggs, muffins, and biscuits with sausage and gravy in a private banquet room at the hotel. *Indianapolis Star* reporters and newspapers from around the state were coming out of the woodwork, trying to get their scoop on this team.

"Should Springs Valley win, it will become the first champion in the history of the tournament that has received more national attention than any state high school event in the history of sport to have never lost a game."

Marvin was reading W.F. Fox Jr's. sports column, "Shootin' 'Em" in the *Indianapolis Star* on the morning of the championship game. "Wow! So, there are sportswriters across the country who are writing about us?" he asked.

"I reckon so," Frankie said. "It sure is a strange feeling to have so many folks talking about our team. I guess winnin' 25 games in a row is kinda unusual."

If the boys hadn't started realizing this was a mighty big deal by now, they never would.

It was a *huge* deal. Every sportswriter by now had done the inevitable comparison with the 1954 Milan team. There was no way to miss the parallels. Even Milan's Bobby Plump, the player who hit the winning shot at the buzzer, said in an interview that he could easily see the similarities.

At last, after all the goings-on back home, the countless interviews, the endless photos, the luxuries offered at the French Lick Sheraton hotel, and now, the overnight stay in the exquisite Sheraton Lincoln Hotel in downtown Indianapolis, game day had finally arrived. They all boarded the team bus. Indianapolis's finest turned on their patrol cars' sirens and led the big yellow Blue Bird bus to the Butler University campus.

But the bus was oddly quiet. There wasn't the usual joking and chatter going on today. The boys rode to the campus in a pensive mood.

Marvin Wood, the Milan coach, had called Rex several times in the past few weeks. Coach Wood was truly able to empathize with what Rex was experiencing—finding himself in the middle of a storm of media coverage. He kept telling Rex, "Just hang in there and try to enjoy this. You know I'm rooting for you guys!"

Just prior to the game, Rex received one more telegram from Coach Wood.

"Coach Wells, please know that we are all with you," it read. *"Never forget that 'Davids' can slay 'Goliaths.' I know this well. I know you can do it! I so hope you win this one! Good luck to all of you!"*

Just as Rex was now, Marvin Wood was 25 years old when he first took Milan to the state finals in 1953 and was beaten by a bigger team, South Bend Central, in the afternoon game. But, the next year, he had led Milan to the state championship.

Doc looked at Rex as the coach was reading the telegram from the Milan coach, and said, "Whatever he wrote to you, believe it. We can win this thing. Our boys are smart, and they know how to play team ball."

Rex just smiled and nodded. He was in very deep thought. After a long pause, Rex answered. "Well, one thing I know for sure. You and I will have the best seats in the house!"

The whole experience still seemed somewhat surreal to the boys, some of whom had never been further from home than Bloomington prior to the season. A couple of the farm boys didn't even have electricity in their homes. They had entered a world they were not accustomed to.

They were escorted to their locker room underneath the ball court to dress for their shoot-around. There were hallways and corridors lined with the huge slabs of limestone that had been used for the building's foundation.

"Man, this is like a cave," Rex noted to Doc as they wended their way to their locker room. Rex went in to talk to his boys and read them a few of the telegrams he'd received. As he began to read, he and the boys heard a lot of commotion just on the other side of their row of lockers. The Ft. Wayne South team had entered to change for the game.

"What?" Rex commented to Doc. "You mean we have to share locker room space with our opponents?" Neither coach could believe it; it was a great surprise and an uncomfortable experience. What coach wants to whisper to his players? Privacy, they felt, should be the order of the day for a game of this magnitude.

As the boys were changing, George Harrison came in with some unusual news.

"You're not going to believe what I just saw," George said. "I wasn't tryin' but I just witnessed that seven-foot Mike McCoy takin' a leak. He was on his knees over the urinal!"

"You're shitting," Marvin said.

"Nope, I was just standin' there. The boys and the coaches laughed. I tell ya, McCoy was peein' on his knees!" George repeated.

"Maybe he just didn't want to splash," Marvin quipped. There was another burst of laughter from the boys, but it subsided to a nervous chuckle when they remembered their opponents were just on the other side of the wall of lockers.

As humorous as it had been to hear this, the boys couldn't help feeling intimidated.

At times they could see Mike McCoy's head sticking up over the top of the row of lockers. Paul, with all his biblical knowledge, spoke in a hushed voice.

"This is like the Israel spies who reported back to Moses just how big those giants were in Canaan . . . when they said that the Israelites were like grasshoppers in comparison."

"Well, we're *not* grasshoppers!" Frankie, practically shouting, exclaimed to the boys. "We took care of that back in September. We're here because we are supposed to be. We was the best team in Southern Indiana! We've won 25 games in a row.

"It don't matter how much bigger Jasper, Huntingburg, Vincennes, or any of the other schools were that we played during the season. We won those games, and we'll win this one!"

Rex heard all this talk and smiled to himself, but he didn't comment. Instead he read Coach Wood's telegram quietly to his players. Sharing the encouragement from fans had become a pre-game tradition last year, when Rex's West Baden team nearly won their sectional.

"I've always thought reading a few of the telegrams gave the team great inspiration," Rex explained in one newspaper article. "When reading through the fans' hopes for us to win, it was very uplifting and motivating. We knew the fans were with us all the way."

But this year, Rex had received nearly 1,000 telegrams.

The boys put on their white home-team uniforms and their newly acquired warm-up suits with the "SV" emblazoned over their hearts. There had been photos taken of them in these uniforms earlier in the week. They looked great. They looked confident. But most of all, they looked happy and ready to play. There was just a little time now before they would head out onto the floor.

Rex addressed his boys one more time.

"Fellas, what can I say at this point? This has been the most inspiring and exciting thing, outside my marriage, that I've ever been a part of. This season has been indescribable. It feels like we've known each other our entire lives. I feel as if we're a family. I know that whatever the outcome of this game is, we will always know each other and recall, with the greatest fondness, our undefeated season. Man, what a season we've had. So many memories made."

He paused, then continued.

"So, go out there and do what you've been doing all year. Play your game. These guys will be more than a handful, but I believe you can overcome their strengths with your smarts! Let's do this. Let's show all of Indiana what you guys are made of. There's a lot of folks rooting for you, supporting you, and wanting you guys to do well today. So, go out there and show 'em what you're made of."

The boys huddled together as Paul led them in a quick prayer.

"Dear Lord, we give you our thanks for this wonderful season. Thank you for being with us from day one and seeing us through such an amazing year.

"Thank you for our coach. Bless him Lord, and bless this team— every member, today, tomorrow, and for the rest of our lives. We give you all the praise and thanks in Jesus' name. Amen."

Marvin hollered "AMEN" as loud as any "Let's Go" after a team huddle. He was ready to play. They all were.

At last, the time had arrived for the big show.

• CHAPTER 18 •

GAME NUMBER 26

"Good Lord Almighty," Bob gasped as he saw Mike McCoy on the other side of the court. "Now I know why he had to kneel down to pee! I'm supposed to keep that guy from getting the ball?"

"You can do it, Bob—don't forget, you're the Enforcer," Butch reminded his fellow forward.

Marvin observed, in his casual and confident way, "Hey, they can't block a jump shot from 20 feet out." Marvin's confidence was contagious, but only slightly. Yes, they could overcome the height advantage. Still, they couldn't help but be a wee bit apprehensive as they looked at their opponents.

It was 1 p.m. Tip-off time. The game was on.

The noise from the crowd of 15,000 was the loudest thing any of the Hawks had ever heard. It was as if they were in a dream. But the cacophony became a kind of white noise, allowing them total concentration and shutting everything else out. It was as if nothing existed but the team, the opposing players, and that ball and basket.

It seemed as if the electricity generated by the fans crammed into Butler Fieldhouse could've powered an entire city. Indiana's state tournament was justifiably famous, and the boys from the little valley were on the biggest stage for high school basketball in the nation. There was some stage fright. They couldn't help it.

Paul was jumping against the tallest high school basketball player in America. But Butch grabbed the tip-off when it glanced off one of the Archers' hands. This was a very good sign.

Mr. Ellis and the other French Lick and West Baden residents who hadn't been able to get tickets to the game listened to their Philco and RCA radios, hearts beating faster and faster as the play-by-play announcer became their eyes.

> *"Schmutzler got the rebound and it's Springs Valley's ball. Number 33, Schumtzler, is in the game playing at the guard position. Schmutzler dribbles across the time line and gets the ball to number 53, Jackie Belcher. Belcher shoots. No good. Radcliff grabs the rebound and shovels it back to Schmutzler, setting up a play. Schmutzler finds the open Marvin Pruett. Pruett takes the ball around the right side, and takes his familiar jump shot. The ball is short, but Pruett got his own rebound and he put up another shot from the foul line. GOOD! The Hawks are the first to put points on the board in this much-anticipated game."*

The color commentator interjected, *"If this is any indication of how this game is going to go, this'll be one for the books!"*

The play-by-play man resumed.

> *"The Archers take the ball out and dribble down court as Valley goes to their man-to-man defense. Oh, my! McCoy just took the pass from Dan Howe, high above every player's head, and he just laid the ball in—not even leaving his feet! Boy, I tell ya, this kid is a giant! The ball game's even, 2-2. I hope the smaller Valley Boys can keep up with that kind of play. They are truly playing among trees!"*

On the second Hawks possession, Jack Belcher sank a free throw, and Valley took the lead, 3-2. That's when the Archers took over and used their "bigs" in the paint to surge on the Hawks, hitting their next three shots from under the basket. On the last Valley possession of the first quarter, Bob took the ball in amongst "the trees" and, with his uncanny ability to make a space for himself, put up the ball, using his body to block out the taller players. The ball rolled in and ended the first period, with the score 12-7.

It's a tribute to the Hawks that their fast and tight defense had kept the score this close. The boys raced to their bench to get instructions from their coach with the two-minute break between quarters.

"Boys, you're doing fine. You're doing fine out there," Coach assured them. "Don't let that front line have their way with you. Get the ball out to Marvin on the perimeter, or Bob or Paul in the corner. Start taking more outside shots. You guys in the paint are having to arch your shots too high to get over them, so keep making that extra pass to the open man for a jumper, and penetrate to the hoop only when you see a decent opening.

"It's going to be a battle under the boards, Bob."

"Boy, you said it, coach!"

The second quarter started with Paul taking the coach's advice, hitting a long one from the right corner to shave the Archers' lead to only three points. The next few possessions for Ft. Wayne South had their center and forwards tipping in rebounded shots, their long arms extending high above Paul and Bob, who were fighting as hard as they possibly could to get position.

Even with blocking out, the Archers' front line could reach over the top without even touching either of the Hawks' forwards. There wasn't one "over the back" call in the first half. The second session went on like this, with Marvin hitting two 15 footers, Butch sinking a 12-footer from the foul line, and Bob sinking a free throw.

At halftime, it was 28-16.

The boys sat down in the Butler Bulldogs locker room, which they shared with the Archers. They knew they had a fight ahead of them, but there was no such thing as "quit" in these guys. Rex didn't say much except to remind them of who they were and what they had already accomplished together as a team.

The Coach didn't want to say anything that their opponents could hear that may sound like the Hawks were worried about imminent defeat. He thought that silence was the appropriate thing. He and the team just sat still for 10 minutes. He knew what they were up against, but he had seen his team come back in so very many games this season. If any team could come back against this oversized Archer team, the Black Hawks could.

"Just keep moving the ball, Butch . . . uh, I mean, Frankie. Jack, you come out, and Butch, you go back to playing forward. We can beat these guys with speed and a lot of hustle 'cause it can't happen under the boards.

"Just keep that ball moving," he went on, "find the open shooter, and use that clock to your advantage, but ya gotta make some stops so you can whittle down their lead. The longer you can keep that ball out of those guys' hands, the better.

"Now, let's go do what we've done so many times before. Hey, and whatever happens in the next half, you know I love you all. You don't know what you mean to me."

Rex knew that he'd gotten a little mushy, especially for high school athletes, but these boys already knew that he loved them, and they loved him.

As Frankie headed onto the court to play in this contest for the first time, he shouted to his teammates.

"Come on, let's get this thing back and show the coach what we can do!"

They all knew that they had to play flawless basketball for the next 16 minutes. Frankie looked over to the Valley Booster section, trying to see Thelma. There were too many people and they were too far away for him to see his gal. But he knew she was smiling, clapping, and jumping up and down with excitement. Her boyfriend was going into the game.

The coach put Frankie in to try to outplay the Archers' guards with his speed, and he did. Frankie put it into high gear, smothering his man on defense, tying up both guards as he switched off with Marvin and continued to keep both Archers playmakers confused.

"Frankie Self managed to be everywhere at once!" one writer observed after the game.

Then Frankie turned to scoring. On the next Hawks possession, Frankie drove to the free throw line, stopped abruptly, and shot a one-handed jumper that went in. He kept giving the Archers' guards fits, knocking the ball out of their hands and getting it back to the Valley side of the court, where he took the ball in for a lay-up.

The announcer was impressed.

"I don't know how that little fella is doing this," he said. *"Maybe they can't see him due to his speed and size! He seems like he's just outmaneuvering them all by himself. This kid ain't goin' down without a fight!"*

The announcer was so right. The regular season had been won, along with seven tournament games, and Frankie was focused on the fact that all the Hawks needed were two more wins.

"If we can just get this thing back close enough," he kept thinking. He believed they would, and he'd decided he was going to be the one to get things started.

On the next Hawks possession, Marvin batted a high pass over the head of the player guarding him, spun around him, and went in for an uncontested lay-in. Frankie hit two more outside jump shots from the side. He was three for three.

"Dang, I should've started Frankie in this game!" Rex told Doc. Frankie was playing his heart out as he always had—the little guy on the little team that could!

Butch found the bottom of the basket and Bob rattled in a free throw. Butch stole the ball and drove the length of the court for a lay-in. The third period went with both teams just trading points—literally. Each team scored 14 points in the third. But the Hawks needed to stop their opponent's onslaught and start outscoring their rivals to erase the Archers' 12-point lead going into the last quarter.

The Hawks came out in the fourth period as determined as ever. They knew they could come back as they always had in the past. One sportswriter put it this way.

"The Black Hawks opened the last quarter with such steam that

the entire fieldhouse perked up. Could they overcome a 12-point deficit against such a team as Ft. Wayne South? Something about their drive made the Valley fans know that if this feat was possible, they would do it."

Marvin stole the ball from the Archer guard and drove in for a lay-up to begin the last eight minutes. Then Frankie stole the ball again. Hinkle Fieldhouse erupted into a frenzy, the likes of which had not been seen since Bobby Plump's last shot in the Milan victory.

The Hawks, however, couldn't capitalize on that steal and the ball went back to the "tree tops." Then Butch found the range and sank a jumper from the right side. Marvin followed suit, doing the same with a fall-away jumper from the right side.

They were still behind, 43-34, but they were now within striking distance. After all, they had been behind by as many as nine, 11, and 13 points in other games during the season. They believed they could do it again. Their speed and tough defense was keeping them in the game. The Archers' coach couldn't believe what he was seeing—a team this small giving his boys just about all they could handle.

Butch grabbed another defensive rebound and got the orange out to Marvin, who dribbled to the right sideline again, and as he was in the air, and falling out of bounds, nailed another one-handed jump shot. The Valley Boys had whittled it down to a seven-point South lead.

Bob was hacked underneath going up with a shot. He went to the line for two foul shots and uncharacteristically missed both. He had been on the receiving end from some very large fellows, having battled all three of them for the entire game.

The deficit was still only seven points. The boys from the valley were still within reach. The Hawks could do the impossible: another Milan, another "David Slays Goliath" story.

Every Springs Valley fan was thinking this way and praying. The folks listening back home had fingers crossed, and were making deals with the Almighty. Little boys were running to their bedrooms, lying on their beds, and praying the most earnest prayer they'd ever prayed.

But the Archers were not going to relinquish one ounce of the fight they still had left in them. They, too, were a talented ball club with an extreme advantage under the boards. There was a good reason they were ranked #1 in the state.

Bob McCracken, who had been such a force under the boards, was always the one with the most rebounds. He had a head-and-ball move under the basket that caused most players to take the pump fake. Bob would act as if he were going up with the ball, then come down and back up. The defending player usually went up with the fake, allowing Bob to put the ball up when his defender was going back down. But this strategy didn't work against someone who didn't need to leave his feet to block Bob's shot. Three times in a row, Bob's shot under the basket was blocked.

The skyscraping Archers hit their next couple of shots and kept the lead. Marvin drained his last jumper as the time dwindled down.

🏀 🏀 🏀

At a minute and a half remaining in the game, with the Archers holding a significant lead, Coach Wells put in the second-string players, so they could experience playing in a Final Four game. It was a once-in-a-lifetime experience, and this was something most coaches would do after realizing there just wasn't enough time on the clock to make a comeback.

He put Jackie back in the game, along with George Harrison, Jim Conrad, Jerry Breedlove, and George Lagenour. The starting five Valley Boys came out, knowing their season had just ended. The second-team Hawks continued to trade basket for basket with the Archers, with the final score, 55-42. Ft. Wayne had been up 12 at the end of the third period, and had added only one more point to that spread in the fourth. The Valley Boys had held their own with the giants from up north in the second half, but it wasn't enough.

The buzzer sounded.

It was over. The winning streak finally ended, and the door was shut on the season to end all seasons. The year of basketball for the

"Twin Cities" was over. The Twin Cities moniker itself was about to go by the wayside. These twins had made up, but their hearts were broken at the end of this game.

Everyone in the Valley realized just how incredible this team had been all season long.

The boys in black and white had certainly grown accustomed to winning, not having tasted defeat for 25 games in a row. No one teaches you how to win; that celebratory feeling of joy comes quite naturally. But losing—that's quite different. It's easy to be gracious in winning, but demonstrating grace and dignity in defeat takes a certain quality of character. Although the Valley Boys and their coach believed with all their heart that they could win the state championship, they accepted their loss with the same humble attitude they had displayed in 25 consecutive victories.

Perspective

Sometimes we just run out of time, it seems, and some dreams simply cannot come true, no matter how much desire there is. Ft. Wayne South, as one writer put it, was "just too big a forest to chop down in 32 minutes." The Hawks, at last, had been defeated after 25 wins. The only time the game was truly close was at the beginning with Valley taking the first lead, but the Archers came on strong and held the lead from there on out. Although the boys from the valley fought hard to get back in the game, they never closed the gap any more than seven points in the last quarter.

As one sportswriter put it in his article, "The glass slipper was finally pulled off" of the Springs Valley Black Hawks. The Cinderella story was indeed over. The clock struck midnight and the magic had disappeared. But that is where the Cinderella metaphor ends. The boys who had reached Hoosier celebrity status in the sports pages had not changed. They had not been turned into anything different, or back into something that they had been prior to being treated as stars.

Receiving so much statewide recognition had not changed them in the least. They started out as good, stand-up country boys and small-town fellas from the hills of Orange County. Heading back home from the big city, they were those same boys they had always been. They were heading home to French Lick and West Baden. The fairytale—yet very real—season had ended.

All the Hawks had played as hard as they could. Bob had fought for rebounds just as he always had. Marvin had hit his jumpers. Frankie played defense "like a demon," as one writer put it. The young sophomores, Belcher and Radcliff, each put in a needed field goal and found the open man for a quick, smart pass.

At the end of the game, Archers coach Don Reichart came over to shake Rex's hand.

"Boy, you had us worried in that fourth quarter," he admitted. "I'm glad this game didn't last any longer, the way your boys were fighting back. I sure can see how you guys won 25 games in a row, the way your boys play with so much heart and discipline."

The Archers coach had just found out what the 25 previous opponents had learned. This was a very clever and special team that had no quit in them.

Rex told reporters he believed his team had not played their best. They'd had much better games of hitting the bottom of the net from outside. It hadn't happened today, so it simply wasn't enough against a very strong team with such a height advantage.

A local news reporter stuck a microphone in Rex's face just after the game.

"We had a chance," the coach explained. "We just ran out of time. I believe if we'd had another two or three minutes we could've done what these boys have done all season: come from behind to win."

Mentally and physically drained, the coach told every reporter wanting a quote this same thing. Every player did his best, but having to heave the ball over the outstretched arms of a 7', 6'5", and 6'4" defender can certainly change one's shot trajectory.

Still, the Hawks' shot percentage wasn't much less than the Archers', with the Hawks hitting 19 of 54 for 35.2 percent and the Archers hitting 23 of 64 tries for a 35.9 percent. The teams had committed the same number of errors. The time just ran out on the Hawks, that's all. They never ran out of will and desire.

"The boys gave it all they had and I'm proud of them," Rex was quoted as saying."They showed they were a basketball team out there. In our case, we just got behind too much and too soon. We came back well in the second half, but the boys just had too much ground to gain."

That pretty much summed it up, but oh, the heartache he was feeling for his players, who had shown so much heart all season long.

The boys accepted defeat as graciously as they did winning 25 games in a row. There were no tears. No heads down. Not one whimper. Those Hawks who could make their way through the celebratory chaos surrounding the Archers congratulated their opponents.

Some of the Ft. Wayne South players came over to shake hands with the Valley Boys as well. In fact, after the game, Mike McCoy walked over to congratulate Bob.

"I'm sorry you lost," he said, "but I've gotta tell you something. You are the toughest little SOB I've ever played."

Disappointed at not winning, but certainly not dejected, the team retreated to the locker room. They had all known that this would be the toughest game of their lives. They also knew that they had nothing to hang their heads about. Rex spoke.

Consolation

"Boys, I'm as proud of you now as I've ever been in any game this year. You may find this hard to accept now, but you will understand this later in your lives: you really learn more about life from losing than winning.

"You guys have certainly learned what it's like to win this season. You've had your fair share, but life is truly a struggle. I think that, in the end, you will take more away from this season by the way things turned out today. Sure, it would've been nice to be the next Milan, as many had hoped. But that's just not what happened with the cards you were dealt.

"You played as hard as you've ever played. You gave it your all and left it all out there on the floor, and that's all I've ever asked of you. You just ran into a bigger team. They got in 10 more field goal attempts than you did—only because they controlled the boards with their big guys, and the 13 points they won by were all put-backs under the basket. If you hadn't been the defensive team that you are, they would've won by a lot more than 13 points."

(In the final game that evening, in fact, Ft. Wayne South smothered Crawfordsville, winning the state championship, 63-34, revealing just how well Valley had played against the Archers in the afternoon game.)

"I still believe you are a better team than Ft. Wayne South," Rex went on, "and on another day, we might have prevailed. You scored even with them for the entire second half."

The boys were feeling a little better about the loss as their beloved coach continued, hoping his words were a healing balm. The coach ended with this:

"Y'know, this team has been playing for a lot more than just a record or a state championship. You've been molding two towns and a consolidated school together into one. And you've really done it, too."

The boys were feeling a rush of emotions from all over the spectrum: heartbreak, pride, gratitude, wistfulness, and much more. Already they were beginning to gain a kind of perspective on their wild ride, glimpsing their season as if from some future vantage point.

At that moment, Principal Katter came into the locker room.

"Boys, I just want you to know that we're all so very proud of you. You guys are champions in all our eyes. You have given Springs Valley such a wonderful basketball season that we will so fondly remember for years and years to come. No, we didn't get the win today, but there are other victories in life, and this season has been one great big 'W' for French Lick and West Baden.

"Don't you ever forget what you have done for Springs Valley," Katter continued. "You made us all one community with one spirit. And that is more important than ever winning a basketball game.

The winners here are the Springs Valley citizens. And they have you boys to thank."

Katter ended his speech. But as he turned to leave, he thought of one more sentiment he wanted to share.

"Oh, and by the way. You all were right about the team name and the school colors. I was wrong. You all knew what you were doing. I, for one, as well as many other folks, learned a great deal during this season. Thank you all.

"Thank you all, very, very much."

• CHAPTER 19 •
BACK HOME AGAIN—IN SOUTHERN INDIANA

The team returned home the next day and received a hero's welcome, complete with a parade. In fact, several schools from Southern Indiana were invited to participate. Huntingburg, Paoli, and Orleans high schools' marching bands gladly accepted the invitation to be in the parade.

That's how special this was. Even schools that Valley had played and pummeled in games earlier in the season had been so taken with this Black Hawks team that they joined in the celebration. Everyone south of Bloomington had been rooting for the Hawks, and the signs along Highway 37, which the team read gratefully on their way home from Indianapolis, reminded the boys of just how many people had been with them all the way. It was a good feeling and brought some comfort.

Although there would be no bonfire or sock hop at the Sheraton Hotel, both town boards declared a "Black Hawk Weekend." All businesses and houses were asked to decorate with black and white. Frank and Bee's, as well as the Five and Dime store down on Maple Street, had a run on black and white crepe paper. There wasn't a roll left in town.

As the boys rode along in the parade, sitting atop the fire wagon and flatbed trucks, they gained some sense of what had just happened over the last few months. The one-and-a-half-mile stretch from

French Lick to West Baden was lined with some 12,000 people, cheering loudly for their hometown heroes. There had never been this big of a turnout for any parade in the past. Nor would there ever be in the future.

The parade extended down College Street, starting at the school, and ended at the Sheraton Hotel, where 800 fans and students had braved the March wind and the chilling rain for a special program at the hotel's outdoor music bowl.

The master of ceremonies congratulated the team and celebrated how the Black Hawks' season-long effort and teamwork had scored a great victory for the consolidated schools. Then Coach Wells was asked to step to the microphone for a few words. Rex shared another of his favorite poems, by Peter Dale Winbrow Sr., which he had memorized long ago.

"The Guy in the Glass"

When you get what you want out of this battle of life
And the world makes you king for a day
Just go to the mirror and look at yourself
To see what that guy has to say
It isn't your mother, your brother, or sister or wife
Whom judgment upon you must pass
But the fellow whose verdict counts most in your life
Is the guy staring back from the glass
You may be like Jack Horner and chisel a plum
You may think you're a wonderful guy
But the guy in the glass will call you a bum
If you can't look him straight in the eye
He's the fellow to please, never mind all the rest
For he is with you clear till the end

And you'll pass your most dangerous and difficult tasks
If the guy in the glass is your friend

You may fool the whole world down the pathway of
years
And get pats on the back as you pass
But your final reward will be heartache and tears
If you've cheated the guy in the glass.

Coach Wells finished the poem, then spoke once more from his heart.

"I know that this team, having looked in that mirror after losing to Ft. Wayne South, could say that they had indeed put out that extra effort," he said proudly. "These boys know they have nothing to be ashamed of. They put out their best effort all season long and that contributed to their great record."

The boys sat in a line behind Rex, all looking down, gazing at the special medals with the team mascot in relief. It was the same black hawk that Rex had asked the Disney cartoonist to draw. This symbol of the team had become a very familiar one to everyone in the Valley. What had once been just an idea in Rex's mind was now a part of the two towns—the representation of this record-setting season and this positive change for the community.

The coach asked the boys to say a few words. Marvin, never one to sugarcoat anything, was the first to approach the microphone.

"Well, you don't really feel so bad when Ft. Wayne just proved they were a better team on Saturday. It's that simple," he said. "They played better than we did."

Frankie passed on the opportunity to speak. He always did his talking on the court. Butch then came up to say one thing.

"At least the Southside Archers are the tallest team in the state."

He seemed to be taking the loss a little harder than the rest of the guys, judging by this vague statement. But everyone knew that was just Butch. He truly was a great ballplayer, but his nonchalant attitude sometimes made it seem like he was somehow disconnected from the rest of the team. This wall between Butch and most of the other boys seemed to be because they came from poor families, while Butch came from a well-to-do one. There was no denying the differences in how they lived their lives; Butch enjoyed certain luxuries that nearly every other player could only dream of. This disparity always seemed to lie just under the surface, no matter how well the boys played ball together.

But the truth is that the co-captain of the Hawks was, for the season, the second-highest field goal scorer on the team, scoring 93 field goals and 35 free throws for a total of 221 total points. Perhaps, having suffered the tragic loss of his father, he had needed this win more than anyone else on the team, having been through so much disappointment and heartache earlier in the season.

The boys all stood up and applauded the fans and thanked them for their support through the season. The fans and students in turn cheered for their coach and team.

But it was cold and wet, and everyone needed to get out of the dreary March rain. Perhaps the weather was fitting for the occasion. It was as if Mickie Sutherland and Ben Schmutzler were looking down on the Hawks from the heavens, shedding tears for the boys in black and white.

But beneath the bravado and stiff upper lips, there were many "what ifs" that the team couldn't help pondering. What if we had played the first half like the second half, when we matched the Archers point for point? What if we hadn't fallen so far behind in the first half? What if they didn't have a seven-foot player?

But the greatest "what if" was this: What if the Black Hawks had not won their first four or five games? What if they had won only a couple of those first games back in November? What if they had not enjoyed the undefeated season, which no other brand-new high school team in Indiana basketball history could claim to have done? What if? *What if?*

If the Hawks hadn't had such an unbelievably successful season, Coach Wells knew, there would have been a lot of second-guessing about the wisdom of merging the two schools. And many imagined that French Lick and West Baden fans would have continued wearing their old school colors for the rest of the season, if not longer, still choosing to cling to their separate pasts.

But instead, they were all drawn into the future with something so positive that even the most die-hard Devils or Sprudels fan could not resist. Everybody loves to win, and winning something greater for this community is what the Springs Valley Black Hawks succeeded in doing. They won back a lost pride and dignity that had somehow disappeared over the years. They bridged a chasm between the towns that had existed for so long. They overshadowed the struggle that both towns had had since the glory days of the hotels had been relegated to the past.

It was a new day, and the Valley Boys ushered this era in with a fiercely competitive team that liked to laugh and have good times while they played the game. To the players on this team, it may have been just a game— but it was a game that had led to one of the greatest experiences of these boys' lives. Still, they just knew that they loved to play basketball, whether on an asphalt court in West Baden or at Butler Fieldhouse.

The pride and excitement generated by this team would carry on for many years to come. Winning goes a long way in a small Southern Indiana town. And in this case of the Twin Cities, winning went twice as far.

The sadness of the loss having worn off a little, the town's welcome home was a great pick-me-up for the Hawks. At first the boys felt as if they'd let all of Southern Indiana down, as well as every little school in the state. But that was not the case at all. What these 10 boys and their coach had accomplished would be remembered for decades to come, and their story would be an inspiration to many other basketball players to follow in their footsteps.

As the congratulatory crowd was dispersing in the rain, Bob gave his coach a hug that was nonetheless way out of Bob's own comfort zone. But he felt compelled to express his emotions. Bob kept up his tough exterior, but he simply wanted to cry—for happiness and sadness. It was bittersweet for the hardest-working Hawk— the Enforcer. Perhaps, having invested so much of himself, he had become more emotionally attached to the team's adventure.

The magical season had come to an end short of a state

championship. Still, Rex knew these boys were all champions. Each was unique, and it took a combination of these different personalities and players, with their special abilities, to create the kind of winning season the Black Hawks experienced.

"Can we give you a ride home, Bob?" Rex asked.

"Naw, Shorty told me he'd give me a lift," Bob said, reassuring his coach that he had a way to get back to his house in the country.

Then the reality hit Bob all at once. He was overwhelmed. A day ago, he was dining in one of the finest hotels in the state capital and playing basketball in the greatest "cathedral of basketball." Today, he would be back on his farm—the farm with no electricity.

Bob thanked his coach, and with a handshake and perhaps a couple of surreptitious tears, they parted ways.

Paul had attended church earlier on this Sunday morning. His parents and the congregation had all praised Paul right after they praised the Lord. Paul knew that his mom and dad had finally understood his love for this game of basketball and that they finally could recognize its importance to him. And they couldn't be prouder of their boy.

But change was coming, for Paul and for the coach, that they never could have guessed at. Paul's dad was retiring for health reasons and moving the family to Ft. Myers, Florida. Another one of Rex's players, Jim Conrad, would also be moving away from the Valley. Jim's dad had been the superintendent at West Baden, and because of the consolidation, he had lost that job.

The coach was losing 40 percent of his next season's starting five.

In 1957–58, all the boys were in the right place at the right time. Had the two fathers made this decision to move away one year prior, there may not have been an undefeated season. It had taken every single one of those 10 boys to make it all happen.

Coach Wells heard the news about Paul. He would later say, "You've never seen a grown man cry more than when I was told that Paul would not be returning next season!"

It seemed that this one special year had simply been predestined.

But for now, all the Valley Boys were back home again in the hills of Southern Indiana, the place where they'd always been quite comfortable. The boys had not known normalcy since last October. They welcomed this return to their everyday lives.

🏀 🏀 🏀

Frankie and Thelma, along with Marvin and Barbara, had already said goodbye to Coach Wells and his wife. As the young couples walked off the hotel grounds, the rain let up, and the sun peeked through the clouds for the first time that day.

Frankie looked up and saw a pair of hawks, that constant sight above the valley.

"We picked a good name for the team, didn't we?" Frankie asked Marvin.

"We sure did, but I think the name picked us," Marvin replied.

A few minutes later, they both looked back up to the clearing sky and counted 10 birds gliding together. Then, an eleventh bird joined the floating, circling flock.

"Hey, that's our team up there!" Frankie exclaimed.

Marvin smiled. "Yeah, I see the coach just joined us."

The two guards who had led the team all year laughed at this coincidence. Or was it? Deep inside they saw themselves in those birds of prey, just as they had all season long.

"Do you think we really accomplished what the coach and those articles have been sayin'—you know, about these two towns comin' together as one community?" Frankie asked.

"I don't know," Marvin answered. "But I do know that I can go into French Lick now, and they treat me like a king instead of wanting to punch me. That must mean something."

The season had indeed changed the school, the team, and the towns forever. The boys had set a very high bar for years to come for every other Black Hawks team.

"Twenty-five wins in a row. That ain't too bad," Marvin suggested.

"I guess we did do somethin' that had never been done before," Frankie answered. It was just beginning to sink in to the boys what had happened this year. And the further they would get from this unusually successful season, the more incredible it would become to them.

As the four walked back to Marvin's car, both girls said at nearly the same time, "Yes, you guys did something very special."

"You started something that will continue on. It took your team to start this school off on the right foot," Thelma added

The two sets of high school sweethearts walked hand in hand. The young couples, each soon to be married for life, felt a certain peace. It was as if this season was a sign for them, telling them to grab for all their dreams, no matter the odds—to take the chance when you hear that small, still voice within that tells you to go for it.

While all four of them sensed that something very special had just occurred in their lives, they did not realize at the time that this season had created life-changing events. There was a feeling of surety that the future would be very good for the two couples. How could it not be with a start like this? They were so very right. They all felt like winners.

At that moment, Coach Wells drove by with his wife, and the two couples waved to Rex and Margaret. Rex rolled down his window and yelled, "We'll get 'em next season. See ya tomorrow at gym class!"

"See you coach!" both boys hollered back.

Just then, they all heard the familiar sound of a car laying rubber and peeling out. Butch was driving out of the hotel parking lot, leaving his "signature" on State Road 56.

There was a pretty girl sitting by his side.

🏀 🏀 🏀

The years went by, and no one could ever forget this monumental basketball season. Little boys continued to hear, from their fathers who had followed the Black Hawks throughout their first season, this story about an exceptional group of mature young men. Ten special ballplayers had come together at a specific time and place, under the right circumstances, to achieve an undefeated season.

In 1957–58, the Springs Valley Black Hawks were born. They set a precedent, as an undefeated first-year team, that could never be topped. But every Hawks team since then has been inspired by the story of these 11 boys and their young coach, who taught two small towns a very big lesson.

🏀 🏀 🏀

A few years later, there was one little boy who loved basketball just as much as the Valley Boys had. Every day he would go out to his basketball goal at the side of his yard and heave up shots from the dirt court. The same shot, over and over.

Later, as he made his grade school and junior high teams, he would go with his mom to watch the Hawks' high school team play. He worked as hard as those boys from 1958 had, and he eventually made his high school team.

Before every game, this boy would look up and see those championship banners from the sectional, regional, and semi-state victories from 1958 hanging from the rafters of a new Springs Valley High School gymnasium. It was part of a new school built just a few years after the magical Black Hawks season—and it had a gym with a regulation-size court.

In those days, the young boy always wondered if he might ever be on a championship team someday. He dreamed big, just like the Valley Boys did. He worked extra hard at his game, just like the Valley Boys. He got better and better, just as the Valley Boys had.

And one day, he became the most famous of the Valley Boys. Today, his retired number is hoisted above the gym floor for all to see and admire.

And printed on the back of that number 33 jersey is a name. "Bird."

The End

EPILOGUE

The basketball season of 1957–58 did indeed change these two towns, but even more so, the lives of these boys and their coach. In the 1958 school yearbook, there is a dedication. It reads: "In unity there is strength. We dedicate this annual to the realization of a dream come true—the CONSOLIDATION of the French Lick and West Baden Schools."

Rex Wells, Coach

Coach Rex Wells stayed on to lead the team for a couple more years. The following season, 1958–59, Rex's brother, Bill, became assistant coach, and Springs Valley was ranked # 8 in the state. Ft. Wayne south was ranked #7. Even though Rex lost two of his starting players, the 1958–59 year was another great season with a record of 18 wins and 4 losses. The Hawks won the first three games of the sectional but were defeated in the fourth contest. It seems that the 1958 "dream team" had existed for that one year for that one purpose—to unite the two towns.

Having been a standout in three sports at Hanover College—baseball, football, and basketball—it's surprising that Coach Wells's coaching career only lasted six years. For a young coach, he compiled an impressive record during the golden era of single-class Indiana basketball. Rex coached championship IHSAA tournament teams, earning two sectional championships, one regional title, and one semi-state championship, and one Final Four state finalist. He coached three schools to sectional final games. Having been named

Coach of the Year in 1958, Rex has maintained that he is only the "custodian" of the trophy, and that the true ownership belongs to the '58 Black Hawks team.

Rex left Springs Valley after Marvin Pruett and Frankie Self graduated. He became the coach of the Greensburg, Indiana, high school team, leading them to the sectional championship after they had won only three games in the previous four years! The town of Greensburg gave Rex the keys to the city.

Upon Rex's success with the Greensburg team, he received a call from Springs Valley, asking him to return. He coached the Black Hawks for one more year, then reluctantly accepted their offer to become principal of the high school. From there, he went on to get his master's degree in education at Colorado State University in 1962. Having spent time at Colorado State University, he and his wife, Margaret ("Margie"), moved to Ft. Collins to make their home there in 1964. In 1970, Rex earned his doctor of education degree from the University of Nebraska.

Rex's professional education career spanned over 30 years that included stints as teacher, basketball coach, athletic director, assistant principal, and principal. He finished his career in Ft. Collins, Colorado, where he was principal of Rocky Mountain High School for 13 years. He has owned his own public accountant business for the past 25 years. Rex and Margie recently celebrated their 60th wedding anniversary. They have three children and five grandchildren. When waxing nostalgic, the coach speaks of moving back to their home town of West Baden for his and his lovely wife's "twilight years."

Warren (Doc) Keyser, Assistant Coach

Doc left the Valley after the '58 season for head coaching jobs in Southern Indiana high schools. He coached at English and Shoals. Most of his long and successful career of more than 30 years was spent teaching and coaching in Seymour, Indiana, where he served as dean of boys and for 12 years as assistant principal. Doc was a lifelong sports official. His education degrees include a BS degree from Indiana Central (now the University of Indianapolis) and an MS degree from Indiana University. Doc and his wife, Doris, reside in Seymour, Indiana. They have been married over 60 years. In retirement, Doc has developed a passion for gardening. Both times I called Doc, he was out on his tractor, bush hogging.

Bob McCracken, 5'11" Co- Captain

The "Enforcer," after his successful senior year of playing basketball, was selected for the Indiana State All-Star team, the first player from Orange County to receive this honor. He received a full scholarship to Utah State University, where he played for one year. He transferred to Casper College, then on to Montana State University. His fourth year, Bob graduated from IUPUI, in Indianapolis after having served three years in the military.

After college, he worked in Indianapolis for the Household Finance Company. After 10 years in the financial field, Bob started his own business, Baby World, a company that sold baby furniture. Bob was president of his company with seven stores in Indiana, Ohio, and Kentucky. Ironically, Bob lived only a few miles from me on Morse Reservoir in Noblesville, Indiana, for nearly 30 years. Wish I'd known that!

Bob and Patsy Zeedyk did not marry just out of high school, the way some of the other boys had married their high school sweethearts. However, in 1999, after many years apart, Bob and Patsy met again at a high school reunion, and they were once again a couple. He still believes she is the prettiest girl from French Lick!

A few years ago, Bob moved back to the same property he grew up on: the farm with no electricity. He built a beautiful home on that acreage where he once hunted squirrels for his breakfast. Bob, an avid golfer, is retired and living quite comfortably these days—with plenty of electricity!

Today, Bob attributes his success to having a coach and friend like Rex Wells. He always said that Coach Wells was more interested in his players becoming winners in life than winning basketball games. "He was my mentor," Bob said. "The father I really never had."

Ronald "Butch" Schmutzler; 6'0", Co-Captain

In December 1978, at the Black Hawks' 20-year reunion, the team and coaches dedicated the gathering to their beloved teammate, who passed away in 1970. At the ceremony held in Butch's honor, a memorial plaque was presented to his wife, Ms. Dorothy Douglas, and daughters, Lisa and Laura of Portland, Oregon.

The plaque and a picture of Butch hang in the Springs Valley Gymnasium as a tribute to an outstanding athlete who contributed so much to the impossible dream of the 1958 Black Hawks. It reads: "Butch" (Ronald) Schmutzler was Springs Valley High School's first basketball team co-captain. Through his leadership and courage and athletic ability, the 1958 Black Hawks recorded one of the most unique chapters in the annals of Indiana High School Athletics. The team completed an undefeated season in 1957–58 and played in the Finals of the Indiana State High School Basketball Tourney. Butch's contribution to the game and his competitive play on the court have been an inspiration to Springs Valley athletes and a tribute to the community."

It was a very sad day for all when Butch passed away at the age of 30. Without question, Ronald "Butch" Schmutzler was the best all-around athlete of the team.

George Lagenour, 6'0" Back-Up Center

George was a hold-over from the French Lick High School team the year prior to this famed season. In his later years, he would comment that his greatest experience during the team's historic season was competing each night in practice against the best center in the state. That was none other than the 6'1" 15-year old sophomore center, Paul Douglas Radcliff. Without question, George was a contributing member of the team and highly respected by his teammates for his diligence and hard work each night in practices.

George attended college in Indianapolis right after high school. He attended Evansville College, which became the University of Evansville while he was a student there. George got his BS degree in computer business and worked for Mead Johnson until the late 60s. He then began his own business in electrical data processing, programming systems for 30 years. George now lives with his wife Vickie in Dubois County, Indiana.

Jerry Breedlove, 5'10", Forward

Jerry was a role player for the Black Hawks first basketball team. Although he did not get a lot of playing time, Jerry understood and accepted his role. He once told me, "I just enjoyed watching those guys play!" Each night in practices, he was committed to making Bob McCracken a better player. He did this by imposing physical competition each night with the roughest and toughest player in Southern Indiana. To this day, Bob McCracken admits that his friend Jerry made him a better competitor rebounding against taller opponents, given Bob's height disadvantage at 5'10".

After graduation, Jerry enlisted in the U.S. Navy for a four-year tour of duty. Honorably discharged in 1963, he returned to the Valley and worked in construction for several years. In the early days of the Vietnam War, Jerry decided again to serve his country by enlisting in the U.S. Navy. He was immediately deployed to Vietnam with a construction battalion (CBs, or "Seabees") who were responsible for building airstrips and military projects.

After Jerry's second tour of service, he came back to the Valley and formed a successful excavation and demolition company with his sons. Sadly, Jerry lost his first wife, Glenda, after a short illness several years ago. Today, he and his wife, Mary Jo, live in the Valley.

Marvin Pruett, 6'1", Co-Captain

A team leader, the All-State junior guard was the team's leading scorer with an average of 18.1 points per game, all the way to the 48th IHSAA basketball state finals in Indianapolis. The next season, under Coach Wells, Marvin averaged 25 points per game. He was selected for the Indiana All-Star team and voted honorary captain for two years. He was selected 1st Team All Sectional in '57, '58, and '59. As a junior, he won 1st Team All Regional, All Semi-State, and All-State honors.

At Evansville College (now the University of Evansville) he was a three-year starter for the Purple Aces in 79 straight games, a record. His total points of 1,122, with a 14.2 average per game, earned him membership in the 1,000-Point Club. He won Little All-American honors in 1963 and was selected to the Evansville College Basketball Hall of Fame in 1990. After college, he taught and coached at Shoals High School in Indiana. He was named to the Indiana High School Basketball Hall of Fame's 1984 Silver Anniversary Team. In March 2015, Marvin joined Larry Bird as the only two Springs Valley high school players to be inducted into the Indiana Basketball Hall of Fame.

The Valley's leading scorer, Marvin was courted by Branch McCracken from Indiana University as well as Adolph Rupp from the University of Kentucky. He ended up playing basketball at Evansville College on a full-ride scholarship, shattering scoring records during his college career. This little school at the southern tip of Indiana would pay the biggest schools in the country to come and play their team. The little Evansville College beat teams from UCLA, Ohio State, Iowa, and Purdue. Marvin had a lot to do with that! After teaching and coaching, he made his career in the insurance business, becoming very successful in that field. Marvin and Barbara now make Newburgh, Indiana, their home. The two high school sweethearts have been married for 53 years.

Frankie Self, 5'7" Co-Captain

Frankie Self married Thelma McFarland and they were inseparable for 55 years. The two had never dated any other person in high school. Frankie, as the hometown boy he was, stayed in West Baden out of high school, working for the *Springs Valley Herald*. After 20 years he was offered a job with the Texas Eastern Oil Company, where he had a successful career until his retirement in 2000. The high school sweethearts had two daughters whom they reared in Springs Valley.

At one of the team reunions where they were being honored, Frankie was asked what game stood out in his mind the most. Most thought that the guard from that famed season would say the most significant game to him was the Vincennes game, where he stole the ball and made the winning shot. Not Frankie. Demonstrating his selflessness again, Frankie thought for a second and said, "I think it was the fourth game at home, when folks started showin' up wearin' our new school colors." That was Frankie! For years, local fans would remind him of his feat of singlehandedly winning the regional game over Vincennes by stealing the ball in the final seconds to score the winning basket. When asked about this, Frankie would say, "They just won't let me forget it."

Sadly, Frankie passed away in 2015. Thelma still lives in the beautiful home they built on a hillside in West Baden. They had a love story like no other. They did everything together and lived a storybook life. When I asked Thelma if she had any photos of herself and Frankie from high school, she left the room for a minute. She came back and handed me Frankie's wallet. She opened it and there inside was her high school senior picture! (I couldn't help but shed a tear.) Oh, how Frankie and Thelma made a life so very full of love. They were truly cut from the same cloth. They may not have inherited the earth, but in their meek and humble way, they each certainly "inherited" what they wanted in life as high school sweethearts, so in love till the very end.

Paul Radcliff, 6'1" Center

Paul was the leading rebounder for the Hawks and scored an average of 10 points per game. His defense skills as a center were outstanding. In spite of his height disadvantage, he kept much taller opposing centers scoring fewer than 20 points a game. This was an amazing feat for a 15-year old sophomore competing against seniors. For his abilities and outstanding tournament play, Paul won All Sectional, All Regional, and First Team All-Semi-State honors.

Paul's family moved to Ft. Myers, Florida, at the end of the 1958 school year and he became an outstanding athlete at Ft. Myers High. One thing that helped Paul adjust to this move to a school so far away from Indiana was the great surprise of seeing two ballplayers from the Hoosier state. One boy, Bob Patton, was from Orleans, Indiana; Paul had played against him with the Black Hawks and played with him in the American Legion ball league. The other was Tom Hayward, from Logansport. The families of Bob Patton and Tom Hayward had moved to Ft. Myers that same summer. The three new Indiana arrivals to the Ft. Myers team were given the name, "the Hoosier Hot Shots." Indiana's reputation for good basketball players was being upheld by these three, who played together for the rest of their high school playing days. After his senior year, Paul was awarded the Florida equivalent of Indiana's "Mr. Basketball" after having led his team to many victories.

Paul attended Kentucky Wesleyan University on a full-ride scholarship, where, again, he excelled on the basketball team. Ironically, Paul became roommates with Roger Benson—the guard from whom Frankie had stolen the ball to win the regional championship game against Vincennes High School. (And Paul never let Roger forget it, either!) And the coach at Wesleyan was T. L. Plain, the former Vincennes coach that Valley had beaten in that unforgettable tournament game.

Paul graduated from Kentucky Wesleyan in 1964 and taught at Davis County High School. He married a Florida girl, Georgia Lawrence, in 1965. He received his master's degree in '66 and began his Ph.D. in '67 at I.U. He then moved back to Florida, where he taught at Edison Junior College for 10 years. He returned to IU in 1970–71 to finish his doctorate, then returned to Florida.

In August 1973, Rex Wells called Paul and asked if he would like to take a position at the new high school Rex was opening in Ft. Collins, Colorado. Unfortunately, Paul couldn't take the offer at that time because of his commitment to finish his contract with Edison Junior College. But in 1977, Rex called Paul again with better results. Paul enjoyed a 26-year career at Rocky Mountain High School as athletic director, then as principal after Rex retired. He and Rex were back together after so many years. They are still very close friends.

Sadly, Paul's wife, Georgia passed away in 2007 after 42 years of marriage. Paul still makes his home in Ft. Collins, Colorado, with his children and grandchildren.

Mike Watson, 5'7", Guard

Mike was a starter in the early season games. Later, he became the important "sixth man" of the team. The spirit he generated and the positive attitude he displayed were enormous contributors to the success of the team. After 60 years, he proudly recalls making that first basket for the brand new Black Hawks team on the night of November 8, 1957. Nearer the end of the season, Mike made the winning basket in one of the most memorable games of the season against Providence.

Mike Watson worked at the Sheraton Hotel, just out of high school, then joined the Marines. Stationed in California, he played basketball, making the team out of 3,000 "Swabbies." He recalls getting a lot of playing time. In his first game, he shot 16 for 16, scoring 32 points.

After Mike's stint in the military, he returned home to French Lick, where he worked at the Kimball furniture factory. From there, he began working for PSI, then for Duke Energy. Mike became supervisor over all of Indiana before retiring. Mike married his high school sweetheart from French Lick, Brenda Dodson. They have been married now for 57 years and make their home in Avon, Indiana.

Jim Conrad, 5'10", Forward

Jim was always called upon to go in the game when the regulars got in foul trouble. After the season, Jim and family moved to Spencer, Indiana, where his father became superintendent. He became an outstanding player for the Spencer Rebels and captain of the team his senior year. Leading his team in scoring and rebounding, he earned 1st Team All-Sectional honors. In addition, he was awarded team MVP honors and selected to the All-Southwest Conference Team by coaches. In 1960, Jim graduated as valedictorian of his class.

Jim Conrad attended Purdue University, where he played basketball as a walk-on. Jim earned his master's degree in economics and business and graduated with distinction. He then attended the University of Kentucky, where he earned his Ph.D. Jim taught college for 30 years at the University of Louisville as a professor of economics, and later became dean of the School of Business at the University of Indianapolis. Ironically, my brother-in-law, Peter Noot (the editor of this book), has known him longer than I, since Peter was the director of publications at that same university his entire career. Small world.

Jack Belcher, 6'1", Forward

Jack Belcher played for Springs Valley for two more seasons. Jackie was captain and leading scorer for the Hawks his senior year and was selected to the Southern Indiana All-Star team in 1960. He was also on the Springs Valley golf team. Thanks to the local resorts, the high school players had access to the Donald Ross course—one of the finest in the United States. Springs Valley put together a very strong golf team, which also made it to the State Finals. Jackie was a gifted athlete.

After high school, he attended Louisiana State University, where he played basketball his freshman year before becoming a starting letterman for three years on the varsity basketball team. He was elected captain of the team his senior year. He also played baseball one year. After graduating, Jack came back home to the Valley and married a girl from West Baden, Peggy Butler. (There seems to be a pattern here.) He became part of the management at the Kimball furniture factory in French Lick. Later, he went into business for himself with his sons in independent office furniture sales. Jack and his wife live in Gambier, Ohio, and have been married for over 50 years.

George Harrison, 6'0"

George Harrison, the player who was called up from the junior varsity team for the Final Four game after Mike Watson's injury, remained in French Lick, where he had a long and successful career at Kimball Pianos. He also built jukeboxes for Rowe International and pool tables for the Brunswick Company. In 2000, George retired after 38 years with Kimball. George lives just outside of French Lick with his wife, Mary Jane.

Bob Trueblood, Student Team Manager

Bob had Coach Wells's complete confidence with his organizational skills and kept accurate and complete team statistics. Prior to the consolidation, Bobby was West Baden High School's statistician for two years. His commitment to carrying out this huge responsibility was exemplary. The task of keeping team and player statistics during this historic season was critical to preserving the records of Springs Valley's inaugural season. Over the years, reference to Bobby's statistics became critical in presenting accurate numbers in various articles on athletics.

After graduation in 1959, Bob enlisted in the U.S. Army, and went on to a long and successful career with the Indiana Telephone Company. In his retirement years, he has become an accomplished bass fisherman, competing and winning professional tournaments all around the country. He and his family reside in Hanover, Indiana.

Billy Rose, Student Team Manager

If a coach ever needed a right-hand man to help manage the many details of each practice and game, it was Billy Rose. The first senior student manager for the Hawks, Billy had been student manager of the French Lick Red Devils the previous three years prior to consolidation of the two schools. Billy, proud of his role on the team, was totally dedicated to performing his duties at this very helpful job and was highly respected by the players and the coaches alike. Coach Wells said, "His contributions to the success of Springs Valley's first historic basketball season were immeasurable."

After Bill's tour of duty in the U.S. Navy, he earned a B.S. degree in education from Oakland City College and an M.S. degree in education administration from Indiana University. He retired as a high school teacher and coach after three decades. Sadly, Billy passed away in 1995. He was 55 years old.

Joseph Ellis, Cheerleader

Joe was a senior cheerleader for the Black Hawks' first three-member cheerleading squad. Upon graduation with honors, he attended Indiana University, where he earned his B.S., M.S., and D.D.S. degrees. Later, he served a tour of duty in the U.S. Navy Health Service. In his successful career, he owned dental practices in North Vernon, Indiana; South Florida; and Phoenix, Arizona. Sadly, Joe lost his wife in 2014, after more than 50 years of marriage. Currently, Joe makes his summer home in Cuzco, Indiana, and his winter home in Florida.

Billy Jo Harris Salyer, Cheerleader

Billy Jo was a senior member of the first cheerleading team for Springs Valley. She was a wonderful individual, respected by all her classmates. She said the highlight of her four years leading cheers had to be the once-in-a-lifetime experience on being on the Butler Fieldhouse court, leading cheers before 16,000 fans. It's easy to overlook the role of the cheerleaders when so much focus is on the team playing the game. But, in the case of the Springs Valley Black Hawks' spirited cheerleading squad, these three individuals contributed so very much energy to each game, and perhaps even helped fire up those Valley Boys in those close fourth-quarter finishes that led the team to 25 straight victories.

Billy Jo passed away in 1989. She was 50 years old.

Beverly Runyon Condra, Cheerleader

Beverly had cheered for the West Baden Sprudels prior to the consolidation. Always popular with the students, she loved her role as spirit leader. In 1958, the students voted her as one of the first Black Hawks cheerleaders. After graduation in 1958, she married Tommy Condra, and for all her married years, she was a homemaker; a loving wife, and mother—the most important job on the planet. The Condra family lives in Terre Haute, Indiana. Heartbreakingly, they lost Beverly in 2018.

Jeff Agan, Mascot

Jeff was the first "little black hawk" mascot. He tells me that he outgrew the outfit after his first year and the mascot suit went to little Suzanne Stanfield. The eight-year-old Jeff became part of the historic season of '58, being there on the sidelines at each game—even when he had chicken pox during the Final Four game!

After graduation from high school and a stint with Merrill Lynch, Jeff took the entrepreneurial route in life. He got a loan from the local bank, his Aunt Harriet vouching for the character of this determined young man.

Jeff's first construction project was a meat packing plant. From that successful venture, Jeff went on to a very successful building career with his own company—Agan Development. He built his office building and began developing shopping centers. Jeff has become one of the premier mall and shopping center developers in the Midwest.

Jeff says he'll never forget that one year of his life when he was the image bearer of the first Springs Valley Black Hawks team. Looking back, he says, "It was quite an honor to have gotten to do this at such an early age."

FROM THE BLEACHERS

I was in eighth grade when French Lick and West Baden high schools consolidated. It was never a real problem for students, once school started. Many adults still held onto their lifetime of hate—at least until basketball season was well under way. My hero early on was Marvin Pruett ("Marvelous Marvin"), and as I told people over the years, he still ranks very high on my list.

A story that I have told many times goes back to my Sacramento Kings coaching stint. We were fortunate enough to beat the (Showtime) L.A. Lakers with Magic, Kareem, Worthy, etc. all on TNT's national TV broadcast! After thwe game, the press conference was fun! One sports news writer asked if this was my "biggest basketball thrill." I instantly said, "Not close. My biggest thrill was when Frankie Self stole the ball against the Vincennes Alices in the Huntingburg regional in the last 11 seconds to win the game for Springs Valley."

I really got a kick out of all the press corps' expressions, as I was certain they felt that Reynolds had actually lost his sanity coaching the Kings! What they could never understand was that it was true. It was great to be a Black Hawk myself and to have watched that special team at a special time."

—*Jerry Reynolds, Former Coach and General Manager of the NBA Sacramento Kings, and current Kings TV analyst*

The 1957–58 basketball season provided me with some of the fondest memories of my life. Our junior high school principal was Mr. Clayton Conrad, father of Jim Conrad, a player on that memorable team. We students assembled every morning in the large study hall where Mr. Conrad would come and give us our daily announcements. It was a second-story room that had creaking floors and a long wooden hall that led to it. As that basketball season progressed I can still remember looking forward to hearing Mr. Conrad walking that long hallway and entering our assembly. There would be a hush when Mr. Conrad would begin. He would always give a summary of the previous week's game and provide his opinion of the upcoming game. After each successful week, the excitement and anticipation grew and grew.

As an older person, I still remember that year and relish the reminiscence of a basketball season that would never be equaled.

—Roger Fisher, former principal and superintendent of Springs Valley Schools

In my 30 years of reporting news about Orange County, Indiana, I have seized every opportunity to revisit the story of the Springs Valley High School Black Hawks of 1958. Once I learned of the path taken by Coach Rex Wells, the players, the cheerleaders and the mascot during that remarkable year of basketball, I was so intrigued I couldn't let it go. Tim Wright's book provided yet another opportunity to look back at a combination of time, place and circumstance that I'm confident has gone unequaled in the annals of Hoosier high school basketball.

—Roger Moon, Bedford Times

The one thing about Indiana basketball in its golden era is how it captured the imagination of the people across the state. I know for our team (the Milan Indians) in 1954, it was estimated that 90 percent of the adult population watched or listened to that game. And everybody thought that this could never happen again. And then, just four years later, here comes little Springs Valley—maybe the first consolidation in Indiana—West Baden and French Lick.

You must be acquainted with Indiana basketball to understand how difficult it was for French Lick and West Baden to come together as a community and support this one team when the citizens of each town were accustomed to supporting their own team against their great rival—the other town's team. The only way that could possibly have been accomplished, except over time, is to have a basketball team that is so successful that the people from both French Lick and West Baden forgot about their former schools and pride in their old traditions after a tenuous start.

This unusually successful basketball season brought those two towns together, and just four years after Milan won it all, Springs Valley went all the way to the State Tournament Final Four. The statewide following the Black Hawks had was amazing. Once again, you'd have to understand the power of Indiana basketball; there weren't any professional teams here and we were drawing close to a million people to the State Tournament each year. And that continued through the 80s until the early 90s.

I remember seeing them warm up on the Friday before the game. I told Bob Collins, the *Indianapolis Star* sportswriter, "Man, these guys can shoot. They're going to make some noise in here tomorrow." What excitement they created in the state of Indiana!

It was the epitome of trying to accomplish the impossible and it looked like Springs Valley could win it all. Everyone was rooting for them to do the same thing that Milan did. Sportswriters dubbed the Black Hawks "the sentimental favorite." Folks across the state believed that the "Milan Miracle" could be repeated with another small-town team.

Many sportswriters believed this same thing, and wrote about this possibility. There's just something so alluring about the small-town team going against the bigger school's team. I, for one, was rooting for the Black Hawks, just as most of the state of Indiana was in 1958.

—*Bobby Plump*

[The boy who hit the shot heard 'round the state in the 1954 IHSAA basketball Final Four game that the film Hoosiers *is based upon.
—Author]*

In the small town of French Lick, Indiana, there was an historic basketball team whose magical season is what dreams are made of and where legends are born.

Todd Marshall – President Springs Valley Educational Foundation - 498 S. Larry Bird Boulevard, French Lick, Indiana, 47432

FROM THE COACH

The Valley Boys is an incredible story of basketball life in the Southern Indiana towns of French Lick and West Baden Springs during the 1957-58 season. Sixty years later, the author has written a powerful human-interest story, based on real people and real events, about an extraordinary high school basketball team whose once-in-a-lifetime sports experience revived the spirits of two towns.

West Baden Springs was my hometown—small-town USA. When folks crossed the Lost River bridge just north of town on Indiana State Highway 56, the first thing they saw was a sign that read "Population 786." I attended West Baden High School and graduated in 1950. I played four years for the Sprudels (the team's nickname) and was co-captain my junior and senior years. I continued to play sports at Hanover College, and after I graduated in 1954, Uncle Sam came calling—just at the same time I was being called up to play for the Washington Senators farm team.

After serving two years in the U.S. Army, I returned to my hometown to begin my teaching and coaching career at the West Baden High School. There were only about 100 students. Little did I know that the 1956-57 school year would be the last for the West Baden and French Lick high schools before the consolidation of the two schools in the summer of 1957.

On August 1, 1957, it was my good fortune to be hired as teacher at the newly formed Springs Valley High School and assigned to coach its first basketball team. At age 24, a hometown boy became part of this extraordinary story. This remarkable season became instrumental in changing the culture of these two towns, promoting a great sense of community and cooperation among the citizens of French Lick and West Baden Springs—now known as "the Valley."

In the fall of 2007, the '58 Black Hawks team gathered at the French Lick Springs Resort to celebrate the 50th anniversary of the school and its first basketball team. It was at this event that I met the author, Tim Wright. To my surprise it was Tim's father, Billy D., who was a star player for the French Lick team when I was in school at West Baden. As we continued reminiscing about our families, Tim told me that he had always been intrigued about the '58 Black Hawks story and that he would like to write a book about this unique team. It was then that I told him about my collection of pictures and newspaper clippings of this historic basketball season. I was extremely honored when Tim asked me to send him the 60-year-old materials.

If ever a basketball team had a rendezvous with destiny, it's Springs Valley's first group of 10 players. Having a variety of backgrounds, the boys responded to the leadership of their young coach. An unbelievable bond was formed between the players and me that continues to this very day. Together, we made history in recording one of the most intriguing chapters in the annals of Indiana high school basketball during the golden era of the one-class IHSAA basketball tournament system.

This saga of the '58 Springs Valley team is much more than a basketball story. Behind the tale of the consolidation of the schools from these "twin towns" lies a tale of a long and tireless effort to combine the two institutions. Tim reminds readers of the fact that not everyone was supportive of unifying the French Lick Red Devils and the West Baden Sprudels into a new team.

The idea of having one school system in the Valley was talked about in prior decades, especially when gambling was in full swing during the first half of the 20th century. Finally, in the spring of 1957, serious action ensued. Differences of opinion were openly debated. Naming the school was a major controversy and became a stumbling block when the time came to vote. Although there were accusations of an illegal election, the vote was taken on June 4, 1957, and passed by a majority of three to one. On August 1 that year, a new seven-member board of education took charge. Springs Valley Community Schools was then adopted.

In later years, residents of the Valley made it clear that it was the team and not the school board that consolidated the two schools. Enthusiastic fans overflowed the old 1,100-seat French Lick gymnasium, and Springs Valley's student body was quick to unite. As the season progressed, consolidation of the schools began looking better and better.

Within the past year, Tim Wright has spent many hours gathering stories from me, interviewing all living players, players' families, and local individuals of the Valley for this book. It has been my honor to contribute to *The Valley Boys*. I highly commend Tim for putting this extraordinary story in writing at last.

—*Rex Wells*

ACKNOWLEDGMENTS

I would first like to thank Rex Wells for being such an immense help to me in writing about this unique basketball season. The many stories he told me, along with the scrapbooks and his own writings, allowed me to put the factual aspects of this book together.

I would also like to thank Todd Marshall for contacting me and urging me to finish the manuscript that had been shelved for nearly 10 years.

My great appreciation goes out to all the living players and coaches from the Springs Valley Black Hawks inaugural season: Marvin Pruett, Bob McCracken, Mike Watson, Jim Conrad, Paul Radcliff, Jack Belcher, Jerry Breedlove, George Lagenour, George Harrison, Warren "Doc" Keyser, and Rex Wells, who talked with me and shared their experiences.

A special thank you goes to Thelma Self, Frankie Self's wife, who was gracious enough to talk with me and share some of her memories and photos.

Thanks to Roger and Brenda Fisher for their help in reading the original manuscript and helping me garner more accurate information.

Bobbie Hale Deremiah, Wayne Ferguson, David Noble, Phil Beaver, Gerald Ritter, Tom Condra, Don Clements, Jerry Copas, Joni Randle, Justin Wininger and Jeff Lane all helped in finding photographs. Art Hampton, owner of the *Springs Valley Herald*, gave his permission to use photos taken by Freedly Rose that were originally published in that newspaper. My thanks go out to them.

My dear friend of many years, George Robinson, read through

the entire manuscript and sat with me, painstakingly going through the entire story, and helping in the editing process.

Lastly, but certainly not least, I must emphasize just how much my brother-in-law, R. Peter Noot, contributed to *The Valley Boys*. His editing skills and knowledge of the written word whipped this story into shape. His amazing ability to restructure a paragraph or simply add the needed word to a sentence and turn a phrase helped to make this a much better read. He is the Max Perkins to my Thomas Wolfe. Thank you, Peter! You are a wizard with words!

ABOUT THE AUTHOR

W. Timothy Wright is a lifelong musician who has performed for the past 45 years with the Wright Brothers Band based in Indianapolis, Indiana. He is the author of Not the Destination, a book detailing the dreams and disappointments that followed his band's career through the maze of the Nashville music recording industry. Wright currently resides in Carmel, Indiana with his wife, Dianne. They have three daughters and 10 grandchildren.

For more information about this book and author, please visit: www.wtimothywright.com